COPING WITH LOSS
THE THERAPEUTIC USE OF LEAVE-TAKING RITUALS

Copyright © 1988 by Irvington Publishers, Inc.

Library of Congress Cataloging-in-Publication Data
Main entry under title:

Coping with loss.

  Bibliography: p.
  Includes index.
  1. Loss (Psychology) 2. Farewells—Therapeutic use.
I. Hart, Onno van der, 1941-   . II. Title: Leave-
taking rituals. [DNLM: 1. Anxiety, Separation—therapy.
2. Ceremonial. 3. Psychotherapy—methods. WM 172 C783]
RC455.4.L67C67 1988   616.85′223   85-23125
ISBN 0-8290-1596-5

Printed in the United States of America

COPING WITH LOSS
THE THERAPEUTIC USE
OF LEAVE-TAKING RITUALS

edited by

Onno van der Hart

translated from the Dutch by

Carol L. Stennes

1988

IRVINGTON PUBLISHERS, INC.
740 Broadway
New York, New York 10003

COPING WITH LOSS
THE THERAPEUTIC USE
OF LEAVE-TAKING RITUALS

Contents

Foreword

Erika Fromm, Ph.D.
University of Chicago

Van der Hart and the contributors to his book create and prescribe rituals of leave-taking as a therapy for patients who have suffered the death of a beloved one; for those who have undergone abuse or have been divorced; for others who remain emotionally preoccupied with a bad interpersonal relationship that in reality already has ended; and for patients suffering post-traumatic stress, such as our Vietnam war veterans.

The technique consists of the therapist's creating a therapeutic myth which leads to a ritual to be enacted together by the patient and the therapist or the patient and a friend. Through the enactment of the ritual the patient is helped in a symbolic manner to separate himself emotionally from people or situations of the past and to leave them behind; so that he or she then can go on to build new and meaningful relationships with others. The underlying idea is that by letting go of what belonged to the beloved deceased or to the abuser, or by divesting oneself of the symbols connected with them and with the emotionally loaded situation, the patient can also take leave from that person or situation and can start a new life of his own.

The type of therapy proposed is short-term strategic therapy. It is clearly directive. The goal the therapist sets himself for the patient is to accomplish success and re-establishment of a normal life after disruptive experiences such as the loss of a loved one, or traumata such as battery have occurred. Directive therapy is action oriented. The authors believe that problematic relationships can be improved more decisively by the patient's taking action that will change his life situation than by merely talking to the therapist about the problem. However, the strategy is not to suggest to the patient straightforwardly and directly how he should handle his real life in the future. Rather, symbolic action, that is, the performance of a ritual, is prescribed by the therapist, who in many cases executes its final phase together with the patient. In others this is done by the patient alone or together with an appropriate partner.

Frequently the first phase of the ritual consists of the patient's being asked to write a letter to the deceased or to the person who has abused him. This letter and the memorabilia reminding the patient of the significant person then are often buried, burned or put away by the patient and the therapist together. This act is to symbolize to the patient his breaking away or distancing of himself from the past in order to free the energy he had invested in the earlier emotional relationship. Thereafter the patient is directed to enjoy a lovely meal in the company of friends, indicating his readiness to invest the freed energy in new interpersonal relationships.

The chapter by George Sargent extends the theme of symbolic leave-taking to situations in which two people live together in a bad marriage. The therapist suggests that, together, as partners, they bury the symbols of their unsatisfactory relationship. Executing this ritual together then enables them to let go of their resentments towards each other, to take leave from their old unpleasant relationship and to start living together in a new, more mature and happier way.

Onno van der Hart, inspired by Mara Selvini Palazzoli and her colleagues in Milan, developed leave-taking rituals as a form of psychotherapy. He is a teleologically oriented strategic psychologist, who is also deeply interested in cultural anthropology and the rituals man used in the past to help himself overcome illness. In the first three chapters of the book Dr. van der Hart gives his theoretical rationale for the ritualistic approaches he has developed in his Leave-Taking Therapy. Eight chapters follow, containing case samples and practical descriptions of when and how to use the creation of parting symbols and rituals as tools of therapeutic intervention. The last three chapters beautifully round out the Gestalt of the book. De Tempe discusses leave-taking rituals from the anthropological, the Seltzers from the sociological, and Gersons from the psychoanalytic point of view. The Seltzers wisely point out that not all rituals are liberating instruments of change (vide the endless repetitive rituals of the obsessive compulsive, which accomplish nothing). They also sound a warning with regard to improper uses of Leave-Taking and other ritual techniques. Gersons looks at Van der Hart and his co-authors' work from the theoretical position of psychoanalysis. He conceives of the therapeutic techniques invented by Van der Hart and his co-authors as strategies that stimulate healthy adaptive mechanisms of defense, showing that the techniques of leave-taking rituals can be used for the benefit of the patient by therapists with widely varying theoretical backgrounds.

The rituals described in this book all have a common structure. However, their form and content are—and must be—individualized to fit the particular patient's life experiences, personality and needs.

Coping with Loss: The Therapeutic Use of Leave-Taking Rituals represents a specific pragmatic approach in psychotherapy. In very practical terms, therapists are shown *how* and *when* to use rituals as tools of intervention. It is a book I can highly recommend to psychiatrists, psychologists, social workers, pastoral counselors, and graduate students in the field of mental health. In addition, people who have suffered the loss of a loved one, or people on whom severe injury has been inflicted by one whom they once loved, may profit greatly from reading it.

Introduction

Onno van der Hart

This book is about people who have had traumatic experiences or have suffered severe losses, the memories of which continue to haunt them, and it is about a therapeutic approach which has been designed to help them. What this involves, in essence, is that by taking leave of the key symbols that keep alive the traumatic memories or the person who is no longer there, the client takes leave of the actual memories or the actual person.

The method presented in this book is not new. Janet (Janet, 1919; Raymond & Janet, 1898) reported two casuistic cases in which taking leave of key symbols was a fundamental part of the treatment. One case involved a 31-year-old woman who had lost her two small children (aged two and one) and her mother in close succession. She lived in constant desperation and suffered from psychosomatic complaints, including severe gastrointestinal cramps and frequent vomiting. Two years after these losses, she had grown so weak that Janet admitted her to his hospital. He noticed that she continually occupied herself with objects that had some relationship to the children, that she cherished keepsakes of them which she wore in the pockets and hems of her dresses—keepsakes such as locks of hair, miniature portraits, ribbons, bows. There was something peculiar about one of the portraits: it was a smooth sheet of metal in which others recognized nothing special, but in which she saw an extremely good likeness of one of her children. These and similar observations made Janet suspect that the woman was hallucinating, and further questions confirmed this: with great regularity, she saw realistic images of the deaths of her children. Janet considered it necessary for her treatment that she take leave of all the "material reminders." The laundry baskets and cribs were to be sold, and anything else she was to hand over to him. "So as not to be too cruel, we destroyed nothing," Janet remarks. He put the package away in a cupboard to be returned to her after treatment. Then he turned his attention to the "inner memories," her hallucinations. These he managed to change using hypnotic suggestion. Although Janet gives no further specifics on the process of change in this case, on the basis of other examples we may assume that his hypnotic suggestions were intended to gradually replace the images of the deaths of her children by images that were less emotion-laden, and that then faded away, for Janet also succeeded in focusing her attention on topics important to her future, such as her midwife training classes. Janet felt this woman's cure was conditional on lessening the material reminders and changing her memories of the deaths of her children.

Janet's second example shows that taking leave of material reminders can be important even when an intimate relationship has been terminated. The woman he describes spent all her time awaiting the arrival of her beloved, who never appeared. Everything was always in readiness to receive him, and she had no interest in anyone else. "When I succeeded in making her burn his letters and his gifts," Janet says, "cease to keep her unending watch for his return, and consent to see other people, she announced that she had quite forgotten the scene during which the engagement had been broken off."

Taking leave temporarily or permanently of material reminders was no less important in Janet's therapies than in contemporary grief therapies. Volkan (1981) asks his patients to leave with him for the duration of the therapy important objects that symbolize the traumatic experiences or the one who is no longer there. He calls them "linking objects."

Basically, the therapeutic approach described in this book involves taking permanent leave of the persons or situations which are the focus of the traumatic memories by taking permanent leave of such objects. This will sometimes mean that they are destroyed, sometimes that they will become less central in the client's life. But the therapy is more than urging the client to throw away key symbols. The actual leave is taken in the form of a leave-taking ritual. It makes up part of a treatment with several facets.

The use of leave-taking rituals as described in this book was inspired by the innovative work of the Milanese family therapist Selvini Palazzoli and her colleagues, and by anthropological studies. Ten years of experience in their use led to the construction of a framework in which the course of such a therapy can be adequately described. To give the reader a concrete impression of therapeutic leave-taking rituals, the varied casuistry is emphasized.

About the contents

In part I, *Groundwork*, Van der Hart goes into the nature and functions of leave-taking rituals and symbols. Chapter 1, *Transitional rituals*, is a brief introduction to the functions of transitional rituals or rites of passage in general and, more specifically, of therapeutic leave-taking rituals. In chapter 2, *Myths and rituals: their use in psychotherapy*, western therapeutic rituals are compared to healing rituals of traditional societies. This chapter describes several aspects of Navajo healing rituals and our therapeutic leave-taking rituals, and shows that both can be described within the same conceptual framework. Leave-taking rituals generally consist of several clearly delineated phases which are discussed in this chapter. Chapter 3, *Symbols in leave-taking rituals*, focuses on the symbolic nature of these rituals. This chapter endeavors to show how symbolic leave-taking can be real leave-taking. By renouncing key symbols, the client also takes leave of what they symbolize: a particular relationship or situation. This chapter, too, explains that the client is in an altered state of consciousness similar to the hypnotic state during the performance of the ritual.

Part II, *Applications*, gives many case descriptions showing how therapeutic leave-taking rituals can be applied in various ways to different problems. In chapter 4, *Freed from oppressive bonds*, Ebbers describes a man with somatic complaints and a depression following a divorce. By means of a ritual, the client assimilates experiences from his youth and marriage and takes his leave of them. The example described here makes it clear that sometimes therapy need not consist of much more than assistance in performing a leave-taking ritual. Chapters 5 and 6 suggest how pastoral or religious counselors might use this approach. They will find a rich source of inspiration to draw on here. In chapter 5, *A consuming fire*, Van Tienen shows how the religious convictions of a client can be tied into the ritual. In the example of a man with unresolved grief, guilt feelings in particular (which are otherwise so very difficult to treat because they are bound up with beliefs or convictions, and these are not under discussion) thus become accessible for therapeutic intervention. In chapter 6, *Forty years on: A study in belated Holocaust mourning*, Herman describes mourning therapy for Jewish survivors of the Holocaust, whose unresolved grief is not for one loss, but often for many dead. Those who are no longer there have no graves, there are no material reminders—unless they are the concentration camps in which they were murdered. This mourning therapy often includes a visit to the camps. Traditional Jewish rituals and symbols help the survivors, including those who have had little or no contact with the Jewish tradition, in their belated grief work. They also help them to break out of their social isolation and to develop a positive sense of belongingness. The case Van der Hart describes in chapter 7, *A ritual in a lengthy psychotherapy*, centers on the fact that the therapist failed to perceive a central affective problem at the start of the therapy. After several years, the treatment could finally come to an end when the client, a young woman whose dissatisfying relationship with her ex-husband was related to unresolved grief over an abortion, finally worked out this problem with the aid of a ritual.

In chapter 8, *A ritual for a young woman with an atypical dissociative disorder*, Van der Velden shows how use is made of psychoanalytic concepts in the diagnostic phase of treatment. It also makes clear that the assessment of problems using psychoanalytic categories does not necessarily lead to an analytically oriented approach in treatment. In contrast to many other examples, the ritual described here does not end with a clearly delineated final ceremony in which dramatic leave is taken of the key symbol. Chapter 9 is entitled *The role of the family members in a leave-taking ritual: an example*. In it, Ebbers describes the therapy of a woman who complains of depression which is apparently connected with previous traumatic experiences but may be related to her present social situation as well. As is customary for systemic therapists, her husband is also invited to attend the first (assessment) sessions. The leave-taking ritual is aimed at resolving the woman's traumatic experiences; the involvement of the other family members in its performance implicitly influences their actual social situation.

In the example described by Sargent in chapter 10, *A burial at sea*, the marital therapy initially took place in the usual manner. But, despite the progress made, the clients could not leave behind them some difficult past events, nor could they let go of the implicit myth that their marriage was "dead." Together they carried out a ritual that helped them to do so. Experience with similar situations shows that this example can serve as a model for many other marital therapies in which past events and obsolete myths continue to distress the partners.

Part III, *Reflections*, gives some considerations about working with therapeutic leave-taking rituals in actual practice from several theoretical perspectives. Drawing on an actual case, Dormaar compares exposure—the basic technique in behavioral re-grief therapy—with the prescription of leave-taking rituals in chapter 11, *Exposure and rituals*. Using this technique, the client is exposed to the stimuli and emotions associated with the deceased (or whatever is gone) until the emotional reactions have been extinguished.

In chapter 12, *Adaptive defense mechanisms in post-traumatic stress disorders*, Gersons investigates the therapeutic effectiveness of leave-taking rituals, based on modern psychoanalytical thinking. Chapters 13 and 14 comprise cultural anthropological views of leave-taking. In chapter 13, *Grief therapy from an anthropological point of view*, De Tempe describes modern western mourning. She explains how a modern grief therapy (in her example, the behavioral re-grief therapy mentioned in chapter 11) may also be regarded as a ritual.

Lastly, in chapter 14, *Culture, leave-taking rituals, and the psychotherapist*, family therapist Wencke Seltzer and anthropologist Michael Seltzer analyze therapeutic leave-taking rituals based on the anthropologically derived concepts of the material and ideational planes of family culture. The main focus is on leave-taking rituals for the disengagement of clients and therapists at the termination of therapy. Specifically they discuss leave-taking rituals involving families in which a child had been hospitalized for treatment of anorexia nervosa and the hospital staff. They conclude this chapter, and this book, with the observation that rituals are powerful instruments of change—for better or for worse—and admonish therapists to use them with wisdom.

Acknowledgements

The origins of this book can be traced to three papers—chapters 2, 4 and 5—which were originally presented at the Symposium on Rituals in Mental Health Care, Utrecht, December 16, 1981, organized by the Dutch Catholic Study Center for Mental Health Care.

Chapters 1, 2, 3, 4, 5, 7, 10, and 11 were previously published in *Afscheidsrituelen in Psychotherapie*, the original Dutch edition, published under the auspices of the Dutch Catholic Center for the Study of Mental Health Care. Chapter 13 is an abridged and translated version of a contribution to G.A. Bancke et al. (eds.), *Gestalten van de dood* (Baarn: Ambo, 1980), and is included with permission of the editors and publisher.

The editor and authors wish to pay tribute to Carol L. Stennes for her excellent translation of all chapters but chapters 6 and 14, which were originally written in English, and for her invaluable editorial assistance. The editor is grateful to Erika Fromm, Ph.D., Brian M. Alman, Ph.D., Louise van Santen, and to his fellow-authors, especially George A. Sargent, who provided helpful comments on earlier drafts of most chapters. Many thanks to Jenny Ravensbergen, Cora M. Jongsma and Ans Hassing-van Duijnhoven for assisting in the preparation of the manuscript. Special appreciation goes to Kate Munro for her dedication and skill in editing the entire manuscript.

PART I
GROUNDWORK

Transitional Rituals

Onno van der Hart

Ouessant is a rugged French island off the coast of Brest, surrounded by a treacherous sea. Despite its twelve lighthouses, many ships have been dashed to pieces on its grim shores. The islanders are fishermen or sailors; many of them have died at sea.

When one of them has drowned and his body is not recovered, the people carry out a ceremony called Proëlla. This is a religious mourning ritual by means of which symbolic leave is taken of the victim six to nine days after his disappearance. For the Proëlla ceremony, a cross is made of white wax. In the home of the missing person, the cross is placed on a table set with white linen and a white cap. The cap is traditionally worn by the women, and now acts as a shroud. Two candles are placed beside the cross. Their glow symbolizes the light of the lighthouses. The family gather around the table. The women are clothed in hooded coats with which they cover their faces as much as possible. Prayers are said, there are long silences, everyone cries and gazes at the small wax cross illuminated by the candles.

The day after this solemn gathering, the priest comes. The wax cross, which is still lying on the cap, is carried to the church in a procession. Just like at an ordinary funeral, a mass is celebrated. After the mass, the cross is laid to rest in a miniature mausoleum that stands amidst the graves in the cemetery.

In many times and places, people have used rituals and ceremonies to mark transitions from one situation to another. Rituals are key scenarios of a culture which aid in making such transitions. They designate the goals, or the desired state of affairs, and the means for reaching them (cf. Ortner, 1973). Rituals are like dramas where those involved are at the same time the actors and the audience.

Frequently transitions concern the course of life of an individual or a family. They relate to the extension of the family group (through a birth, for example), its diminution (such as a child's leaving home, divorce/separation, death), or a change in the activities of the individual family members (such as taking a new job, going to a new school, promotion, retirement).

In our culture, certain transitions are clearly marked by rituals. Wedding ceremonies, for instance, are the key scenarios for marriage, and mourning rituals designate how leave can be taken of a deceased person and how he can be mourned. Other transitions, such as a child's leaving home, are often much less ritualized. People who are faced with such situations must find their own expression for them.

Other cultures have rituals unfamiliar to us. For instance, they have puberty ceremonies in which the transition from child to adolescent takes place. These rituals are often the symbolic expression of the fact that the old situation, that of being a child, has died, and that the person is reborn in the new state, that of adolescence. Nor do we have explicit healing rituals. Healing rituals are dramas in which the symbolic actions of the healer, the patient, and the family members remove the disease and restore a healthy and harmonious situation. Of course our culture, too, has key scenarios for healing, but we do not tend to view them as rituals.

If we must take leave of a deceased person, our culture offers death, burial, and mourning rituals for this purpose. These traditional forms enable the survivors to cope with their loss. Together they can express their grief and feel the support of their environment. After successful leave-taking rituals, they are in a position to make a new beginning in life.

There are also people for whom the traditional mourning rituals offer insufficient comfort and support. Sometimes a person has been taken away too suddenly. Sometimes 'too much has happened' between the survivors and the deceased. In any case, they are unable to live with the situation and the loss. To them, the traditional rituals are inadequate for dealing with their emotions and for organizing their lives in a different way. It must be added that mourning rituals in our culture often provide only a means for dealing with positive feelings, and leave too little room for the expression of ambivalent feelings toward the deceased person.

Others are unable to cope with the loss of the deceased because they did not take part in the rituals. For instance, they did not attend the funeral, as they were advised to stay home, being the most closely affected; or for one reason or another they were not informed in time (cf. Fortuin, 1980). Or the official ritual my have been so repugnant to them that they could not manage to enter into it. For rituals work only if we do not remain the audience, but also become actors.

Our culture does not provide special rituals for coping with another type of loss or traumatic experience. Apart from the legal divorce proceedings, there is no leave-taking ritual for partners who separate. A material separation does take place, and this has a ritual character, but there is no emotional separation. Similarly, there are no rituals for people who lose their jobs, lose a limb, who have to leave their home and familiar surroundings. Fortunately, many people are able to fashion their own private scenarios to cope with their losses and to take leave. But others remain so emotionally attached to the old situation that the transition cannot be successful.

For persons who have suffered a loss, whatever its nature, and do not succeed in dealing with it themselves or with friends or family, there are therapeutic scenarios varying from self-help groups to individual psychotherapy. This book presents a scenario that corresponds in form and content to the traditional leave-taking ritual: the *therapeutic* leave-taking ritual. It consists of symbolic actions which form an ordered whole, with the aid of which the person, the couple or the family can take their leave of something and make a new beginning in life. In fact, the therapeutic leave-taking ritual shows the most correspondence with a traditional ceremony such as Proëlla, in which leave is taken of a *symbol* of the deceased. The therapeutic leave-taking ritual is indicated not only for working through a loss, but sometimes, too, to obtain a perspective on other traumatic experiences: past experiences which haunt the person or persons and prevent them from orienting themselves to the present and the future. If it is successful, the ritual helps to wind up the past.

People who carry out a traditional ritual generally know where they stand with one another, what they can expect, and what is expected of them. Traditional rituals are highly predictable and, if they fit into the world view and perception of those involved in them, they are almost automatic: *this* is how it is done and *this* is good. A therapeutic leave-taking ritual is specially designed for the unique situation of the client; it is a unique and one-time private event. There is nothing automatic about it, not for the client, nor for the therapist, who is working with it for the first time. Both of them may perceive the ritual as a mechanical device, making it difficult to enter into it. By the way, this is also a danger with traditional rituals (cf. Moore & Myerhoff, 1977; Myerhoff, 1980, p. 86).

Most chapters in this book give actual cases of examples. They show both the unique nature of each leave-taking ritual, and also the basic structure which the rituals described have in common. Readers who are unfamiliar with this approach are thus provided with a sort of "tradition" which can be of use if they want to design rituals themselves.

All the same, this tradition must not be regarded as an integral set of rules which must be kept to at all costs. It can better be regarded as a source of inspiration, a challenge if you wish, to invent and to carry out that which is suited to the unique situation of the person who wants to take leave. For example, the beautiful and extremely effective ritual that the famous American psychiatrist Milton H. Erickson (cf. Zeig, 1980a, p. 287) prescribed for working through an unusually difficult loss differs from most examples presented in this book.

A rancher brought his depressed and suicidal wife to Erickson. She had severe arthritis and for this reason the doctors had strongly advised against her becoming pregnant. Erickson realized how much she longed for a child and in what physical and mental condition she was. He advised her to become pregnant as soon as possible, and to enjoy her pregnancy, if need be spending the last months in bed. The woman soon became pregnant. Her arthritis improved and she was no longer depressed. She had a little girl, Cynthia, with whom she and her husband were very happy. Cynthia died when she was six months old, a crib death. A few months after that the man once again brought his wife to Erickson and said that she was worse than ever. Erickson talked to her seriously about her wish to end her life: by doing so, she would also destroy the memories of the happiest time of her life. He told her to go home again with her husband. He was to find a eucalyptus sapling for her and plant it according to her instructions. Eucalyptus trees grow very rapidly in Arizona. "I want you to name that eucalyptus sapling 'Cynthia'. I want you to watch Cynthia grow. I want you to look forward to the day when you can sit in the shade of Cynthia." Erickson visited the woman a year later. The tree had grown very rapidly. The woman was much better, both physically and mentally. She had many flower beds and showed all of them to Erickson. Erickson later remarked: "Every flower she grew reminded her of Cynthia, as did the Eucalyptus tree that I named Cynthia."

Myths and Rituals: Their Use in Psychotherapy

Onno van der Hart

The treatment of persons suffering from psychosocial and psychosomatic complaints varies widely from culture to culture. But however different such treatment may be, we always find the same elementary structure. The causes of the complaints and the reasons they persist are first translated into the terms of a therapeutic myth, and then treatment takes place in the symbolic realm of the myth. The treatment serves to bring about transformations in the myth which correspond to changes in the apperception of the client or patient and in the functioning of the social group of which s/he is a member.

In old societies strongly bound by tradition, the treatment takes the form of healing rituals. We have numerous different types of therapy which are the western counterparts of such rituals. And rituals are beginning to find a place in directive forms of therapy—rituals which differ greatly from the traditional healing rituals in form, content, and complexity.

The chief difference between traditional and western rituals is the cultural context in which they are prescribed and carried out. Traditional healing rituals are based on a mythological world view and a corresponding religious myth shared by the healer, the patient, his family and friends. Western therapy is usually nowhere near so extensive. In strategic or directive therapy, the therapist tries to construct the therapeutic myth, ordinarily secular, in terms of the world view of the client, and to adapt treatment to it.

This chapter compares traditional healing rituals with western therapeutic rituals, based on a description of religious healing rituals in Navajo society and leave-taking rituals in western directive therapy. An important principle in strategic or directive therapy is adapting treatment to the client's experience. In certain cases, this may also imply an adaptation to the existing religious myths of the client, while the leave-taking ritual may derive its form and content from them.

Navajo myths and rituals

The Navajo Indians, in the southwestern part of the United States, have a wealth of traditional myths and rituals. Their traditional healers, the medicine men, fulfil many roles simultaneously. The medicine man is doctor, psychologist, priest, and historial rolled into one. The Navajos make no distinction between a church and a hospital.

Today, Navajos will make use of the facilities of a modern western hospital if necessary, and their medicine men regularly refer people with somatic complaints to white doctors. Conversely, the doctors, such as surgeons and psychiatrists, also send patients to the medicine man. When a surgeon has performed an operation and has given the necessary medical care, he may discharge a patient with the words: "We've done all we can do for you. Now you can do the rest of the healing with your own ceremonies." (Fields, 1976, p. 18). The Navajos are more keenly aware than white people of the fact that illness and an operation disturb a person's equilibrium. The patient is not recovered if the wound heals nicely; treatment of his "mental wound" is also required and this is what the traditional healing rituals provide.

The Navajo medicine men believe in the power of the mind over the body. Official medical practitioners have come to regard them more and more as experts in the prevention and treatment of psychosomatic illnesses, emotional disturbances, and psychoses. It has been shown that their healing rituals provide more solace for Indians with such difficulties than conventional psychiatric treatment. This is particularly true of people who are depressed by a prolonged mourning process and who take a traditional attitude toward life (Fields, 1976, p. 16). A central concept to the Navajo view of life is that the universe is an orderly whole. It consists of supernaturals, people and other living beings, and non-living nature. Everything that happens is interrelated. In the world view of the

Navajos, the natural and the supernatural must be a coherent system in equilibrium. According to this idea, when expected rainfall does not come, this is not only associated with other meteorological data, but also with the fact that "people have become too mean" or because "whites are selling liquor to the Navajos" (Kluckhohn, 1968, p. 679). Illness, too, points to a disturbance in the harmony of the universe. The goal of healing rituals is to restore this harmony and, along with it, the health of the patient (Murray, 1977, p. 215); as a Navajo put it, "To be healed is to become whole and to be whole one must be in harmony with family, friends, and nature" (Fields, 1976, p. 13).

Before someone who is ill can be helped, a diagnosis must be made. To this end a diviner is consulted who does so in terms of the following: the patient became ill because he saw an animal being struck by lightning; because he has been in contact with a disease-causing animal (such as a bear, a jackal, or an eagle); because he failed to observe ritual rules; or because he had some involvement with ghosts and witches.

The diagnosis determines the choice of the healing ritual. The cause of the illness may be very complex, so there is always the chance that an incorrect diagnosis was made. The Navajos take this possibility into account as follows: before a patient commits himself to carrying out a demanding and costly healing ritual, he first carries out one small part of it. If he improves, then the diagnosis was correct and the choice of the ritual as well (cf. Kluckhohn, 1968, p. 680).

A Navajo healing ritual—usually called a chant or a sing, because singing is one of the main activities—takes from one to nine nights plus the days in between (Reichard, 1963, p. xxxiv). A ritual is an extremely complex event which includes singing and praying, offering prayersticks, bodily cleansing, and making sandpaintings.

Each ritual has its own myth that tells the story of the ritual's origin. The myth also contains numerous references to other myths, the most important of which tells about the supernaturals and the origins of the Navajo people. The ritual thus forms an integrated part of the total view of life of the Navajos. For a particular ritual, the myth indicates the most important supernaturals in the chant, the meanings of the songs in the ritual, and the origins and meanings of the objects used in the ritual (Lamphere, 1969, p. 285; Murray, 1977, p. 212).

The myth recounts the family life of the supernaturals. Frictions between brothers and sisters are extensively related, and the previously scorned or neglected child ultimately wins over the child who was favored.

The symbolic nature of such tales becomes clear if we realize that many conflicts and tensions occur in the Navajo tribe or clan which may not be expressed openly or directly. The group norms emphasize harmony and solidarity. Those who suffer the most under these tensions but may not talk about them directly start to feel anxious or guilty, become frustrated or confused, and report that "they feel sick all over" (Reichard, 1963, p. 285). Thus the plot of the myth contains a symbolic solution to interpersonal problems—not only those between brothers and sisters—that often occur among the Navajos.

Of course the existence of interpersonal tensions is not actually denied by the Navajos. But their cosmology, of which the myths are a part, gives them the opportunity to do something about them in a safe way. It does not threaten the continuity of the group, as a direct discussion of the conflicts would: ". . . the trouble was just that he [the patient] was on hand when lightning struck. The proper rite can straighten this out" (Kluckhohn & Leighton, 1974, p. 238). The rectification in fact also includes the resolution of social problems which disturbed the stability of the group.

Roughly speaking, Navajo healing rituals operate on three levels: (1) they impart to the participants the Navajo model of the natural and the supernatural world; (2) they consist of symbolic objects and acts which restore the patient to health; and (3) through the participation of family members and friends, they help restore the harmony in the social group. Troubled relationships are improved by acting, not by talking.

This chapter focuses on the activities with the purpose of healing the patient. If they are to have the desired effect on him, then he must be extremely concentrated on their performance. This concentration requires that he be in a sort of trance (cf. Murray, 1977, p. 213; chapter 3) in which he enters into the symbolic event and at the same time experiences the security and support of the ritual and of the presence of family and friends.

During the chant three sorts of acts are performed with the ritual objects. Together, their goal is to counteract the "actions" which were undertaken against the patient, to remove the "ugly conditions" from him and to make him immune to malevolent influences, in order to thus create "pleasant conditions" (Lamphere, 1969, p. 269).

The first sort of symbolic act, the making of *prestations* (sacrifices or offerings), involves offering prayersticks to appropriate supernaturals. This obliges them to help the patient, for instance by giving their assurance that the ritual objects and acts will product immunity.

A second sort of symbolic action is aimed at the patient's *identifying* himself with the supernaturals whose power can heal him. This might be accomplished by the patient's giving expression to appropriate scenes from the myth which goes with the ritual in dramatizations and in sand-paintings. An example would be the most important and favorite my-thological figure of the Navajo, Changing Woman, who is always out to promote the welfare of the people. In one of the myths she is reju-venated. If the patient gives expression to the circumstances and the ritual details in which she regained her youth and beauty, he identifies himself with the rejuvenation she underwent (Reichard, 1963, p. 115). Identi-fication with supernaturals may also take place by ritual acts which sym-bolically bring the body of the patient into contact with them. Symbolic objects which already possess this power are pressed against the body and certain medicines derived from supernaturals are taken in (Lamphere, 1969, p. 296).

A third type of ritual acts are those aimed at *removing* the "ugly conditions," or the malevolent powers which are making the patient sick. These powers may be located in the stomach or, represented by arrows, in the flesh. Both sorts are taken out by sweat-emetic rites (Reichard, 1963, p. 108; Lamphere, 1969, p. 297). Such cleansing rites also put the patient into a state which attracts Goodness, or benevolent powers.

Briefly summarized, the main symbolic actions with the purpose of healing the patient are: the making of prestations, the identification of the patient with the positive powers of supernaturals, and the removal of malevolent influences. These themes are repeated in every subritual, in every prayer, and in every song cycle. One of the themes may dominate or be emphasized in a subritual (Lamphere, 1969, p. 301). Together the symbolic actions bring about the removal of "ugly conditions" in the patient and ensure that "pleasant conditions" come in their stead. The unity or harmony is restored, not only in the patient's mind and body, but also in his relationships to the natural and supernatural environment and in the relationships in the group of which he is a member.

The basic structure of healing rituals

However amazingly complicated the performance of a Navajo chant may be, its basic structure is particularly simple, and this is equally true of the healing rituals of many other peoples. A healing ritual is actually a complex of myth and ritual (Munn, 1969; 1973; cf. Kluckhohn, 1942). To obtain some insight into this complex, we must first look into the question of what myths are.

Myths are *stories* which, in the society in which they are told, are regarded as truthful accounts of an early history (Bascom, 1965; Fontenrose, 1966, p. 54). Myths describe how one state of affairs turned into a different one, how chaos became the cosmos, how an uninhabited world became inhabited, how androgynous beings became men and women, how sin and death came into the world, and so on (cf. Turner, 1968). It is characteristic of myths that a limited number of elements occur: myths are always a closed system, while the actual history of humanity, of a people or of an individual is an open system in which an unlimited number of elements take part (cf. Lévi-Strauss, 1979, p. 40).

In a complex of myth and ritual, the negative experiences of the patient are first recounted in terms of the myth. The myth tells how the accident, the affliction, or the illness came about and why it remains. It is the medium through which the complaints are given expression in a symbolic manner. The second phase of the healing process consists of the ritual actions which are carried out by the healer, the other members of the society, and the patient. These symbolic actions dispel the negative images which were given expression in mythical stories or transform them into positive images (Munn, 1973, p. 595). They bring about a symbolic transformation or reorganization so that a transformation can take place in the apperception of the patient and his complaints can disappear. They can also change the social relationships between all persons involved.

We have seen how the Navajos have three main themes in their totality of ritual actions: the prestations, the identification of the patient with appropriate supernaturals, and the removal of malevolent powers from his body.

If a myth is to act as a language in which the complaints of the patient can be expressed, then it must form a subjective reality which is shared by the patient, his family and friends, and by the medicine man, and which shows a relationship to the objective reality of those involved. Referring to a ritual for a difficult childbirth among the Cuna Indians, Lévi-Strauss (1963, p. 197; cf. Van der Hart, 1983a, p. 60) remarks:

> That the mythology of the shaman does not correspond to an objective reality does not matter. The sick woman believes in the myth and belongs to a society which believes in it. The tutelary

spirits and the malevolent spirits, the supernatural monsters and magical animals, are all part of a coherent system on which the native conception of the universe is founded. The sick woman accepts these mythical beings or, more accurately, she has never questioned their existence. What she does not accept are the incoherent and arbitrary pains, which are an alien element in her system but which the shaman, calling upon myth, will re-integrate within a whole where everything is meaningful.

The ritual transforms, or brings about changes, in the events of the myth, and along with it, in the subjective experience of the patient. His experience as he perceives it consists not only of his physical complaints, but also of his feelings of conflict towards the other members of his group. And since they also take part in the ritual, it is quite conceivable that social relationships are transformed as well. The Navajos express this in the following metaphor: "Since power is (. . .) like a wave in a pool, always effective though becoming weaker the farther it radiates from chanter and patient, each person in attendance derives benefit from what is done in proportion to his proximity to the ritual" (Reichard, 1963, p. xxxvii). In western terms, this implies that the symbols and symbolic actions of the ritual reflect and change physical complaints as well as personal feelings and cognitions and social relationships.

Myth and ritual in modern psychotherapy

The modern western forms of psychotherapy also possess the basic structure of a therapeutic myth which translates the complaint into its terms and explains its origin, while the treatment also takes place in the realm of the myth. And what is true for the myth accompanying a Navajo healing ritual is equally true for a modern therapeutic myth: if it is to be effective, then the myth must be ". . . compatible with the cultural world view shared by patient and therapist . . ." (Frank, 1973, p. 328).

If people seek help from a therapist, they are distressed. They are troubled by anxieties and uncertainties, they experience conflicts, tensions, and disappointments, they complain about the chaos in their existence or about the meaninglessness of life. For them, the therapeutic myth is an acceptable account of the origins of their complaints; it is a story that explains what went wrong, and may even point to a way of restoring unity. Ideally, the myth offers a grip and a perspective on the situation.

Modern therapeutic myths differ from traditional myths in that they are secular and fragmentary. They make no references to prehistoric times, and supernatural beings play no part in them. They are not founded upon a view of life, a single world view shared by therapist and client, whereas in traditional societies such as the Navajos they are.

If the modern therapeutic myth is to provide the client a grip and a perspective, then often he must be educated in and converted to the world view of the therapist (cf. De Swaan et al., 1979). Traditional myths are explicit; they are stories. Modern therapeutic myths are often implicit; they consist of ". . . meaningful but not fully developed elements of a potential story . . ." (Waardenburg, 1980, p. 55).

Even though they may differ as to form and content from traditional healing rituals, the modern forms of psychotherapy, family therapy, etc. are their western equivalents. They often even seem to be substitutes for traditional rites of passage (cf. Van Gennep, 1909; 1960). Traditional coming of age rituals, for instance, help children to become young adults and help their parents to see them as such. Our family therapy not infrequently takes on this function (cf. Haley, 1973).

In directive or strategic therapy, the therapist endeavors as best he can to adapt himself to the world view of the client. He or she tries to speak the client's language and to express the therapeutic myth in the client's words. An oft-used model in directive therapy, the life cycle of family or individual, is excellently suited to this. Here complaints or symptoms are generally described as reactions to the fact that the family or individual was unsuccessful in making certain transitions in their life cycle or in resolving certain crises (Haley, 1973). Common transitions, such as leaving the parental home, getting married, giving birth, or changing jobs take place at expected moments. Crises, such as an accident, losing one's job, a serious illness, or death, generally take place suddenly. Both predictable transitions and sudden life crises require a redefinition of existing relationships and changes in the way in which people get along together (cf. Van der Hart, 1980). If a certain transition was made well, but a person does not know how to perform the tasks that the new role entails, this may result in the same type of complaint as well.

The directive therapist's goal is to be successful in doing something about the complaints of the individual or family, and to see to it that the necessary transition or adaptation to the new life phase takes place after all. Very briefly, the goal of the therapy is "to restore normal life" (Ter Horst, 1977). Once the client and the therapist share a therapeutic myth, the treatment on this basis generally takes place through actions. Directive therapy is action-oriented. One form in which the client can solve problems and can remake or conclude a transition is by performing a ritual.

Rituals in directive therapy differ in numerous respects from the traditional healing rituals such as the Navajos have. They never constitute the treatment in itself, but only a part of it; they are secular and based on a fragmentary world view and on a therapeutic myth constructed especially for and with the client or the family. I define rituals as prescribed symbolic actions that must be performed in a certain way and in a certain order, and may or may not be accompanied by verbal formulas (Van der Hart, 1983a, p. 5). One assumption we make is that therapeutic rituals are more effective the more absorbed those involved are in their performance.

It was the Italian group of family therapists led by Selvini Palazzoli (Selvini Palazzoli et al., 1974, 1977, 1978) who first started prescribing rituals in family therapy and saw that they could be an extremely effective means of bringing about change. Initially these therapists designed each ritual separately, a method which demanded a great deal of creativity and often even depended on "flashes of genius" (Selvini Palazzoli, 1974). Today they also have a number of standard rituals which can be prescribed in certain situations.

Therapeutic leave-taking rituals

Many complaints and problems can be indications for a therapeutic ritual (cf. Levick et al., 1981; Rey et al., 1981; Selvini Palazzoli et al., 1974; 1977; 1978; Van der Hart, 1983a; Papp, 1976; Van der Hart & Ebbers, 1981; Seltzer & Seltzer, 1983). My personal experience relates primarily to designing and prescribing leave-taking rituals. For the client, carrying out a leave-taking ritual is a sort of re-grief therapy in which a symbolic leave is taken of persons or situations from the past. If it is as it should be, the ritual also helps the client to make a new start in life, just as traditional mourning customs do. The therapeutic leave-taking ritual is a rite of passage with the aid of which the client leaves behind him a certain unhappy situation and effects a new situation.

Like traditional mourning customs, the therapeutic ritual at first attenuates the leave-taking. It enables the bereaved, for a while, to give the dead person as central a place in his or her life as (s)he had before, yet at the same time the ritual emphasizes death as a crucial event whose implications must be acknowledged (Marris, 1974; Bowlby, 1980).

In the Navajo healing rituals, tradition determines the form and a large part of the content, and a certain tradition is beginning to develop in work with leave-taking rituals. The design of the rituals no longer depends on the therapist's inspiration. Their basic structure is known and the therapist can learn the various forms they may take from the literature, for instance. The actual form of the ritual must be determined together with the client; it must be adapted to the client's experience and his desires must make up its fabric. The tradition can best be regarded as a source of inspiration, not as a norm to be complied with.

The structure of leave-taking rituals consists of several phases. First there is the *preparatory phase* in which the therapist explains how performing a ritual might be of help to the client. In this phase it might be a good idea to show the client several actual examples. One thing this indicates is that there is a sort of tradition—the client is not being used as a guinea pig—and that other people have found help in this manner. It can strengthen the client's belief in progress, which is viewed as a nonspecific therapeutic factor (cf. Frank, 1973; Rabkin, 1977).

This is followed by the *reorganization phase* in which the client carries out certain concrete tasks which stimulate the internal process of working through and keep it going until a conclusion has been reached. The client may make or create things to serve as symbols of the relationship he or she still has with the person in question. These might be drawings, paintings, statues or figurines, poems or stories. One particular form is the "continuous letter" (Rubinstein, 1977; cf. Van der Hart, 1983a), in which the client puts down on paper each day whatever he or she still has to say to the person. The writing is done in a circumscribed ritual setting. For instance, it must be done at a fixed time and place, and a possible arrangement might be that the client put a picture of the person he or she is writing to on the desk. While carrying out this task, the client often spontaneously starts writing to other people out of the past: people to whom no real goodbye has ever been said. The continuous letter may also be written, but never sent, to someone with whom the client still has dealings, perhaps a father or mother, when a thoroughgoing discussion of the past is not feasible or just plain useless. In this phase, the client collects any existing symbolic objects, things which Volkan (1981; cf. Volkan & Josephthal, 1980) call "linking objects." The client may attribute magical powers to them which enable them to bring him into contact with the person he or she has lost (cf. chapter 3).

The activities in the reorganization phase can evoke powerful feelings and emotions. The task of the therapist consists of aiding and supporting the client in these activities and helping him or her to allow the feelings to come to the fore within the safe and clearly delineated limits of the ritual. In this way the mourning process can reach its conclusion.

When it is clear that the reorganization phase has come to an end, the *finalization phase* can begin: the client carries out the leave-taking ceremony in which a solemn and stately farewell is said to the symbols, both self-made and gathered. Often this is done by burying them, or first burning and then burying them. Transforming and parting with the material symbolize taking leave of the person. During a symbolic burial, usually carried out in a quiet spot somewhere in the country, the client can go through the same sort of experience as at a real funeral. It may be useful for the therapist to be present at the ritual, so that it can take place without any distraction.

After the "burial" or "cremation" a sort of *cleansing ritual* takes place, perhaps in the form of a shower or a bath. This is followed by an *incorporation ritual* together with the partner, with friends or with family. This ceremony often takes the form of a meal, giving symbolic expression to the client's most important relationships in his new phase of life. The incorporation ritual embraces a new start.

In conclusion: leave-taking rituals consist of more than just the final ceremony. This ceremony can fulfill its therapeutic function by virtue of the preceding process of change. The course described here will be encountered in nearly all leave-taking rituals. As the following example (Van der Hart, 1983a) will illustrate, the structure must always be adapted to the unique characteristics and circumstances of the client.

Case description

Marjan is a 32-year-old married woman. She was referred by her physician because she is afraid she will kill her 1½-year-old son, Jeroen. Moreover, she has developed so many fears that she hardly ever leaves the house.

Marjan's symptoms appear to be related to a traumatic event that took place a few years earlier. She had been married before and had a little girl. Johan, her first husband, and her daughter, Marijke, were killed in a traffic accident. Marijke, just one year old, was killed instantly; Johan died later in the hospital. Marjan could not get over this tragedy. She realized that both of them were dead, but they were still alive in her imagination.

A few years after the accident—and still very much depressed—she met Theo, whom she married because he could accept the fact that he came second in her life. Modest as he was, Theo could lay no claims on Marjan, who was still preoccupied with such a loss.

It is clear that Marjan's unresolved grief has been a great burden, from the beginning, to the relationship between her and Theo and to their ties with Jeroen. In addition, both have problems with Marjan's family, with whom they have intensive contact. Theo has broken off almost all contact with his parents. (There were several unresolved issues behind this.)

But besides all these difficulties, the therapist encounters positive aspects; perhaps the most important is that Marjan and Theo love each other and their son very much and have a mutual bond that can withstand a good deal of strain. And despite all their symptoms, both of them give the impression that they can take quite a bit individually.

In Marjan and Theo's therapy, which lasted two years, the problems with their respective families were worked on intensively and with good results. We will not discuss this aspect, but will focus on the grief work, which took place during the first six months of therapy. When, at the first session, Marjan's tragic past and both their attitudes towards it are brought up, the therapist remarks that a part of Marjan seems to live at home with Theo and Jeroen, while the other part dwells on the past with Johan and Marijke. Marjan agrees. When the therapist says that it is as if there is an empty chair and an empty highchair in their house and that they must say farewell, both Marjan and Theo are shocked. The therapist talks about carrying out a separation ritual as a re-grief therapy, and gives some examples. He asks Marjan and Theo to think it over and talk about it in the weeks to come.

At the next session, Marjan says that she has been through a difficult period. Just thinking about a possible separation from Johan and Marijke caused her many problems. All kinds of memories kept running through her mind, and she felt very emotional. She plans to make a painting of each of them, and then to bury them. She would like to start out as soon as possible. The therapist discusses with Marjan and Theo how she can make room and time for this, considering the family circumstances, so that she can express her emotions freely. He makes an appointment with them for the following week and urges Marjan to call him up if she feels the need. As Marjan begins to paint (while her mother-in-law or Theo cares for Jeroen) she cries for hours: "bawls," as she puts it. But she keeps at it and works very hard. She starts farewell letters to Johan and Marijke. The first few days she is busy for hours on end, and later for shorter periods.

Marjan sets aside everything for her re-grief therapy. Her symptoms—her fears that she might do something to Jeroen in her obsession—do not disappear immediately, but she feels she is on the right track. After a month, she indicates that she thinks she has worked through most of it. The paintings are finished, the letters are almost completed. She says that she does not want to start a concluding ceremony yet because she may have something to add to the letters. The therapist accepts this—rightly or wrongly.

Four months pass in which therapy focuses on other problem areas. Then Theo suddenly tells Marjan that it is beginning to bother him that she has not concluded her farewell to Johan and Marijke. Marjan reacts vehemently. She gathers together the paintings, the farewell letters, and all the keepsakes. She chooses the keepsakes she wants to give to Johan's family and what she wants to keep herself. At a quiet spot in the country, she buries the paintings, letters, and the keepsakes she chose.

She puts in a plastic bag what is still to be discarded and throws it into a collecting bin. She buries a special memento of Johan by his grave and another she throws in the water near the hospital where he died. After she has done all this, she throws away the clothes she has been wearing. She talks about the entire ritualistic event with Theo, and together they discuss what it means to both of them. The intimate contact following this becomes their own incorporation ritual.

In the next few days, Marjan writes several farewell letters to some of Johan's family and sends them the keepsakes that she chose for them. She indicates that her grief work is terminated. After this she works successfully on various other problems.

What was the complex of myth and ritual in this example? The client sought help for her anxieties and her concern that she would do some injury to her child. These complaints were brought into relation with her unworked through grief (caused by the death of her first husband and her little girl). We can call this reconstruction an implicit therapeutic myth; the myth was not developed into a complete story. It was clear that the therapist and the clients believed it was true. On the basis of this myth, an important goal of the treatment was achieved through the performance of a suitable ritual.

We might ask ourselves if the three main themes of the Navajo healing rituals—prestation, identification, and removal—are also somehow operative in our therapeutic leave-taking rituals. The making of prestations by the Navajos consisted of offering prayersticks to supernaturals. Perhaps writing the leave-taking letters could be compared to this. But Marjan did not need to assume that they really existed "somewhere." Her writing was "pretending." The second activity, identification with positive powers, is quite unrepresented in this example. But if we might call the state of unresolved mourning, in accordance with the Navajo usage, an "ugly condition," then the removal of ugly conditions played a main role in this therapy.

In the reorganization phase of the leave-taking ritual, one thing the client must do is express what he or she still has to say to the person in question, and this is often accompanied by powerful emotions. By taking leave of the objects which symbolize a relationship with others, the client also loses something of his or her inner experience. This is even more accentuated in the psychoanalytic terminology used by Volkan and Josephthal (1980, p. 126): the client carries the deceased with him as an *introject*—"a foreign body in my breast," as one of their clients put it. Whatever the client does not wish to assimilate, to integrate, is rejected and must be removed.

Expressing hindersome emotions within the bounds of the ritual and carrying out a leave-taking ritual provide the leeway to develop more "pleasant conditions." The cleansing ritual once again underlines this: being clean is being troubled by nothing, according to a traditional view (De Vries, 1968, p. 281). The Navajos feel that a person in such a state attracts Goodness. The incorporation ritual, in the form of a dinner or sexual intimacy, seems, too, to be directly aimed at promoting pleasant conditions. It is a model *of* that condition and is at the same time a model *for* future occasions involving the same people (cf. Geertz, 1973, p. 93).

Psychotherapy and the religious dimension

Peacock (1975, p. 224; cf. Geertz, 1973) describes the symbolic entity of religion as something one can hold on to, as a structure with the aid of which one can see order and sense in the course of events.

Formulated in such abstract terms, the therapeutic myth appears to serve the same functions as religion.

The myth the therapist offers the client and which he or she accepts does not lead a life of its own, isolated from the client's other experiences. If the client is religious, then it is quite possible that he relates the therapeutic myth to his religious views and experiences. The therapeutic myth will be more effective the more strongly it is supported by the more extensive religious perspective and its myths. So for the pastoral counselor, it is better not only to approach clients in a reflective, nondirective manner, but also in terms of their religious myths.

Chapter 3 describes the leave-taking ritual of Mrs. Jansen. She was a religious woman who had had an unhappy life. A leave-taking ritual would help her to leave the painful experiences from the past behind her and start out on a more satisfying life. The therapist wanted to reinforce the significance and the power of the ritual by adapting his therapeutic myths to her religious experience. He asked her to make fourteen drawings of the most important moments in her life, corresponding to the fourteen stations of the cross. This later became four drawings, after the four evangelists who each had a message.

To an outsider these comparisons may seem quite arbitrary. But to Mrs. Jansen, they put her suffering into a broader context, giving meaning and significance to her task and providing her with support and something to hold on to during the execution of the task.

In secular psychotherapy, situations can also occur where a religious myth is more effective than the secular therapeutic one. A final example, which also makes it clear that an appropriate myth can sometimes lead to a simple and effective directive, will illustrate this. After a stay in a psychiatric hospital, Mr. Verkooyen, a 70-year-old widower, became very withdrawn and was put into socio-psychiatric follow-up care. The hospital stay had resulted from his constant preoccupation with adultery he had committed 40 years earlier. He felt it was a betrayal of his wife and of Christ. The therapist did not try to help Mr. Verkooyen take some perspective on his guilt feelings, but reconstructed his life story in such a way that it would be logical for him to carry out a sort of atonement ritual (cf. Van der Hart, 1983a, p. 90). They agreed that Mr. Verkooyen would think this over in the coming week. Next time he came, he told the therapist that after their talk he had gone to a priest whom he had always wanted to consult, but never had. He had told the priest the same story. The priest had told him that he had indeed betrayed Christ. But if he would tell his story to Christ, then Christ would ask him, "Do you love me?'' The priest asked Mr. Verkooyen what he would reply. ''Yes, Lord, I love you.'' ''Then Christ says to you,'' continued the priest, ''tend my sheep, protect my lambs. And do you know who the sheep and the lambs are?'' ''They are my children and my grandchildren and my office.'' ''Then Christ says to you that you must once again take upon you the care for them.''

This had a great appeal for Mr. Verkooyen. He sought contact with his children and grandchildren and returned to his business. An atonement ritual or another sort of therapy was no longer necessary. Perhaps this example illustrates, too, that a therapy need not resort to a ritual too hastily. A ritual is no simple task for a client to fulfil.

In conclusion

Be it a traditional healing ritual of the Navajos or some modern form of psychotherapy (not only directive therapy), we always find the following basic structure: first the complaints for which help is sought are translated into the terms of a therapeutic myth, and then treatment takes place to correct or transform the story of the myth. The treatment restores as much as possible whatever went wrong in terms of the myth. For the Navajos, treatment takes the form of a healing ritual; we have the various types of individual, group, and family therapy. Rituals, especially leave-taking rituals, can be a particularly effective form of treatment as an adjunct to directive types of therapy.

Therapy is a secular activity. Sometimes the therapeutic myth can take on religious content within this context. Whether the myth is secular or religious, it is always essential for the success of the therapy that it is compatible with the client's experience and that it is meaningful, both for the client and for the therapist. The myth must be able to serve as a symbolic context for the client's complaints and symptoms and it must offer a link to the ritual so that it can provide for correction or transformation. In this we must always be keenly aware that a ritual works not only because it is a ritual, but primarily because it acts as a *vehicle*, as a suitable framework for the necessary processes of change.

3

Symbols in Leave-Taking Rituals

Onno van der Hart

Leave-taking rituals revolve around the fact that the client, in taking leave of a symbol, also takes leave of what it symbolizes: a certain relationship, feelings for a person or a situation. The ritual is a form of *make believe*, so to speak. This chapter is an attempt to show how "pretending" can be just as effective as "really doing," how symbolic leave-taking can be genuine leave-taking. First, two examples of actual cases are described. This is followed by a general indication of the state of mind during the execution of a ritual. Then, several aspects of symbols and symbolic actions are covered, including the concept of symbolic identification and the principles of similarity and contiguity which are the basis of the formal relation between the symbol and what it symbolizes. The view of leave-taking rituals expounded here is compared and contrasted to a view in which the concept *cue conditioning* plays a main role. Lastly, attention is devoted to possible harmful effects of leave-taking rituals.

Examples

Mrs. Jansen, 48, a divorcée, carries out a leave-taking ritual (in the presence of her therapist) to rid herself of her constant preoccupation with the past.* She had a terrible childhood followed by two broken

---

*This therapy was done by Jos Ebbers. This example and the next one are described in more detail in Van der Hart and Ebbers (1981).

marriages in which excessive drinking and violence by the husbands played a major role.

Availing himself of the fact that she is a practicing Catholic, the therapist asks Mrs. Jansen to make fourteen drawings of the most important moments in her life, corresponding to the fourteen stations of the cross. In this way she can once again bear witness to her life. When each drawing is finished, she can talk with the therapist about the thoughts and feelings which were aroused in her by the making of the drawing. After she has made all fourteen, the therapist wants to discuss with her how she can take leave of her martyrdom in a symbolic way.

Mrs. Jansen accepts the therapist's suggestion, but thinks that fourteen drawings will be too great a burden for her. The next time, when she tells how much pain the first drawing caused her and that she can never go through this fourteen times, the therapist agrees. He then suggests that she make four drawings, corresponding with the four evangelists who each had a message.

After she has made four drawings, the therapist discusses with Mrs. Jansen what they symbolize and how she can take leave of them. She feels it would be best to burn them, along with some letters, books, and pictures. The burning takes place out-of-doors, in the presence of the therapist. At first the books do not seem to want to catch fire, which makes her despair about the success of the ritual. But when finally everything is burned after all, she burries the remains there. At home, a very saddened Mrs. Jansen goes through the whole ritual once more with the therapist. She tells him that, while she was burning the symbols, she quite spontaneously saw many images before her of important events in her life. After the therapist leaves, she carries out a cleansing ritual, and then goes to eat with a friend.

In the period after the leave-taking ritual, Mrs. Jansen is considerably more cheerful than before. She makes more contacts with other people and is very busy building up a new life. She does encounter difficulties, but she learns to get along with them better and better. Three months after the ritual, the therapy is terminated. After this she has very occasional talks with the therapist.

Marga, 24, is a single young woman who was referred by her physician for nervousness, depression, and strong feelings of hate. For four years she had lived with Henk, who repeatedly abused and raped her. She also had good times with him, but the physical violence became more and more dominant.

One of the first interventions by the therapist is to suggest to Marga that she write Henk a "continuous leave-taking letter" (Rubinstein, 1977; Van der Hart, 1983a), a letter in which she puts down what is on her mind each day. She need not actually mail it, but she ought to carry out a final ceremony with it.

After a few weeks of writing, Marga sometimes feels somewhat relieved and even a little happy. But, to her chagrin, she does not seem to be able to rid herself of the "ghost" of Henk.

The therapist asks her if the ring she is wearing on her finger was a present from Henk. Marga says it was. The therapist suspects that this ring symbolizes the sexual relationship between the two, and that Marga has not been able to break it off entirely in her mind.

The therapist talks about carrying out a leave-taking ritual, in which Marga not only ought to destroy her continuous letter, but other symbols of the relationship with Henk as well (such as this ring). The idea appeals to Marga. Together they discuss the form the leave-taking ritual should take.

On the day the ritual is to be carried out, Marga arrives with a bag of odds and ends and a bag full of tools. She and the therapist go to a quiet place, where she smashes the ring flat, breaks some other things, tosses it all onto one big pile and sets it on fire.

Marga gazes at the fire a long time. Then she asks the therapist to go back with her. On the way back, she says, "It's like coming from a funeral!" In the therapist's office she starts to cry—for the first time with someone else present. After twenty minutes she says that it surprised her that "those dead things" still meant so much to her. She thinks it is a little frightening that she saw Henk himself burning with all the other things. Nevertheless, it had gratified her: "Just what he deserved." When she goes back home, Marga takes a bath. She throws away the clothes she wore during the ritual. That evening she goes out to eat with a friend.

After carrying out the ritual, Marga feels more and more distance from Henk and the terrible episodes with him. She is no longer depressed and she develops contacts with several nice people. After four individual talks over a period of two months, she goes into group therapy. This therapy will deal with problems in relationships in the family she was raised in.

Rituals and trance

While Mrs. Jansen concentrated on burning the symbols which represented her tragic past, she spontaneously saw all kinds of images of important events from her life. She realized later, she said, that she had also taken leave of those events.

Seeing or hallucinating those images was a result of the fact that Mrs. Jansen was really absorbed in the execution of her task. In association with the goal of the ritual, the leave-taking, spontaneous processes took place in her imagination which were of assistance in achieving that goal.

With Marga, too, similar processes occurred. Mrs. Jansen and Marga were in a *trance*, an altered state of consciousness, described by Erickson & Rossi (1979, p. 2) as "a period during which patients are able to break out of their limited frameworks and belief systems so they can experience other patterns of functioning within themselves."

Not only does this altered state of consciousness play a role in the final ceremony, but in the preparatory period of the ritual as well (cf. Steens, 1982; Van der Hart, 1983b). For instance, a person can start on the continuous letter fairly uninspired, while at a later stage the writing takes on a more autonomous nature: the client no longer directs the contents, but follows whatever enters his or her mind. Spontaneous emotional and physical reactions occur, such as crying and headaches that come on and go away again. In dreams, too, this process of taking leave is continued.

Perhaps the basis of the trance is that the client is concentrated on the execution of the task and on its goal. The stronger this concentration is, the more easily autonomous, or unconscious, mental activities are set in motion which help the client to work through the process of leave-taking.

The assumption has repeatedly been expressed in the literature that in a state of trance, the functioning of the right half of the brain is dominant. The function of the right hemisphere is spatial and tonal perception; it is specialized in recognizing patterns and in synthesizing thoughts, and it regulates analogical forms of communication. The left hemisphere is specialized in language and in linear, analytical thought (cf. Bandler & Grinder, 1975; Erickson et al., 1976; Lex, 1979; Watzlawick, 1978). We need not go into this any further. But it will become clear below that the analogical manner of information processing characteristic of the right hemisphere is vital in carrying out leave-taking rituals.

Symbols and symbolic actions

Turner (1967, p. 19) calls a symbol "the smallest unit of ritual behavior which still retains the specific properties of ritual behavior."

Turner is somewhat vague here: he does not distinguish between symbol and symbolic action. It is a symbolic action which is the smallest unit of a ritual. In this context we restrict the definition of a symbolic action to: the manipulation of a symbol. Skorupski (1976, p. 135) gives a formal definition:

> Some form of change is produced in an object, *s*, which is taken as standing for, or "re-presenting," the goal object, *g*. So, *s* "is" *g*. Therefore the same change is produced in *g*.

A symbolic action is an *analogical* action. The way in which one treats a symbol is analogical to the way in which one would treat what it symbolizes. Cherishing symbols means cherishing the link with a person: dusting off the picture each day, being constantly preoccupied with the crib and the clothes of a dead baby, setting the table for someone who is no longer there. In short, symbolic action is make believe.

In this chapter, the most important example of this is the final ceremony of a leave-taking ritual: parting with (burying, throwing into the sea) objects which symbolize the relationship with someone means taking leave of him or her.

From the foregoing it will be clear that a symbol is a thing that refers to something other than itself. More than that, it replaces what it symbolizes, it substitutes for it (Skorupski, 1976). It represents it and makes it tangible. It often symbolizes something immaterial; for instance, a personal relationship, or the feelings for and perceptions of someone else. What it symbolizes, according to Beattie (1964), is generally affectively charged. One tends to accord the same affective charge to the symbol. As Marga remarked after the execution of her leave-taking ritual, it surprised her how much "those dead things still meant to her."

Ritual symbols are condensed symbols: they refer to more than one subject. And besides they can easily take on or evoke new meanings. "The image, the form, is there concretely before us, and it can thus expand, evoking within the prepared viewer a whole complex of abstract, intuitive notions or states of being—qualities, associations and relationships which cannot be described or defined but only experienced" (Lawlor, 1978). If the sight of a symbol alone can bring this about, how much more will that be the case when changes take place in such a symbol. In Mailer (1980, p. 1017/8) we find the example of a young woman who had not been able to mourn the violent death of her friend adequately. A few months after his death, she is sitting in the kitchen drinking coffee with a friend. As she reaches to pick something up from the table, her hand suddenly looks strange to her. She sees that the ring of Osiris, which she got from her friend, is broken. She has had herself under control all that time, but now she feels so much pain that she has to sob. She has not cried so hard in ages. Mailer describes the effect of this experience as follows: "She was not sure there was any such thing any more as Gary (. . .) He was a lot out of her mind. He might really be dead." What occurred spontaneously in this example is achieved purposely and in a structured manner in therapeutic leave-taking rituals.

Symbolic identification

The essence of symbolic identification seems to me to be that symbols are the outward forms of subjective experiences and states of consciousness. It is not simply the equation of symbol to person or event.

Tylor (1878, 1964; cf. Skorupski, 1976) says, on the other hand: ". . . the symbol substitutes for the thing symbolized." According to Tylor, if symbolic identification takes place, the one is equated with the other. Sticking pins in the picture of a man would make the man sick, according to this principle; burying pictures or souvenirs of the person from whom one is taking leave would then imply the burial of that person.

Sometimes it does seem that the client experiences it like this. For instance, Marga, at the ceremony with the symbols of her relationship to her ex-friend, not only saw those objects burning, but also her ex-friend. And yet she knew at the same time, as she said later, "that it wasn't him."

To my mind, symbols are inseparably bound up (or must be identified) with the feelings and thoughts fostered by the client about the person or event. The actions which transform the symbols run parallel with changes in the client's experience. They evoke new experiences and at the same time give form to them. They are models *for* and *of* those experiences (cf. Geertz, 1973, p. 94).

An example will illustrate this: a young woman has been hesitating for a long time about breaking her engagement. At a certain point she is walking across a bridge. She stands still, stares over the water. She takes off her engagement ring, flings it into the water, and knows that this has irrevocably put an end to the relationship with her fiancé.

Choosing symbols

A list of symbols often used in therapeutic leave-taking rituals would include: wedding rings, letters, pieces of furniture, pictures, all kinds of presents, articles of clothing (Van der Hart, 1983a, p. 118). All these objects were in one way or another suitable to symbolize the relationship with the person in question and are therefore called *key symbols*. They are frequently objects which belonged to the deceased person, and they are cherished after his death or departure.

Jones (1967) points out the importance nearly all mourners attach to an object that calls the deceased to mind. And Pollock (1961) remarks that old letters, souvenirs, portraits, eyeglasses, locks of hair, clothing, and other intimate possessions are treated as continual reminders of the existence of one who is no longer there. In Pollock's view, this is an expression of the denial of the loss.

Volkan observed how mourners attribute magic powers to certain material reminders: thus endowed, these objects maintain their contact with the person they have lost (Volkan, 1970, 1972, 1981). Volkan (1972) terms them *linking objects*. In his study of "pathological mourning" and its psychodynamic treatment (Volkan, 1981), he devotes attention to the way in which people with mourning complications deal with these symbols.

The survivor selects the key symbol of the person who was dear to him soon after his death. Rather than using the object for its intended purpose (for instance, using a camera to take pictures), he puts it away in a safe place, generally out of sight. He can go for a long time without seeing the symbol, but he must know for certain that it is there. Volkan mentions the example of the patient who kept such an object in his car. After an accident, he went to great lengths to retrieve it from the wreckage; it was the only thing he saved. The mourner might also institute a rite—we could call it a substantiation ritual—by taking out the object from time to time and giving free rein to thoughts, imaginings, and feelings that have no place in reality.

Among the various sorts of objects Volkan encountered in his practice, there is one that deserves special mention: something that was simply there when the mourner first heard of the death or last saw the body. Volkan calls this a *last minute object*. One of his examples is a man who was just about to play his favorite records when he was informed by telephone that his half-brother had drowned. The records became his last minute objects.

Although Volkan does not say so, sometimes the grave of the deceased can act as a key symbol or linking object. Or it might be some other place, such as the hospital where the person in question died (cf. chapter 2). And, as the examples in this chapter have shown, key symbols are used not only for a deceased person, but for a person from whom one has been divorced or with whom a relationship has been terminated, as well.

We can distinguish two formal principles on the basis of which these objects are bound up with the person from whom leave is being taken, and therefore can act as key symbols for the relationship.

a. The principle of similarity. The picture of the ex-husband or ex-wife, the bust of the dead daughter, the drawing of a difficult episode in the past are all symbols which bear a resemblance to what they symbolize. We might call these symbols *icons* (cf. Firth, 1973). The resemblance may be very striking, as is the case with the wooden bust of a child. It may involve only one quality which the symbol and what it symbolizes have in common: a cactus can represent someone with a somewhat prickly nature, and the drawing of a jail can symbolize being trapped in a relationship. The principle of similarity also plays a role in our use of language. It is the basis of *metaphors*.

b. The principle of contiguity. Articles of clothing, rings, furniture, are symbols which are bound up with what they symbolize on the principle of contiguity. Everything that in one way or another derives from the person or has been in contact with him or her can act as a symbol for the relationship with him or her. Rosner provides an interesting example involving her ex-lover: "He went back to his wife. I didn't shed a single tear when we said goodbye, which is not at all like me. A few days later I found a hair on my pillow, one of *his* hairs. His hair was dark but it was thinning and there were a lot of white ones, too. That hair unleashed my tears. I cried and cried, until I realized that it wasn't one of his hairs at all, but one of my cat's" (Bibeb, 1984, p. 7). The principle of contiguity also occurs in our use of language: it is the basis of *metonyomy*, a "figure of speech consisting of the use of the name of one thing for that of another of which it is an attribute or with which it is associated (as in lands belonging to the *crown*)" (Webster's Seventh New Collegiate Dictionary, 1976).

In general, both principles perform the same function. Both belong to the same class of relations: that of symbolic identification.

Similarity and contiguity in symbolic actions

Symbolic actions were defined as analogical actions. The way in which the symbol is dealt with is analogical to the way in which what is symbolizes can be dealt with. We can say that the principle of similarity is the basis of the actions. Tearing up, burning, burying pictures or letters has the quality of *parting with, taking leave* in common with what goes on in the client's perception of the person or event. At night in bed, hugging the pillow where someone used to sleep who is no longer there resembles (and gives expression to) the need to be closer to him or her.

The principle of similarity is dominant in leave-taking rituals, but the principle of contiguity can be applied in them as well, often on a *pars pro toto* principle: whatever affects a part of a whole also influences the whole. (Watzlawick (1978) uses the *pars pro toto* principle in another way. He uses it to mean the immediate recognition (perception) of a whole on the basis of only one characteristic part.) A widow still had so many reminders of her deceased husband that she carried out a burial ritual with only a few of them. She put the rest out with the garbage. On the basis of the *pars pro toto* principle, she still found that she had taken a worthy leave of him like this.

The principle of similarity is dominant in the Proëlla on the French island of Ouessant. The following quotation from a 14th-century Chinese novel demonstrates that this was also the case, in certain circumstances, in quite another culture:

> Tung Cho's followers (. . .) did not forget their leader. They sought his corpse for burial, but only a few fragments were discoverable. Then they graved an image of fragrant wood in his likeness, laid that out in a princely coffin for burial. They selected Meiwu for his tomb and, having found an auspicious day, conveyed the coffin thither. (Lo Kuan-Chung, 1959, p. 92).

Discussion

1. This chapter focused on the symbolic nature of therapeutic rituals. The main point is that, in these rituals, the principle of symbolic identification operates. Rosenblatt et al. (1976) give a supplementary inter-

pretation of comparable traditional customs, the *tie-breaking customs*. These customs, part of mourning rituals, involve destroying, giving away, or temporarily setting aside personal possessions of the deceased, observing a taboo on the name of the deceased, and moving (p. 68).

In a comparatively lasting relationship, such as a marriage, various modes of conduct suitable to the relationship are associated with stimuli from the surroundings of the relationship. This phenomenon is called *cue conditioning*. After a death or another form of separation, the relationship must be regarded as ended and one must develop new patterns of behavior. The stimuli make it more difficult for change to take place, because they evoke old dispositions. *Tie-breaking customs* are intended to remove or to change the stimuli or *cues*, and thus to facilitate change (p. 67/8). Rosenblatt et al. feel these customs are primarily important if the person left behind were to build up a new relationship: the reminders of the previous marriage would otherwise interfere with this.

We have seen this happen more than once in therapy. Marga, after writing a continuous leave-taking letter, remarked that she still had not gotten rid of the "ghost" of her ex-friend. It was as if he was still with her in the house. Everything he had done there—built-ins, wall paper, painting, everything he had given her or made for her, still made Marga think of him. Her leave-taking ritual had to include parting with most of these reminders and refurnishing her house. Another example is the case of a young woman who had been treated by her physician—without success—in her mourning for the death of her father, the loss of her friend, and the abortion she had had. During a house call the doctor discovered the stimulus, which was also the chief symbol, that stood in the way of her further development: "In the corner of the room there stood a crib all made up, intended for her baby that had never been born" (Kemeling, 1979).

Besides their symbolic function, therapeutic leave-taking rituals can also perform the function described by Rosenblatt et al. But rituals have also been carried out in therapy in which this function was not present. The client had gotten stuck in a mourning process, but material reminders of the relationship no longer existed. He created them himself—for example, by writing a leave-taking letter or making a drawing—or went to a lot of trouble to find something after all.

2. Making symbols for a leave-taking ritual as opposed to the use of existing symbols has another important aspect that deserves attention. We might wonder whether the destruction of objects which belonged to or came from the person in question would not produce guilt feelings.

It would theoretically be possible for the client to feel that he destroyed the person symbolically, on the *pars pro toto* principle. Marga, for instance, "saw" her ex-friend burning, instead of letters and pictures. Might she not be haunted by such an image later? In her case, nothing of the kind became apparent in a follow-up talk two years after the ritual.

The way in which a leave-taking ritual continues working depends on the intention with which it was carried out (cf. Van der Hart, 1983a, p. 139). Existing symbols which are the outward forms of inner experiences can be used to take leave in a dignified, respectful way from someone, not to take revenge on a person. This is possible if fairly extensive preparation takes place beforehand and the ritual is carried out entirely according to the agreement. A leave-taking ritual is a final ceremony, a winding up.

There are also clients to whom the idea of choosing existing objects which have to do with the relationship does not appeal. They prefer to carry out a ritual with self-made symbols: with paintings, drawings, busts, poems, letters, stories, or even a collection of shells. What they have made themselves, they want to destroy or transform. If reminders do exist of the person in question, then a decision must be made as to what will happen with them, for they can continue to act as stimuli which call up old responses.

3. The two examples of leave-taking rituals presented here both had to do with breaking off a relationship which had a highly unpleasant nature for the client. This meant that the emphasis was entirely on destroying the objects which acted as symbols of the relationship. We need not always assume that leave must be taken from each and every symbol (see Van der Hart, 1983a, p. 119). If leave must be taken of someone precious, or if a relationship had positive aspects, it may be very important to the client that some objects be kept as keepsakes. No matter what is done with the key symbols, the goal is always to help the client withdraw his or her emotional attachment from the person who is no longer there, thus making it possible to reinvest emotions back into new relationships (cf. Worden, 1982).

PART II
APPLICATIONS

4

Freed from Oppressive Bonds

Jos Ebbers

Many people seek help for complaints or difficulties which are related to unresolved grief. The therapist can help them design and carry out a leave-taking ritual or some other form of grief therapy. The choice of a ritual or some other approach depends not only on characteristics of the client. The personal preference of the therapist and the circumstances in which he or she works also play a large role. A social psychiatric counseling center, for instance, with its heavy case load, offers almost no leeway for intensive regrief therapy as propagated by Ramsay.

In this chapter I would first like to describe how my personal background influenced my choice to design and to prescribe therapeutic rituals in appropriate situations. This is followed by an example. It is particularly interesting that the ritual not only helps the client to work through the separation from his wife and children, but also helps him to cope with several painful events from his childhood.

Personal background

I was raised a Catholic and was an altar boy for years. The Catholic church has been simplified in many respects, but I remember clearly the many rituals and symbols from my time as an altar boy and later, too, at seminary. What went on during masses and funerals made a deep impression on me. I have seen and felt what the church rites and symbols mean to people, and how they are influenced by them, particularly emotionally. Later I could not pass off these symbols and rituals as empty and meaningless, but neither could I allot them a role in my private life and in my work.

Stories I read or heard about therapeutic rituals appealed to me, they elicited a response. My earlier experiences were fertile ground on which my own wish to work with rituals in therapy could grow. Now, when I develop a ritual with a client, I often see before me images of the church services: the many candles and flowers, and the "proselytizing" on All Souls' Day. Sometimes, when I think back to the funeral services I attended as an altar boy, I can practically smell the incense. If I am present when a therapeutic ritual is carried out, I see images of the funerals and the accompanying rites which I so often went through. While the form of a therapeutic ritual differs from that of a church rite, what strikes me is how strong the resemblance is in the perception of those involved. People were emotional and very moved during the funeral service and the burial, but afterwards, at the reception, a sort of calm prevailed. Sometimes they even joked. It was as if most of the leave-taking had already been accomplished. I have come across a similar process in leave-taking rituals in therapy.

The idea of constructing a ritual together with a client also had another appeal to me. As a psychotherapist I was trained in directive forms of therapy (cf. Van der Velden, 1977, 1980). I also prefer to employ them because they call so directly on the therapist's creativity. Directive therapy also regularly requires creativity on the part of the client. The same is definitely true in developing leave-taking rituals. This involves finding a form in which the client can work through and take leave of events from the past in his own unique way.

In short, my earlier experiences with traditional church rites and symbols and my practical experience with forms of directive therapy made the idea of employing rituals in therapy very attractive to me. On the one hand, there was something very familiar about it, and on the other hand, it was very adventurous.

Client compatibility

Of course the question of rituals may not simply be decided by the therapist's tastes. In the first place, the ritual must answer to the complaints or difficulties of the client and to the way in which he perceives his situation. A leave-taking ritual would seem to be indicated if the complaints can be described in terms of a transition which was poorly made or not completed, and the client's word choice will reflect this. Formulations characteristic of such a situation would be:

> "I carry a heavy burden on my shoulders; I would like to lay it down."
> "Somehow I haven't really buried my father yet."
> "My life up to now has been one bad fairy tale that just hasn't ended yet."
> "If only I could give all these troubles back to the past."

In general, the therapist is wise if he conforms to the client's use of language. This is of essential importance when he makes the suggestion to develop a ritual. The idea of making a transition over again with the help of a ritual must come across to the client as somehow natural. If the client, too, has an affinity with religious or secular rituals and symbols, there is a good chance that the therapist's suggestion will appeal to him. After hearing the function of rituals explained, the client often indicates that he sees a possible manner of resolving his problems. Reading material about therapeutic rituals can also motivate the client to solve his problems in a similar manner.

The following example shows how the client's story inspires the therapist to suggest a ritual and how he conforms to the client's word choice. It puts some stress on motivating the client and it makes clear how the design of a ritual concerns both of them.

The example

Jan Kok was a 45-year-old man who had been under treatment by various specialists for headaches and backaches for several years. But the treatment had not had the desired result. Jan was also bothered by depressions which he felt were inexplicable. They regularly prevented him from performing his tasks properly at the company where he worked. Besides, he could no longer keep his mind on his work. After having a talk with Jan, his physician referred him for psychotherapy.

Case history

Jan comes from a family of four children in which father was a factory worker and mother brought up the children. The war years were difficult for this family. Apart from this, there were many tensions between the two parents as a result of which Jan often fled the house. His upbringing was more or less taken over by his friends on the street. His school marks were poor, but because of the pressure his parents exerted on him, he managed to obtain his high school diploma.

After he had been working a while, he was drafted. Here he acquired many friends and he went out regularly. Having tasted this freedom, he could not readjust to the rules at home and he went to live alone. He was able to provide for himself with his job as a bank clerk. He soon met Marja, and they started dating. A few years later they got married.

According to Jan, the first years of their marriage went well, but after the birth of their child their relationship worsened. Jan felt that Marja paid too little attention to him; Marja was disappointed because he was not on the way to becoming a big businessman as she had hoped. They fought constantly. According to Jan, they had a love-hate relationship. Marja became pregnant with a second child, leading to more tensions. Five days after the birth of this child, Jan made his decision and left his wife and children.

After that he had a very difficult time, developed physical complaints, and felt very guilty because of having left his children in the lurch. He did try to get back in touch with Marja, to conclude a visiting arrangement, but because they worked at cross-purposes, and Marja had a new boyfriend she had met shortly after the divorce, nothing came of it. When Jan came in for therapy a few years after their divorce, he still could not see his children.

The treatment

The mental health center Jan came to started out by working on his psychosomatic complaints. He was put in a group of people with similar complaints. Here he learned to exert some influence on his symptoms, but it offered no solution for his depressions. Assertiveness training also had little effect. A few months after this he asked for individual therapy.

In one of the first individual talks, he said that the rash way he had left his family haunted him. It allowed him no peace of mind. He kept asking himself how things could have gone so far. His worrying did not solve anything, it only gave him constant headaches. He had consulted all kinds of psychology books to find an answer, but he never found what he was looking for.

During the talks, Jan started to become aware of the fact that his psychosomatic complaints, his problems at work, and his difficulty in making social contacts were related to an unresolved past: the traumatic leaving of his wife and children, his difficult marriage, and the problems at home earlier.

The therapist suspected that Jan would benefit by a leave-taking ritual in which he could work through and leave behind him various events from the past. But the time was not yet ripe to suggest it. The first step would have to be agreeing with Jan's view that he so strongly felt his past to be chaos.

The therapist suggested that Jan write an autobiography, to put some order into his life story. In order that Jan be able to relive episodes from the past as vividly as possible in an emotional respect, it was suggested that he visit several places that played an important part in his autobiography. The significance the writing and the visits were later to take on for him is shown by the end of his autobiography:

> It was a historic excursion which was to prove extremely discomfiting and disconcerting, because it evoked many negative feelings and emotions. I will have to break old shackles and heal still open wounds. Life is a negative memory, a painful failure; it is very hard to shut it out of my mind. It gives me the strong feeling that I am too maladjusted and obstinate to be able to get along positively with myself and with others. Why do I punish myself like this? When will I learn either to carry the cross or to put it down?

Introducing the ritual

At the next session Jan told what he had gone through during the writing and the visits and he showed the therapist his autobiography. The therapist felt that the time was now ripe for a ritual. In his autobiography, Jan gave a clear picture of the difficult transitions he had had to make.

He had left his parental home too hastily. He had also left his wife and children too hastily; the divorce was a poorly made transition. Jan still lived in a sort of historic present tense; he was incapable of building up a life of his own with which he could feel satisfied. He did not yet have any idea how to orient himself toward the future.

The therapist introduced the idea of a ritual and used Jan's own words as much as possible. "When we look at the course of someone's life, we can distinguish several important events such as birth, marriage, and death. These are important transitions to which people must give great care and attention. These transitions are often ritualized, which gives them the special attention they need. But so many people just don't seem to allow themselves the time for them. Take you, it seems like you are still carrying all kinds of negative feelings from the past like a burden on your shoulders. The physical pain constantly reminds you that you still have not been able to free yourself from the oppressive bonds of the past. Do you think that the time is now ripe to take leave of the negative feelings and to conclude your past by means of a ritual?" Jan felt that the time was ripe for it. He had carried his heavy burden long enough, he said.

After this the therapist talked a little about the function of symbols and rituals and about the forms a leave-taking ritual might take. He suggested that Jan write down the negative experiences from his youth and his marriage for one last time, and in this manner arrive at as good a conclusion of the past as possible. Then, with the help of the leave-taking ritual, he would be able to part with the negative experiences set down on paper and the symbols associated with them. If Jan were to carry out the ritual, the therapist wanted to suggest writing in the form of the "continuous letter" (Rubinstein, 1977). The therapist's account appealed to Jan; he said he would like to set to work in that way. The therapist advised him not to decide right away, but first to think things over well once more.

At the next session Jan said he wanted to carry out a ritual. He wanted to write his story on recycled paper. The paper would symbolize his life: even if it has been written on and crumpled up, it can be reprocessed and used once again.

To expedite Jan's execution of the ritual, the therapist advised him to choose a place in his house where he would be able to work on his leave-taking letters without being disturbed. Jan thought his own study would be the most suitable place.

So that Jan would quickly get into the right mood during his writing sessions, it was agreed that he would create or invent a symbol to represent his life. Symbols can fulfil the same function for a leave-taking ritual as photographs do for a vacation. When you look at the pictures later, you can relive the same emotions you had on the vacation. It is like pretending to be on vacation again.

It was also agreed that the therapist would call up the medical officer of Jan's company to suggest that he not call Jan in for a checkup for the duration of the ritual. It seemed to the therapist that it would be better if the whole process were not disturbed by Jan's resuming work. The medical officer complied.

At the next session Jan said he had not yet started writing. He did show some objects he had made which symbolized the past, the present, and the future to him. A *cross* symbolized his burden from the past. A *picture* of him looking at himself in the mirror stood for the present. "Because of my past, I don't dare to look myself in the face," was a common remark of his. For the future he had chosen a *drawing* with the text "faith—hope—charity": faith, hope, and charity he needed to have a firm basis in the future.

Jan and the therapist agreed that he would write only in the evenings between seven and nine. He felt best at this time of day. He did not yet know to whom he would address himself in his letters. He just wanted to sit down at the agreed time and wait and see who came into his thoughts.

For seven weeks Jan wrote about his past experiences evening after evening. In his letters to his parents, he told them they had paid too little attention to him and that he always had to prove himself to them. In the letters to his wife, he described how he had arrived at his decision to leave her and the children. To the children he wrote how he lived with his guilt and that he hoped they would understand when they grew up.

During the first weeks his depressions got worse and he received medicinal support for the most difficult moments. All the while he was writing there were regular talks to discuss his experiences. At these sessions it was also discussed how he wanted to part with his leave-taking letters and the symbols he had made. The therapist told him how other clients had performed their leave-taking rituals. The more his letters progressed, the stronger he felt he was becoming and the stronger his need became to conclude the ritual and his past.

The therapist and Jan agreed that on the evening before the ritual he would lay out all the things he wanted to take leave of. He would also put together in one place all the objects he wanted to keep, so that after the leave-taking ritual he could assign them new places in his home. The next morning he would drive to the North Sea and throw the hand-written pages one by one into the water. This would be a symbolic way of giving his heavy load from the past and his guilt back to nature, so that he would be liberated and could get down to work on a new future. After this, he would throw into the water the cross he had made (symbol of the past) and the picture of him looking at himself (symbol of the present). The symbol of the future, the drawing with the text "faith—hope—charity" he wanted to take home again to give it a place of its own.

The desirability of a ritual cleansing to mark the end of the leave-taking ritual was discussed with Jan. At the therapist's advice he would take a shower at home after the ritual, and then he would throw out his underclothes.

After these acts, attention would again be directed toward the present and the future. To celebrate his new state and the success of the therapy, he would fix himself a festive meal. He preferred to eat it alone, for in reality he was alone. But after this he would go and have a drink to the special occasion with a neighbor woman who was informed about the entire process.

Jan carried out the ritual according to the plan. Later he said that he had felt strange, confused, and abstracted on his way to the sea. When he got there, he waded into the water to carry out the acts as agreed. This took about half an hour. After he had seen everything disappear in the waves, he felt that his tenseness and his uneasiness had disappeared. He felt like he was floating. He later described this state as follows: "It was as if the power of the mighty sea surged into me." On his way to the sea and during the ritual, Jan seems to have been in an altered state of consciousness, a trance, corresponding to the state of mind of a client in hypnotherapy (cf. chapter 3).

After that he had driven home to carry out the cleansing ritual, a good shower. There he had thrown out his underclothes. After the shower, he prepared and ate the dinner, and then went over to his neighbor's for the drink. He talked the whole ritual over with her and gave her a present to show his appreciation for her moral support during the ritual.

After that he went home to put the pictures of his children, a few childhood photographs, and a wooden box (which reminded him of his marriage) in their new places. He realized that these symbols had acquired a different emotional value.

Aftermath

The first few weeks after the ritual Jan and the therapist still saw each other regularly. He went on feeling relaxed, but the most important realization was that he no longer needed to take on so much. Driven by the idea that he still had so much to do, before the ritual he had scarcely been able to find time to relax. He got in touch with the medical officer about going back to work. His return to work caused many difficulties, because a reorganization had taken place in the company. The personnel manager suggested that he simply continue drawing sickness benefits. John put up a strong resistance to this.

The therapy sessions were concluded four weeks after the end of the ritual. John told the therapist that he would keep him informed of developments. In his last letter, four months after the ritual, he wrote that he still felt very good and that he had succeeded in keeping his own job in the company. He had not yet been able to build up a circle of friends, but he did not yet feel much need of it. Jan showed that his self-confidence had increased. He considered himself more capable of tackling problems in his life constructively.

In conclusion

The example described here illustrates how leave-taking rituals can help people to reexperience poorly made transitions from the past and to conclude them successfully. A leave-taking ritual is an entity of symbolic acts. If the acts are to be effective, they must have a certain attraction for the client, and the symbols to be used must have special significance for him or her. The example described here shows this very well.

We might wonder whether a form of family therapy—the client with his parents or the client with his ex-wife and the children—would not have been more appropriate. Would it not have been preferable to talk things over directly with the others involved? In the early stages of individual therapy the client had indicated that he did not want to talk with his parents. Attempts to talk with his ex-wife had proved unsuccessful. For this reason he had no confidence that things would turn out differently in a therapeutic setting.

The client wanted to come to terms with himself. For him, a leave-taking ritual was the appropriate framework. In this way he could address himself to his parents, his ex-wife, and his children in a symbolic manner. The therapist had suggested he actually send the letters, or at least parts of them, but he had not been willing. In the letter to his ex-wife, he indicated that he wanted no more contact at all with her. He gave symbolic expression to this wish by tearing up the letter and throwing it into the sea.

A Consuming Fire

F. J. van Tienen

The basis of a good therapy lies in the fact that the therapist is able to accommodate in it the experience of the client. If clients describe the situation that is troubling them in terms of their religious experience, then it is a good idea for therapists to take them up on this (cf. chapter 2). Clergymen are in the fortunate situation that those who come to them for help can also address them, implicitly or explicitly, on this religious dimension, and they are entitled to an answer on this aspect.

This chapter describes the contact I had as a clergyman with a man who was referred for serious mourning problems (in which guilt feelings played a large role). He did not practice his religion, but had been raised in the Dutch Reformed church. In keeping with the way in which the client spoke about his difficulties, the initial conversations were of a secular, therapeutic nature. At a later stage the religious dimension came more to the forefront; sin and forgiveness became key concepts which opened the way to jointly developing and carrying out a healing ritual in a religious context.

The client

Wim Jansen, 34 years old, was very depressed when he first came to see me. His wife, Marianne, had died 16 months before of cancer which had started as breast cancer. He was left alone—their marriage had been childless—and he had not been able to work through this loss. Nearly a year earlier, he had been admitted to the psychiatric ward of a general hospital for an attempted suicide with an overdose of sleeping pills, and he had been discharged after two weeks. His employer was very understanding of his situation; he had made an agreement with him that Wim could come to work whenever he wanted. His job would be there for him. The couple next door usually took care of his meals and clothes and the housecleaning. When they saw that not a single positive development took place in Wim's situation, and felt that it was becoming high time that something did, they managed to motivate him to seek therapeutic help. He did it to please them—he did not see the point of it for himself.

The conversations

Wim started out by saying that there was no point in talking. He wanted to die. His life had no meaning at all any more. At home, the ghost of his deceased wife was still so compellingly present that he could not get around his guilt in her death. Later in the session, Wim said very sadly that he not only felt guilty about the death of his wife, but also about the abortion that she had had. At first he had been strongly against it, but finally he had agreed to it. At the end of the talk, Wim agreed to my suggestion to talk about his experiences with Marianne a few times.

In the course of a few conversations, it became clearer clearer to Wim how his wife had kept him on a leash in a very charming way, and how he had always accepted it. He learned to express what he had continually concealed from her, his irritations and his anger. He once again began to see a few extra-marital adventures of his which were laden with guilt feelings as he had seen them when Marianne was still alive: attempts to get a little breathing space outside of the reach of Mother Marianne. The depression gradually turned into grief. Instead of being weighed down by his misery, he could look it in the eye, so to speak. The world had not collapsed, but he had lost his wife: his wife, who was sweet but dominating; who had taste, but could not handle money; who, like himself, could romp and play with children, but who had twice had an abortion; who was sexy, but who had a sort of coolness he did not understand; who guarded over his health, but refused angrily to go to the doctor whenever he brought up the lumps in her breasts. His depression tapered down to manageable grief for the loss of a real person.

Things did not go so easily with his guilt feelings. They became less unwieldy, but turned out to have deep roots. Wim did not practice his religion, although he had been brought up Dutch Reformed. I therefore hesitated to take the step from guilt feelings to awareness of sin. I knew that awareness of sin is not so much a religious and ecclesiastical category as a religious dynamic, a common human given. I rationalized my hesitation by saying to myself that I did not know what the words "sin" and "forgiveness" meant in his background, nor what feelings they would evoke in him.

During the next two conversations nothing remarkable happened, and I waited, half suspecting, half knowing that my note, "we have reached a level of assimilation," was an escape.

In our next talk Wim took the initiative: "I thought over everything I did wrong, and I made a list of it." In three minutes he mentioned everything. There was a sort of repetitious monotony to the story. When he had summed up everything, it was quiet for a while. Then he said, "This is my confession." Again there was silence. Then he told me he had walked into a church last Saturday and had confessed the same thing. The priest had replied, "My son, that is a great deal of sorrow. So God has forgiven you for it." But for some reason or another, this had given him no feeling of forgiveness. From stories Wim had told me earlier, I knew that he, because of his childhood, did not have much reason to trust his fellow human beings. In the past, he had always had to "buy" affection. Two divorces and three fathers in his family had left their marks. With such a damaged father concept, how had he been able to find a workable god concept?

Wim's discontent put us before a double task. On the one hand, he had not gone through the old sacramental triad of repentance, confession, and satisfaction. It became clear to us that his confession was unsatisfactory to him because he felt it was mere lip service. On the other hand, he had no good concept of a forgiving, merciful Father that I could employ.

Wim was a man who was very expressive in his speech and thinking, who often wanted to render his actions meaningful through symbols. For instance, on her birthday, he had always given Marianne as many red roses as she was years old and had always added to them enough white ones to make 75. Then he had always said, "Honey, we'll make all of them red in the coming years." I saw a way of capitalizing on this. It might appeal very much to Wim if I were to suggest working through his guilt feelings by means of a ritual, an entity of symbolic actions. In this way he would be able to straighten things out for himself.

The preparations for the ritual

I suggested to Wim that we design for him something more tangible than that verbal confession. I told him that rituals work because they are symbolic actions; rituals are ways of taking action. The idea did appeal to him. In that same talk, I asked him what kind of father he would have been for his children. He would have been a loyal, lenient father, he said.

In the talks we had after this we read several passages from the Bible—almost archetypal stories in which Wim could easily recognize himself and the Lord as he hoped for Him. We first read the parable of the prodigal son (Luke 15: 11–32), then the reconciliation of Jesus with Peter (John 21: 1–19), and finally the story of Elijah comforted by an angel (I Kings 19: 1–18).

We talked about the ritual, too, which was gradually taking shape. I wanted to forge a link to some important remarks Wim had made earlier. In our first talks, he had said that he wanted to be burned off the face of the earth. In the course of our contact, he had transformed this into the wish that his sins with and against Marianne be burned away. I suggested to him that he should write down for once and for all everything that was troubling him. When he was through, he would take the letter to church. There I would build a large fire where he could put the letter. We would make the arrangements together.

Unexpectedly a problem arose, at least for me as a theologian. Wim wanted to put $500 in the envelope as a sort of offering of atonement. As I was raised in the firm belief that there must be a clear discrepancy between the confession and the atonement, in order to avoid even suggesting that one can buy off sins, I was unhappy with this amount of money. Apart from this, I wondered if it was advisable to allow Wim to continue his old pattern of buying affection. When we talked about my misgivings, it turned out that Wim was quite capable of rejecting the idea of correspondence between sin and reparation. At my suggestion to give the money to the mission, he announced that he had already donated that amount by bank. I don't know whether he actually did put money in the envelope. I suspect he did.

The ritual

On a certain day, five months after our first talk, Wim said he had finished writing. The ritual took place a few days later, on Sunday at six o'clock in the evening. Wim's next-door neighbors were there. In the past weeks he had kept them informed of his progress. Witnesses for the prosecution or the defense, I wondered at first. Wim saw them differently: as allies of Marianne and himself.

Before the altar I had placed a large copper holy water container filled with salt and denatured alcohol. Above it I had piled dry pin branches, in which I had hung two pieces of incense. Between the altar and the holy water container stood the burning paschal candle, symbol of the new life given by death. Only the spotlight on the large altar cross was on. I had decided not to wear any vestments because I felt I was only a distant attendant in this ritual of personal meeting.

When the four of us walked into the dim church, Wim was a little nervous. We walked forward in silence. At the altar, I read Romans 13: 11–12:

> And think, knowing the season, that now it is high time for you to awake out of sleep: for now is salvation nearer to us than when we first believed. The night is far spent, and the day is at hand: let us therefore cast off the works of darkness, and let us put on the armor of light.

Then Wim took the envelope out of his inner pocket and very calmly prayed Psalm 130:

> Out of the depths have I cried unto thee, O Lord.
> Lord, hear my voice: let thine ears be attentive to the voice of my supplications.
> If thou, Lord, shouldest mark iniquities, O Lord, who shall stand?
> But there is forgiveness with thee, that thou mayest be feared.
>
> I wait for the Lord, my soul doth wait, and in his word do I hope.
> My soul waiteth for the Lord more than they that watch for the morning: I say, more than they that watch for the morning.
> Let Israel hope in the Lord: for with the Lord there is mercy, and with him is plenteous redemption.
> And he shall redeem Israel from all his iniquities.

Hebrews 12: 28–29 was then the obvious choice:

> Wherefore we receiving a kingdom which cannot be moved,
> let us have grace, whereby we may serve God acceptably
> with reverence and godly fear:
> For our God is a consuming fire.

After that I removed the paschal candle from the standard and set fire to the alcohol. A three-foot flame. We waited until the pine boughs were crackling and the incense clouds started rising. Then Wim put his letter into the flames. We waited again until it had burned up completely.

We were all moved. I had intended to read Luke 15: 1–10, about the lost sheep and the lost drachma. I was glad that I got as far as verse 7. I never got to the drachma.

After that, we sang away our emotions in the hymn "Great God, we give thee thanks." When we walked out of the church, I saw that the ceremony had lasted 35 minutes.

As we sat drinking coffee, it was a little quiet at first, but then the tension broke and we all talked rather jubilantly. At the dinner afterwards, Wim ordered a bottle of champagne as an aperitif. "That's what my father did, too, when I was born. My mother thought it was exaggerated. But I know now what my father felt then. He was right."

Follow-up

Several years have since passed. I let Wim read this text two years after the ritual. He had no objection to publication. When he read that I suspected that he had put $500 into the envelope after all, he looked at me and laughed but said nothing. At any rate, he did not share my theological objections. I realized that we had become equals in our relationship at the moment when I was formulating my misgivings during the preparation of the ritual. He had thrown off his bonds and could stand on his own two feet.

This follow-up talk made it clear that Wim was really doing well. He had remarried and was happy in his relationship with his wife. He had long since started working full-time again.

Discussion

1. In the therapy described here, the talks started out in a more or less Rogerian fashion. In this way the client's depression could more easily develop into genuine grief. But the treatment of the guilt feelings needed more than this. Given the family background of this client, one might be inclined towards a psychoanalytical approach. But a more directive approach seemed to be indicated with this expressive man, who was also beginning to get impatient. A ritual stressing *action* was entirely appropriate; it was carried out after 15 talks. This example illustrates that the design and execution of a ritual is not a type of therapy in a class apart, but that it can be an appropriate method as part of a more comprehensive approach.

2. In chapter 2 it was indicated that it is sometimes a good idea, with religious clients, for ecclesiastical therapists to allow the secular therapeutic myth to adapt to the religious experience of the client. This is clearly what happened in the example described here. The resulting ritual had a highly religious nature as well. We may assume that this ritual not only influenced the religious experience of the client, but that it, as a symbolic process, also led to positive changes at other levels.

3. In this reconciliation ritual, we encounter in general form the structure of leave-taking rituals described in chapter 2. There was a reorganization phase, which had actually started long before the ritual was introduced. The presence of the neighbors at the ceremony in the church also lent it aspects of a reunion ritual, which gives form to a new start in life. This reunion ritual took on a more secular character at the coffee and the dinner which followed.

Forty Years On: A Study in Belated Holocaust Mourning

Sonny Herman

"Death waits for me

As eternity overtakes it." Jacques Brel

The death of a loved one leaves an emptiness that can never be wholly filled. The physical form of the loved person no longer exists. Continuities are broken. Systems, once taken for granted, are disrupted. Sources of love and attention are lost.

In various forms and shapes death comes, and only its finality is common to all. As survivors, how we cope with such loss depends on our unique circumstances, the irreparable nature of the loss, and the support or lack of it from family and friends. Though one can only lose what one believed to have possessed, loss is loss, whether factual or fantasied.

When death enters our lives we wonder how we can survive it, even whether to survive at all. At such times the attitudes of others towards us may radically change. Those who were formerly friendly and helpful may become reserved or distant, due to their own difficulty in dealing with our loss. Though there may be no lack of helpful suggestions, these may be impossible to implement without further support. Often too, letters, cards, even visits seem to have a terribly hollow ring to them.

In this chapter, in describing the mourning processes and leave-taking rituals of survivors of the Holocaust, a few of the more important therapeutic principles and techniques will be briefly outlined, and their effects illustrated through the experiences of three victims of the Holocaust. Though in some ways the losses experienced by survivors of the Holocaust are comparable to losses suffered under more natural conditions, in other ways these are quite incomparable. By comparing and contrasting them, their differences are highlighted.

Natural death and the mourning experience

From time immemorial, people have mourned their dead. Mourning is a process which, to paraphrase Freud, is meant to counteract the melancholy lurking in us all. Through this process endured hurt may be alleviated, and the danger of damage to one's self becoming permanent, avoided. Mourning is a way of paying homage to the dead, and should give comfort to the survivor. In surviving the death of a loved person, one may pass through the whole gamut of emotions, and may experience for the first time what it means to be a whole person, truly human, mortal, and time-bound. For life implies death, as death implies life. Death, the destroyer of life, is a stark reality that is never further than a heartbeat away. This knowledge quickens in some of us a longing for immortality, and in others, a desire to live life to the hilt so that death may be denied. Living on can thus become an act of confirmation of creative energy and a continuing life force and, in thus perpetuating one's life, become a sign of faithfulness to the loved, dead one.

Rituals of mourning and symbols of death serve to facilitate the survivor experience and the integration of the pain of loss into the totality of life. In one of his creations, the Dutch painter Vincent van Gogh symbolized Death as the Reaper, with a big sun and the cutting edge of the scythe. In Van Gogh's portrayal, there is little that is frightening or sad about the presence of death in life. Death is described by him as ''working in broad daylight, with a sun flooding everything with a light of pure gold'' (Van Gogh, 1958).

The Holocaust and the Jewish experience

In contrast, those who survived the death camps of the Nazi regime saw death working in mud, faeces and starvation. Van Gogh's Reaper had become the cold scythe of Mengele's curt order: "left" or "right." The smoke-filled night, the glow of blazing chimneys, the smell of burning flesh held nothing of "the light of pure gold." For the survivors of the Holocaust, the ugly Death of the concentration camps made the loss of their beloved ones who were blatantly murdered a terrifying, unintegratible experience.

Many first- and second-generation survivors of the Holocaust have been unable to mourn these dead, whose only crime was to be born Jewish; a fact which made them, by Nazi law, subject to extermination. Without corpse, grave, or funeral rite, mourning became difficult, if not impossible. After the war, most of the survivors felt an overriding need to take up their lives once more among the living, to marry quickly and raise families as a way of compensating for their cataclysmic losses. With the passing of times, however, the urge to mourn their loved ones properly and with dignity has become pressing. For some, despite the lapse of forty years, this need has not lessened but grown, fuelled by psychical energy erupting from long suppressed feeling.

Mourning therapy is indicated when normal grief channels are blocked, or when no organized structure of rituals and symbols exists to assist those in need of them. The therapy to be described here offers these survivors a chance to mourn at long last. That is, to go from painful, pathological conditions which often include deep depression, social dysfunction, and withdrawal from life, work, and interests to states of being in which a more purposeful, creative potential can be activated. The framework of this therapy is determined by my personal orientation, which is partly grounded in psychoanalytic theory and practice, partly in a rabbinical training. All my patients have in common what is known as "the survivor syndrome" or one of its variants.

The Survivor Syndrome

Lifton (1979) found that survivors of the Holocaust are in general filled with indelible and grotesque images of death, guilt, psychic numbness, and diminished capacity to feel, resulting in withdrawal, apathy, depression, and despair. He also noted their fearfulness, suspicion of counterfeit nurturance, and sense of alienation from a world that had allowed such atrocities to happen. Krystal (1968) stressed the disturbances in object relations found in such persons and the difficulties in communication of affect other than angry demandingness. Hoppe (1962) noted too the lameness of affect and chronic depression, which contained both depressive and persecutory elements. Close emotional attachments were difficult for the survivors to form when they had lost everyone and everything. Instead, they tended to regard their children as possessions meant to compensate them for what they had lost. In deep mourning for their murdered family members, their mourning process was extended, incomplete, and impaired, shorn as it was of the usual rituals and institutions usually available to work through grief and loss.

The Concentration Camp Syndrome or KZ-syndrome may be defined in the following terms (ICODO Commission, 1981):

1. diminished psychical buoyancy;
2. a feeling of chronic anxiety, sometimes bound to certain (phobic) representations, sometimes diffusely present and manifesting itself in a chronic feeling of expectant doom, sleep disturbances with nightmares and aggressive expression as efforts to keep anxiety at bay;
3. a deeply rooted feeling of lack of desire (dysphoria), with feelings of guilt, of personal unworthiness, and of unworthiness of the entire world;
4. profound pessimism with apathy, hypochondric symptoms, and avoidance behavior. This behavior shows clearly masochistic features.

In some survivors the first phase of a KZ-syndrome starts immediately after or shortly after the war. This phase is followed by a period, which can be relatively long, of apparent improvement which is generally related to success in society. However, at the height of one's career and eventually when family and conjugal life is over, a second phase may follow in which the syndrome is reactivated: the so-called "late consequences of persecution and resistance."

The term *KZ-syndrome* usually applies to symptomatology in persons who survived one of the concentration camps. The term *Survivor syndrome* applies to symptomatology in those who survived the camps, as well as in first and second generation survivors. Since my patients come from both categories of survivors, the latter term is employed here.

Therapeutic principles and techniques for belated mourning

Working mainly within the surviving Dutch Jewish community in Holland, I was commissioned to help those who experienced hurt and pain as a result of first- or second-hand encounters with the Nazi occupation of Europe. Coupling the disciplines of theology and psychotherapy, my approach is close to that of Jackson (1959) who suggests that "surviving means surviving those 'who are and who are not.' " Facing the fact of death at the physical level with a firm sense of reality, the therapist and/or religious counselor must encourage a healthy expression of feeling in his clients, and induce them to reinvest their emotional capital to reap the highest benefit.

For psychotherapists, the first rule is to create a relationship of trust and security through which the patient is enabled to express and freely experience the whole spectrum of emotions. This relationship of trust and security is absolutely vital to success with these survivors. The variety of feelings which come out in an atmosphere of acceptance ranges from self-condemnation to high self-esteem, from normal grief to extreme expressions of guilt and unworthiness. But not only the patient's feelings are involved. Perhaps more so than in other therapies, with this particular group of patients, therapists may suffer much from feelings of guilt, shame, and self-condemnation in the course of the therapy. In confronting the suffering of these patients, they are brought face to face with their own feelings of impotence, indifference, unworthiness, even of responsibility for man's injustice to man. Because very deep layers of transference and countertransference may be tapped in these confrontations, the feelings, reactions, and cathartic processes of the therapist as much determine whether therapy will have a successful outcome as the processes taking place in the patient.

In the second place, the therapist must have a genuine respect for the patient's integrating capacity, and for the pace at which integration can be achieved. Short-term therapy with these patients can take much more time than the therapist may bank on. A contractual undertaking for minimally two sessions a week for a period of ten months is about a minimum for these therapies. Treatment is concluded when two conditions are met: (1) the patient no longer suffers from symptoms, and (2) the therapist is assured that enough material has been made conscious, internal resistances overcome, and transformation and recovery achieved. The ultimate aim of therapy is to bring about in the patient a certain degree of insight, self-understanding, and a positive reorientation of the self.

Three phases can be distinguished in the *process* of mourning (cf. stages—Bowlby, 1980; Hodge, 1972; components—Siggins, 1966; sequences—Ramsay, 1977). The first phase is characterized by expressions of disbelief, a ventilation (catharsis) of feelings of anger, guilt and distress at the loss, or pining. In the second phase the survivor, in evaluating and elucidating his or her experiences, tends toward idealization of the one who is dead, and feelings of insecurity and the threat of ego-loss come to the fore. The third, and final phase is characterized by depression and the desire to give up one's hold on life. But if the therapist takes the time and care to help the patient work these and other newly arising symptoms through systematically and carefully, then these become suddenly transformed, and recovery takes place.

In stimulating and evoking the process of mourning in these survivors, I developed several techniques which proved useful in the healing process. By supplementing the linear technique of the Freudian school (that is, following chains of memory so as to advance from the manifest to the latent content) with the Jungian concentric method of amplification (that is, careful and conscious illumination of interconnected associations objectively grouped around particular images), the individuation process, which had become impaired, is given a new impulse. As Fordham (1978) notes, the individuation process generally starts in the unconscious, gains expression in dreams and imagery (especially active imagination), and seems to direct the individual's consciousness toward a greater awareness of himself as an individual person at once separate from and yet also a part of society as a whole.

The principle is to follow the goal-directedness of the psyche, picking up the hidden messages to the therapist which indicate what the patient wishes to consciously express but dare not, for fear of the fantasied consequences. Ezriel's (1956) model of the wished-for but avoided relationships has helped me to seek out that portion of the message that asks for recognition. We begin a process of sensitization to bring hidden feelings and anxieties into awareness. This permits an advance toward the experiencing of loss and the survival that comes after, but in a new way (Alexander's "corrective emotional experience"; cf. Alexander & French, 1974).

During the therapeutic process, use is made of many of the traditional Jewish rituals and symbols of mourning. The Jewish way of life, even for those long divorced from it, still has deep resounding rituals and symbols that afford links with the past and present, and which go beyond the rational and the explicable. The tradition expresses a form of "Love that does not die" (the I-Thou relationship.* These leave-taking rituals

---

*Emil Fakenheim (1970) describes this living of life in the deepest and most intense way so as to deny death as "the 614th commandment."

and symbols, which are described below in some detail, have been
evolved within the Jewish cultural pattern for the purpose of guarding
against permanent ego-loss.

Jewish leave-taking rituals and symbols

Helping to mourn the many by the few

The concept of *Kiddush Hashem* is now applied to the approximately
six million murdered Jews in Europe during the Nazi regime. The "High
Season" in this group-focused mourning takes place in January with the
commemoration of the liberation of Auschwitz. This yearly reunion begins with a visit to the cemetery in Amsterdam and the placing of flowers
on the monument of Remembrance. The monument is designed as, and
made of a broken mirror. In its reflection even the sky is shattered. For
it, too, will never be the same. The scars go deeper than the human eye
can pierce. Each face that is reflected in this mirror becomes distorted.
Looking, we realize that the horror of Auschwitz has forever changed
our perspective on life. Life after Auschwitz is living with megadeath,
death which can never, ever be fully mourned.

Rituals for individual mourning

Group-focused rituals, even when directly participated in, do not
always help the individual mourner. For the individual mourner there are
a number of rituals and symbols which may be utilized to facilitate
mourning and leave-taking processes. Not all of the rituals described
below are, however, necessarily carried out by a particular individual.
Besides, many of my patients are Jewish only by the accident of birth.
Nonetheless, they have some semblance of residual knowledge concerning cultural patterns which help them to make links to the past; to a time
that is no longer theirs. In the mourning process our search is for a life-
giving force, for meanings for living, and the discovery of purpose. Our
search is always for what is meaningful for the seeker, rather than what
is dogma for the guide. The saying of *Kaddish*, visiting the cemetery,

establishing a formal date of death, abstaining from sexual contact for a limited period, attending a funeral and, for a limited number of persons, actually visiting the death camp Auschwitz and climbing through the wreckage of the gas chamber, are leave-taking rituals which can and do help to facilitate the processes of transformation and recovery. For some mourners, walking the same roads that were taken by their lost families, being actually confronted with the place of their parents' destruction, and being able to go home again after this confrontation, has been vitally effective in freeing their blocked-off energy and feelings for their adult offspring. It is as though, through this meeting in the place of destruction, an otherwise homeless soul can come home to rest. With it a vitalizing image is incorporated into the survivor. A patient described this experience as though he, himself, had followed a Jewish pattern of old: ''Once again the descent into Egyptian slavery and back into a new life.'' His experience ''in the wilderness,'' the death of a whole generation, became a symbol of survivor continuity, and of immortality.

For the benefit of those readers who are unfamiliar with Jewish rituals and symbols of mourning, a brief description follows of those symbols and rituals which are referred to in the text.

Kiddush Hashem (Act of Holiness) symbolizing martyrdom, is usually used in all cases of martyrdom.

Kaddish (Hallowed is the name of God) is a mourner's prayer. This doxology does not mention death at all but confirms the glory of God, Creator of Peace and the Godly Kingdom of the Messianic future yet to come. The traditional understanding of the messianic period includes the awakening from their sleep (in the dust) of the dead to participate in eternal life.

Eyl Maleh Rachamim (God full of Compassion) is a prayer used either on anniversaries or at burials.

Keriah is the tearing of clothes to signify the tearing of one's own flesh and blood (the blood ties of family).

Washing of hands. A symbol of dis-infection from death.

Sitting on low chair or floor. A sign of humility, acceptance of man's smallness and powerlessness in the face of death.

Eating of mourner's meal, to include a hardboiled egg and round shaped, individual (bread) roll, to signify the cycle of life and death.

Shivah. Seven days of separation from normal daily work and communal responsibilities. Space for absorbing slack time in which to be counselled by others. Occasion for reflection and feeling. One stays at home (own home or that of the deceased) and is visited by ''counsellors.''

Kabalat Shabat. On the Friday evening of the Shivah period, mourners are "received" in the synagogue and are greeted by the community, all standing as a sign of respect, who also verbally express their sharing in the event by reciting a Hebrew formula.

Lighting of candles. Candles are to be burned during the whole week of mourning, as symbol of light in darkness, the delicate nature of life.

Abstention from conjugal relations. During the Shivah period of mourning sexual contact between partners is avoided.

Abstention from meat dishes. During the Shivah period the eating of meet is avoided, as a token form of loss.

Case descriptions

In the following the three phases in the process of mourning, as these unfolded in the dynamic interaction with three survivors of the Holocaust during therapy, are described. These three cases illustrate in different ways how the more abstract principles and techniques of therapy earlier outlined take on body and obtain meaning for the person.

The precipitating factors in these therapies are sometimes of an external nature (for instance, a recent death in the family), sometimes of an internal one (for instance, the uprush of hitherto repressed material via dreams or nightmares) and sometimes external and internal.

The curative factors and the form that healing takes differ from individual to individual. But in all cases one can observe that the possibility to enter into a very deep and trusting relationship with the therapist, the chance to experience and give full vent to positive and negative feelings, without loss of love or understanding, and the time and the room to reintegrate old, and often till now unacceptable aspects of oneself, but at a new and more realistic level of being, brought about transformation and recovery. The mourning processes with which we are concerned here are of a very special kind, without the normal requisites: corpse, grave, funeral rite, or other concretizing symbols. Mourning, moreover, of the death of loved ones which took place almost forty years ago.

Anne

Anne was born in 1933 in Holland in the year that Hitler came to power in Germany and put Jewish lives under threat. Born of a Jewish mother and a non-Jewish father, this mixed parentage would save her time and again from transport and death in an extermination camp during the Nazi occupation of the Netherlands from 1940–45. Since she was not obliged to wear a Yellow Star she was free to wander the streets, and so witnessed razzias ("collection actions") by the Nazi Green Police. Picked up several times and interrogated, she was released each time when her papers confirmed her mixed parentage. During the occupation, the street in which she lived was inhabited mostly by Jewish families. By mid 1943, as more and more of its inhabitants were picked up and transported to concentration camps in the east of Europe, he street had become a "ghost street."

Years after the war, Anne began therapy because of extreme moods of depression, alternating with fierce outbursts of aggression. She felt an uncontrollable need to inquire into the background of each person she would meet, and suffered a near-paranoid fear that she was discriminated against by Jew and non-Jew alike. Her husband, who was also of mixed parentage had, like her, survived the Occupation. Their only son was a source of great joy but of much anxiety too, because of a consuming fear that he might one day "face the threat of annihilation in this anti-Semitic world." Recently their son had married a Catholic girl, and a son had been born to them. The grandparents were overjoyed but anxious as well. As his grandmother, Anne felt torn between two conflicting desires: to acquaint the child with his Jewish background and all that this implied, and to spare him any knowledge of the terrible past. What she would like to do but dared not, was to tell the child of all that they had suffered because of the terrible transports, of the long wait for those who had never returned, of the anguish and the strain and uncertainty, which was still unresolved even after forty years of waiting. To speak of the terror of living through all this, and the shame of escaping the fate of those who had not returned, thereby constrained to keep the worlds of life and death separate.

In reconstructing during therapy the period following the liberation in 1945 Anne gave poignant expression to these feelings: "In the first months we held our breaths at every step in the street, and listened for the ring of the bell at the front door. Even when mother received notice from the Red Cross that all her immediate family, some fifty persons in all, had not survived the camps, we could not believe that the authorities were not mistaken. When all waiting proved fruitless, we took to walking the streets at regular times, looking into the faces of people passing, hoping to recognize one of our own family. Later on, we read advertisements in the newspapers, hoping that one of our family would be among those advertising and seeking contact with lost family. We watched the post for news, convinced that one or more of our relatives, an uncle, a cousin, or an even more distant relative might have survived, reached America or Israel. Time passed, and no one returned. Visits to Israel and a search at *Yad Vashem* (memorial in Jerusalem to the Holocaust) could not destroy our belief that someone must have survived.''

In probing the sources of her depression and anger in the course of therapy, two important incidents were relived again and again. In the first Anne recalls her memory of an aunt who had come with her young child to stay at her parents' house, seeking temporary refuge and possible contact with the underground, in the hope of avoiding the transportations.

"It is afternoon. My aunt is peeling potatoes at the kitchen table, the baby is in the high-chair. Suddenly a razzia begins. The doorbell rings, the sound of jack-boots climbing the stairs, a knock on our front door. My aunt tells my younger brother and me to go and hide in the cupboard on the veranda. A little while later, only the sound of silence. Creeping out of our hiding place, peeping through the veranda door, I see a pile of half-peeled potatoes on the table, the high-chair is empty, and my mother is standing by the window, tears streaming down her cheeks.'' Anne joins her mother, looks out the window and sees a truck moving away with its tear-laden contents. Later that evening, her mother, who wants to join the transport voluntarily to be with her family, is prevented by her father from doing so, who pleads "think of the children.''

In one session Anne implied that her father, in preventing her mother from doing what she felt was the honorable thing to do, to identify with her own people even if this meant death, had made unfair use of the children.

A second, indelible incident took place when she went out shopping during curfew hours: the shocking experience of being confronted with anti-Semitic outbursts from people whom she had known and trusted all her life. "The same, homely shopkeepers suddenly became vile enemies of the Jewish families in our street, and best friends of the Occupying Power, our enemies and persecutors.'' From that time on, her mother never went out, even when permitted to do so, since she would have to wear her Yellow Star, once a symbol of honor, the Star of David, now a badge of ridicule and dishonor.

These two incidents bring out clearly the concrete source of Anne's feelings of anger and impotence in the face of an indescribable and unjust

Fate, feelings so fierce that they had to be repressed, and her subsequent depression.

During the course of therapy, Anne's father became seriously ill. It was clear that he would soon die from terminal cancer. His approaching death and Anne's over-involvement with it was a sign for me that much more was going on than normally takes place at the death of a parent. This event released a floodgate of emotions in Anne, opening up the way to a resolution of her conflicts.

After the war her parents had divorced. Her father had left home and remarried, but had kept up contact with his children from his first marriage. Now, as his death approached, a tremendous amount of stored-up energy was released in Anne. This first became apparent in physical overactivity. She visited her father twice, sometimes thrice daily, for hours on end. His death soon took on an all-consuming character. Together we discovered that, through his death, "the others could finally die too." The guilt of having parents who had survived the "great Death" had prevented the death of the others from becoming a fact of reality for her. Anne had lived with the memories of former years frozen in her mind, unable to say farewell to her aunt and cousin, who had become a symbol of all those who had disappeared without a trace. During her father's dying, faces of those others came back with increasing clarity. Names that had formerly been forgotten were suddenly remembered, as the mental attic, full of memorabilia, came to life. Family anecdotes and jokes surfaced, and even the face of a once lively and jolly mother reemerged.

At the death of her father, rituals of leave-taking were extended to incorporate the loss of all the others too. A systematic roll call of all those departed took place and, with it, fantasies of how they might have looked, had they lived to maturity and old age. One by one we said farewell to them, giving expression to guilt feelings and feelings of pain at surviving them. Coupling the fortune of survival to feelings of unworthiness was, at first, extremely painful for her. The half-peeled potatoes, the empty high-chair were transformed into an invitation to build a future. Into the high-chair we mentally put her own grandson, and set her daughter-in-law to continue peeling the potatoes at the table. Thus they became links between the past and the future. To complete these symbolic acts, she decided to have her grandson circumcised. Later, trees were planted in Israel to honor her dead relatives. By thus reliving and transforming these painful experiences, a layer of guilt and shame was uncovered, expiated, and integrated. Her extreme outbursts of (projected) aggression now abated. With this laying to rest of the lost family members, the necessity to inquire into the background and identity of every stranger dissolved. Jewish symbols of identity became more integrated into life at home and her feeling of general well-being increased. In accepting Death as eternal, outside of time, and in realizing that people who grow old and die enter into Eternity, life took on a new meaning and became more liveable.

Esther

In 1980 Esther's husband died. He was seventy-one and she, sixty-nine. After the war, in 1946, they had married and a son had been born a year later. Their son, the apple of their eyes, had now been married for five years and, to their great delight, their daughter-in-law was pregnant for the first time. That the pregnancy coincided with the time of her husband's death seemed to Esther a small, but important and consoling fact.

Esther's mourning did not follow the traditional Jewish rules. To begin with, she had had her husband cremated, a fact the more surprising when one considered that she had been incarcerated in a Nazi camp, and had seen many of her fellow prisoners exit life through the chimneys of the exterminating ovens.

Her ostensible reason for consulting me, six months after the death of her husband, was her deep depression. She felt full of shame, she said, because she was unable to get over her husband's death. Those around her, including her son, felt she was taking too long to recover. After all, he had lived to a ripe old age and their life together had been a good one.

During the first interview, when speaking about her late husband and the circumstances of his death, something in the way she told the story made it seem unreal, as if she were recounting what had happened to someone else. Clinically, this process of distancing oneself from one's feelings, treating them as if belonging to another person, is called depersonalization. Suddenly, and completely out of context, she mentioned the name of a man which was neither that of her husband, nor of any current acquaintance. Without remarking on this slip of the tongue, I continued to try to understand her immediate predicament: her need to express her pain to an extent that was frowned on in her intimate family circle.

Four days later, on her second visit to me, I approached with some caution the subject of the name that had slipped out in the first interview. She was startled to find that I seemed to have information about her former marriage, knowledge of which she had withheld from all who knew her now, even from her late husband. When I told her that she had told me of this, she could not believe it. She was silent for about fifteen minutes, and then burst into tears. Through tearful eyes she told me about the circumstances of her first marriage and how they were torn apart. It had been such a painful experience that she had spoken to no one of it, not even her late husband. Locking it away in the past, eternalizing her first marriage by splitting it off as past history, she had replaced her first husband by the second. But the death of the second husband had revived the death of the first, and now she was faced with a double death. This seemed to explain why her mourning took such a difficult course, causing her so much added pain and suffering.

At the age of eighteen she had married in full Jewish traditional style, a handsome young man, who had come to work in her parents' business. They were very happy together but the marriage had been childless in spite of all their efforts. This caused some difficulty within the family. Coming from an orthodox background, after ten years of childless marriage they had been given the opportunity to end the marriage with the sanction of the religious authorities. They had actually considered doing so, but at that point the approaching threat of Nazism to Jewish life drew them closer together. They decided against separation. When the time came, clinging close to one another, they reported with the rest of the family for transport to the east; and, like so many others, experienced the hell of the long journey.

For several days and nights they were shipped around Europe in freight cars. Her husband suffered a heart attack in her arms. She held him close until they arrived at their fateful destination, where she asked for medical help. In line with the policy then of not wishing to sow panic, the "reception committee" took the body of her husband, placed it on a stretcher, and promised to inform her later on his condition. She never saw him again. Nor did she ever hear anything from the so-called medical team. Like so many others, she searched continuously for his face among the crowds of prisoners. When she thought that she saw his face among them, he was always just too far off to be spoken to directly or greeted.

On her return after the war, she waited for news of his release; in vain. Eventually she received a Red Cross notification of his death. With this news, she moved to another city, quickly found an eligible husband, married, and soon became pregnant. Replacing her first husband by the new one, she put the past out of her mind. In her immediate surroundings no one had known her before the war, so this replacement was complete. Until her second husband died. Then she was faced with the travail of having to mourn two persons, instead of one, one whose death had occurred forty years before.

Following her associations and thoughts, she now became terribly shocked that she had permitted her husband to be cremated, even though it had been his own wish. In this way he could be united with his murdered family whose end had been through the chimneys of the extermination camp. As ashes and dust, he had felt that he would be closer to them in death. In secret, Esther had held the fantasy that both her husbands would meet and discover her infidelity, and the special success of her second marriage in bearing a child. Careful and delicate re-activation of her feelings of helplessness at her first husband's death, and exposure of these feelings of inadequacy and shame about the childless marriage, were very helpful to her.

In making us of leave-taking rituals in mourning both her dead, I helped her to listen to the voices of the two husbands which she carried in her. She decided to buy a plot of ground in a cemetery in which to bury the ashes of her second husband, instead of leaving the urn unattended on a shelf. She selected two separate dates from the Jewish calendar to be named as remembrance days, so that the two men could be honourably separated in time and in name, allowing their lives to take on separate meanings for their one surviving wife. During the course of therapy, a grandson was born and was given the names of both deceased men. This was a source of great joy for her, since this new life could be seen, not as a denial of the deaths that had preceded it, but as a new chapter in an ongoing life history that had seemed to come to an end twice before.

Ada

Married, and the mother of three strapping boys (fifteen, thirteen and eleven years old), Ada was referred to me by a local rabbi. She wished to join the Jewish community, being the daughter of Jewish parents. But she was haunted by nightmares about her foster parents, who had both died within the past four years.

Her own parents had been transported to a death camp in 1943. As a baby, she was placed in a family temporarily, who hid her for a while and then passed her on to another address. Eventually she was adopted by a non-Jewish family where she remained, and grew up as their only daughter. She was educated as a Christian, baptised and, despite her very dark and Jewish appearance, expected to enjoy a completely integrated life within a close-knit Christian community. Through a chance meeting with a concerned christian, she became more and more interested in what had happened during the war, and her feelings of being strange in the foster family setting increased.

On a trip to Israel with members of her Christian community, she discovered that her background might have been a Jewish one. When she inquired about this, her adopted parents told her that this was indeed so but they had refrained from telling her because they had not wished to burden her with the terrible history of the Holocaust. At that time she was preparing to marry a non-Jew and had no contacts with the Jewish community. She went through with the marriage in church with all the trimmings, and settled down to build a family life.

Gradually, though, she became obsessed with the war and the exterminations, and began to have dreams at regular intervals about the deaths of her real parents. Trying to put this out of her mind, she invested a lot of energy in raising her children, in being a good Christian wife and a dutiful adopted daughter.

On the death of her adopted mother, she listened at the funeral to the preacher telling of the woman's bravery in risking her life by taking a child into her home, thereby winning a soul for Christianity. Greatly puzzled by these words, she nonetheless refrained from discussing it with anyone. On the death of her adopted father, the Christian charity of both parents toward her was lauded even more highly. From all sides she was told how grateful she must be, and must remain to their memory for having saved her life. Were it not for them, she too would have perished in the gas chambers at Sobibor.

These remarks made her increasingly uncomfortable. It was required of her to remain a faithful Christian because her life was saved from this fate; but her true parents were dead merely because they were born Jews. She now began to question the justice of her parents' deaths. Feelings of guilt, shame, and betrayal of her parents' heritage began to overtake her. It was as though being Jewish had been regarded in her Christian family as a crime, with the right to survive the scythe of Nazi destruction accorded only to Christians.

As time passed she became more and more involved in the background of her parents and other family members whom she had never known, and who were also dead. She was the sole survivor of a family of some thirty people over three generations, from grandparents to grandchildren. Her dreams got worse, became filled with aggressive images. She was overcome by feelings of hate directed at her deceased adoptive parents. This hate took on an obsessive character. Anything to do with Christianity became identified with them and rejected, as her hate for the community and their way of life increased. The exaggerated forms that her feelings took were seen by the interviewing rabbi as pathological.

As we looked into the matter, Ada and I discovered that her anger and frustration were as much directed to her real parents as to her foster parents. In her own words: "Because they did not take me with them, they left me at the mercy of these hypocrites. It is better to be dead than alone with strangers who have made me into something that doesn't fit. I am a misnomer, a fish out of water."

A number of sessions followed in which we spent much time trying to formulate the connection between the deaths of both sets of parents, the real and the adoptive ones. What Ada would have liked to have happen was that the adoptive parents should have died as her real parents had, and her real parents have been spared the indignity of their murder. But chronology cannot be reversed, although the subjective chronology of the individual can be revitalized. Ada had no conscious memories of her parents but through the aid of friends and contacts, passport-size photographs of them were obtained. With these photos and photos of her adoptive parents, we began to set matters right, despite the passing of years and the absence of the people concerned.

Ada's mourning process. Ada could not permit herself to say aloud what she would have liked to have been able to say to her foster parents. The nasty remarks could not pass her lips, because she had been taught always to be grateful to them and to speak kindly of them. To speak unkindly about them would bring her into contact with demonic forces. She had been told by the pastor to respect her parents, whatever they might do or say, because of the commandment to "Honor thy father and mother that thy days might be long upon the land which the Lord thy God giveth thee."

The first step was to ascertain which of the two sets of parents, according to the Bible, was Ada's father and mother. She decided: "Those who died at Sobibor." They then were to be honored. But how to honor parents in their death? Normally one has them buried according to the ritual. A prescribed period of mourning is kept, the Kaddish prayer is said, and a date reserved for a yearly memorial. The difficulty of mourning someone whom one has never known presents a problem. The photographs showed two young people. Ada felt that she could not say farewell to parents who looked as young as they did. Together we built up older faces, attributing to them the characteristics, familiar traits, and manner that they might have had. Each step was carefully checked to guard against over-idealization, each feature made realistic. As the personalities of the real parents emerged, I pointed out to her that they seemed to represent overcompensations of her adoptive parents. It was as if they had to possess only good qualities to make amends for the bad ones of her adoptive parents. On reflecting on this, Ada realized that this was indeed the case. Gradually, more realistic profiles of her real parents emerged. When these were achieved, we then set out to say farewell to them by means of leave-taking rituals. For a period of one week Ada refrained from eating meat. In the material of one of her dresses she made a small slash on the left side, to symbolize on her clothing her broken heart (*Keriah*). Together we read the prayer *Eyl Maleh Rachamim*, and said the Kaddish prayer one after the other. As a mark of her at-one-ment with her deceased parents, Ada then undertook to speak to her husband and children about her real parents, and about their attitudes and possible feelings toward these two people whom they had never known.

Concluding Remarks

Perhaps these examples may convey the false impression that therapies of this kind are rather mechanical, and depend only upon the introduction of formal rituals at the correct time in order to effect a "cure." This is far from being the case. In fact, very much more may be demanded of the therapist, in the sense of personal involvement and active participation in the healing process, while at the same time remaining sufficiently objective and impartial to allow the patient to observe and experience him or herself as it were through the eyes of the other (the therapist). These patients, having suffered indescribable losses, seeing their dearest and nearest savagely mowed down by an (in)human scythe before which they were completely powerless, left with not even the bodies of their loved ones to mourn, have now to enter into a very deep, trusting relationship with a stranger, their therapist.

Most of them have learned to trust no one, that trust does not exist. As one patient said: "The whole of life is made up of people who are out to deceive you." Even the Jewish authorities during the period of Nazi occupation became suspect. The synagogues were distributing centers for Yellow Stars; the address lists of members of the communities were used as the main source for the organized roundups.

During the course of therapy these patients need to experience the full force of their repressed feelings: from hate, fury, anger, to despair, and eventually, love. For a large number of people the inability to do so, the *not* letting go of their Holocaust dead has seriously hindered their possibility to invest energy in new, deep relationships. Many families can only express loving relationships in material terms. Experiencing intimacy, expressing tender or comforting feelings have become taboo. Yet, if they are to recover, these feelings, and the bitter ones too, have to be let out, ventilated, experienced, made conscious, and integrated. The attitude of the therapist is vital to this process. This must be one of complete acceptance, warmth, empathic understanding if trust is to be reestablished.

But it is just at this point that the therapist may become the butt of serious negative feelings that the patient needs to express. Because when death strikes, this is often experienced as a loss of love through the loss of life, as a break in the chain of being, and anger erupts. The therapist can become the target of serious attacks of aggression. Even the small number of therapists who themselves survived the death camps are not exempt from such aggressive attacks by patients. These attacks can dishearten even the most compassionate therapist temporarily. In order to prevail in therapy, the therapist should not loss sight of the existential aspect of this suffering. Beyond the overt communications of all of the patients in this survivor group is the problem of man's inhumanity to man, the problem of suffering inherent in the very nature of being. It is the task of the therapist to enter into a relationship despite feelings of being inadequate to the task. Often he or she may be overcome by depths of despair, by the enormous demands for love and attention that these starved patients crave. How can the therapist be firm and yet loving, help the patient in his reality-testing by withstanding the inordinate demands without rejecting them, by understanding to the point of not being able to understand? To show the person how to express his or her feelings in a congruent, authentic way, to learn to recognize that life is at times unfair and unjust and that one must, ultimately, take responsibility for one's life and actions. To help the patient to achieve insight, learning that one's likes and dislikes of others have their roots in reasons that have more to do with oneself than the other; learning that how one feels today is related to experiences in early childhood and in one's later development, learning that others recover and that one can do so, too.

By the attitude and behavior of the therapist in the dynamic interaction with the patient, the patient is given another chance to identify with more adequate figures, model his or her behavior on these, and aim at more realistic goals. When this is achieved, the process of transformation and recovery is completed.

None of these journeys into the psyche of the other leaves the therapist the same as he was before. An old rabbi once explained: "From my teachers I learned much, from my colleagues even more, but most of all I learned from my pupils." Paraphrasing this, I would like to suggest that the patient's psyche has a way of teaching the therapist how to help the patient best. The inner forms of psychic structure and the various compensatory forces thrusting themselves to the fore for recognition, the inner re-organization processes and the symbolic forms that arise as signposts in a seemingly chaotic manner, all educate and transform the therapist.

We are often taught that it is the patient's basic trust that must be developed before therapy can really take place. Perhaps it is time for the therapist to question this assumption of "basic trust in the patient's own contribution to the therapeutic process," and give priority to developing his own trust in the patient's creative qualities. Through our patients we can meet the evil, the catastrophe and, above all, the death that lies in wait for us all. Only Eternity will triumph over it.

A Ritual as Part of a Longer Psychotherapy

Onno van der Hart

Designing and prescribing a therapeutic leave-taking ritual is not a separate type of therapy. It is a way of approaching certain problems and it is part of a wider therapeutic framework. Sometimes the treatment need not consist of much more than the ritual. But more often—at least that is my experience—the ritual is either the beginning or the termination of a lengthier therapy.

If it is carried out in the final phase of a therapy, then what came before the ritual can be interpreted in at least two ways:

a. it was the necessary preparation for the ritual: the prior treatment has enabled the client to take leave both of an unworked through situation from the past and of the therapy and the therapist by means of the ritual.

b. in an earlier stage, the therapist underestimated the central affective problem which was ultimately solved with the aid of the ritual.

This chapter reports a lengthy treatment which is brought to a close by a leave-taking ritual. The first purpose of this description is to illustrate how a ritual can fit into a therapy in which other methods had been employed before it. The second purpose is to show that, in this case, hindsight is not better than foresight—in retrospect, it is no simple matter to determine whether the therapy needed to last so long or whether the ritual would have been appropriate earlier.

Case history

When she first comes to the therapist, Sandra is a recently divorced 30-year-old woman. She does her utmost to make something of her life, but with very little success. She feels very unstable and she makes it understood that, even after some six years of psychiatric help, she still cannot manage on her own.

Sandra is the only child—unwanted—of a marriage between two older people who had a hard time getting along together. They only managed to give their daughter a minimum of attention. The father has since died; the very elderly mother lives in a nursing home. One reason for the constant tension between father and daughter was that her outgoing behavior annoyed him. Sandra completed secondary school and soon afterwards went to live on her own. She managed well by herself and had a job she liked very much.

When she was 20, she met Jaap, who was two years older, and they were married within six months. From that moment on there were tensions between them. Sandra and Jaap had a lot of fights, at first about his drinking, later about all kinds of things. The fights regularly led to such deep depressions in one or both of them that admission to the emergency ward of a psychiatric hospital ensued. The fights and her hospital stays together resulted in Sandra's having to give up her job. When they were not in the hospital, the two of them received outpatient psychiatric treatment, but this was not of any help.

Sandra had had one miscarriage and one abortion, the latter despite the fact that she had badly wanted to become a mother. The abortion took place when their relationship had reached its lowest point. After this, too, both of them had to be admitted to the hospital. Upon being discharged, Sandra filed for a divorce. When Sandra comes to the therapist, she has been living alone for two years but the divorce has only recently become final.

The first course of therapy

A colleague introduces Sandra to the therapist. She has been in therapy with the colleague for some time. They have come to the conclusion that a different therapist might be able to help her more. The first thing that strikes the therapist about Sandra is her comely appearance: the fashionable clothes, the very well-groomed hair and the makeup. Although he does not make it a habit to comment on a person's appearance, this time he gives in to his impulse to do just that. Apparently a well-groomed appearance is very important to Sandra, who is very poor at taking care of herself in many other respects. He tells her she looks nice. Sandra immediately remarks that she is very conscious of her appearance and thinks nothing is right about it. She has felt this way ever since her adolescence. She uses clothes, makeup, jewelry, and hairstyles to camouflage or to correct what she feels is unattractive. She even experiences her own body so negatively that she avoids all contact with men. Recently she went to a plastic surgeon but he saw no reason to operate. She is now trying to be referred to a different one.

Sandra tells about her childhood and about her marriage, when the real troubles began. She mentions the miscarriage and the abortion and the fact that the two of them afterwards had to be admitted to the hospital. Since the divorce, things have been going slightly better with her than with Jaap, who still often has to be admitted to a psychiatric hospital.

Sandra wants to make something of her life, but she often feels anxious and uncertain; she cannot manage alone yet. Everything that happened in her unsuccessful marriage and all the psychiatric interventions have given her a low opinion of herself. Sandra and Jaap still see each other often: they may not be able to get along together, but they cannot get along without each other either. For this reason, Jaap's therapist took the two of them into marriage counselling, the goal being insight into the backgrounds of their strong and ambivalent attachment. Sandra feels the marriage counselling talks are inadequate for the difficulties she is presently encountering in building up her own existence: her fears and uncertainties, the low opinion she has of herself, difficulties in social contacts, and in looking for a job.

Generally speaking, the therapist is not in favor of an individual therapy alongside marriage counselling. For Sandra he feels an individual therapy is necessary; but he also feels that the marriage counselling can do more good than harm. There Sandra can focus on the unresolved aspects of her relationship to Jaap. In the individual therapy, emphasis can lie on building up her own life. Here he sees her negative self-image and her uncertainty as important problems. If she developed a positive self-image, then she would probably dare to come into contact with other people, she would be better able to assert herself, and she would generally be in a more favorable position to do what is necessary in order to lead a satisfying life.

The therapist wonders what the best approach to this would be. He believes that changing Sandra's negative body image might be the best way. He sees this body image as a *metaphor* for her mental and social problems (cf. Haley, 1973). Since Sandra has an open and responsive attitude and a well-developed imaginative faculty, the therapist feels that hypnotherapy will do her a lot of good. He suggests to Sandra that they start out by working on a more positive body image using hypnosis and explains how he wants to accomplish it; she gladly takes him up on it.

The second session starts with the induction of hypnosis. Sandra reacts readily to the therapist's suggestions. He had thought he would give her some time to get used to hypnosis before actually starting the hypnotherapy. After having been in a trance for five minutes, Sandra suddenly starts to cry. The therapy is initiated immediately. She remembers the dream she had the night before. In the dream she was pregnant, and she had twins. She was very happy with the babies and she felt very strong and capable of taking care of them. When she woke up, she realized that it was only a dream and she was dejected.

The therapist manages to relate the agreed therapeutic goal, the correction of Sandra's negative body image, to this dream. But, in doing so, he overlooks the fact that Sandra's dream probably indicates that she has not yet worked through the loss she suffered from her miscarriage and her abortion. It will be a few years before she comes back to this subject herself.

The therapist asks Sandra to imagine that the pregnant woman in her dream is on her left. Then he asks her to imagine on her right the woman she would like to look like. The left-hand woman turns out to be wiser and calmer, the right-hand woman is younger and more exuberant. The left-hand woman has dark hair, the right-hand one has flashy blond hair. Sandra is asked to observe how the two women meet each other and start talking. There is something about each of them that attracts the other, but initially they do not feel at ease. They are so different. They decide to do something together: clean up a room. When that is finished, Sandra says it is enough for one time.

Sandra comes to the next appointment with light blond hair. Under hypnosis, the theme from the previous session is continued and again a dialogue takes place between the two women. Sandra identifies herself more strongly with the younger, active woman, who, as she puts it, "is running away from herself and making a mess of her life with all her activities." The older, wiser woman shows warmth and understanding and stimulates the other one to give herself more leeway and not to be so hard on herself. Then the two of them have some coffee together and the mood is pleasant.

Before Sandra comes out of the trance, the therapist says it is not necessary for her to consciously analyze her hypnotic experiences. She can concentrate on her everyday life, while her hypnotic experiences steadily take effect in a positive manner.

During the third session Sandra says things are going better with her. She has had her hair colored a shade darker. Recently she has become aware that she feels a lot of anger towards her ex-husband Jaap and several other people. When she is under hypnosis, the therapist asks her to meet these people one at a time and to tell all of them exactly what she thinks. She does, with great fervor, to her father, to her mother, and finally to Jaap. After an hour of intense inner activity she says, with a sigh of relief, that she has done enough and feels very calm.

The therapist has the impression that Sandra is actively working on the things that come up in the sessions. Considering this, it seems to him a good idea to go along with what she brings up instead of determining the subject and the direction of the talk himself. This is also an implicit indication that Sandra herself can determine the direction of her life.

In the sessions that follow several aspects of Sandra's everyday life are discussed: what will she do if Jaap asks for her help with his personal difficulties and she knows he will only react with ingratitude? How will she behave toward men? Will she look for a full-time or a part-time job? She realizes that she can still go in all directions in choosing a profession. She is happy to see that nothing is yet final in her life.

Sandra also mentions that there is a lot that still bothers her about Jaap and her parents. The therapist shows her how to write a "continuous letter" to each of them. She writes the letters, which she will not send, at home, and this takes a few months. In her therapy sessions, Sandra imagines several times that she is talking with someone and that she gives him or her a piece of her mind.

As time passes, things go better and better for Sandra. She conducts herself more and more in a way which she feels is suited to her. For a while she acted like a seventeen-year-old—that was how she felt and in that way she could catch up on what she had missed earlier. She sometimes sees Jaap and when she does, she has a better perspective on him. She is seeing another man intermittently and has a pleasant relationship with him. She now knows what she really wants to be—a masseuse—and she has started taking a course in it. The talks are terminated after 12 sessions spread over nine months.

A follow-up talk takes place nine months later. Sandra impresses the therapist as a warm, friendly adult woman. She is functioning well in her course and in her social contacts. She has had several conversations with Jaap and his therapist. She feels that she was able to make good use of those talks for herself by telling him straight out everything that had always bothered her. She has now worked through a large part of her relationship to him, and she regards Jaap as a good friend. She is grateful to him for the fact that he urged her to register for the course she is now taking. His urging also made her feel that not ''all men in the world are bent on getting in the way of my development''—her father had always done this.

Three months later Sandra calls the therapist to tell him that she passed the first year of her course in massage. Her life is going like she wants it to. She has finally gotten her house furnished to her own taste, well-kept, with bright colors and more plants. To her surprise she has discovered that she looks exactly as she had always wanted to. She has made several good friends who appreciate her. She can express to them what she does and does not want. She does not yet feel capable of living with someone else, but even if she never does, she feels she can accept this. She is satisfied with her life as she now leads it. She has put Jaap at more of a distance; she quit going to sessions at his therapist's because she got the feeling she was wasting her time.

Second course

Two years after terminating the therapy, Sandra calls for an appointment. Things have gone well for her the past two years. Over and over again she has realized that she can do things herself, that she is someone, too. She has developed well in her work as a masseuse and she knows that she has a lot of capacity for it. But she would like to have a few more talks with the therapist, because she feels she is becoming a little uncertain in the face of upcoming changes—a new job, a different house. Besides, she still experiences difficulties in her relationships with men. She would like to work through several aspects of her relationship to her now deceased father. Her thoughts keep coming back to these kinds of things and hypnosis seems to her the best way of tackling them. The therapist agrees.

In the first session she quickly goes into a trance. She spontaneously observes herself in a sort of concentration camp, but it does not rouse her anxiety. When the therapist goes along with her with suggestions of peace and relaxation, the concentration camp changes quite naturally into a deer park, serene and lovely. Sandra feels at her ease. She is enjoying the sunshine and there is no one else around to bother her.

At the end of the session the therapist gives the post-hypnotic suggestion that these experiences will continue to have positive effects in many ways. Sandra comes out of hypnosis relaxed and refreshed.

At the next session two weeks later Sandra says that a lot has happened. She had the urge to go out and enjoy herself and to dance and she did just that. She feels that she has a great deal of energy and that she can have strong influence on other people. She realizes, she says, that fun is not the only thing in life, but that she must also work for her own development and the things she wants to achieve. Now she wants to resolve the problems with her father.

In a trance, she soon observes herself in a room sitting at a desk. She is studying. Her lessons are lying on the desk. Her father comes into the room and tries to get her away from the desk. He always sabotaged her desire to learn. If she showed an interest in a course, his reaction was always: "It's a waste of money. You won't finish it anyway." Now, too, he says so. But Sandra does not put up with it this time. She tells him that is absolutely not true. Whatever he has allowed her to do she has always completed successfully. And even then he always had to make it hard for her. He never stimulated her. Father's first reaction is to dodge her remarks, and he tries to disconcert her. But she persists, and slowly but surely he begins to show more and more understanding of what she says. This does her good, and she is able to terminate the conversation in a satisfying manner.

A month later Sandra says that she has had a talk with Jaap. It was during this talk that she realized how much she had been afraid of men in the past. Although this roused strong feelings in her, she feels that the fear has already diminished. She has also realized now much she rebelled against her father by studying and working, while he thought it was all a waste of time. But studying and working are important to her too, apart from her father. Sandra feels the need to do some more work on this in hypnosis.

She observes herself working calmly and pleasantly in her own home which, in her trance, consists of private living space and an office. (In actuality this is not yet true.) The woman she is helping is grateful to her for her help which she has given in a very personal manner. Then she goes into the living room and changes the furniture so there is better light. When she has gone through some more of these experiences, she is finished, and the therapist gives the post-hypnotic suggestion that these experiences will go on working in a positive manner in her everyday life.

Sandra expresses the opinion that she can go on by herself for a while, at her own pace. She and the therapist agree that she will call if she ever again feels she wants his help.

The third course

Sandra calls again six months later. She brings up the relationship with Jaap. Even though she has her own life, she still cannot sever the emotional ties to him. This also becomes apparent from the telephone call that the therapist receives from Jaap just before the appointment. Rather heatedly, Jaap asks what is happening to Sandra in the therapy. The therapist does not go into this; he tells Jaap to ask her himself if he wants to know. Jaap then shows how ambivalent his attitude towards Sandra is. He hopes that the therapist continues to work with her, because he has seen how much she has already achieved.

The therapist mentions the telephone call to Sandra. She says that after all that has happened, she still wants to be friends with Jaap, even though their relationship is often a mother-child one.

The therapist realizes that there is still something that keeps Sandra and Jaap bound to each other. Since Sandra has no idea what that might be, he suggests a task that can help her discover what keeps her tied to Jaap. He asks Sandra if she would like to find a stone that can symbolize Jaap. She might paint the stone if she wanted, to make the resemblance to Jaap greater still. The idea is that she carry the stone with her constantly the next few weeks (Zeig, 1980b). If she wants, at the next session she can tell about what she has gone through with the stone.

Sandra accepts the suggestion and the next time she arrives with a plastic bag which contains the stone. She shows the therapist the stone and says that there is a large ugly side to it that mostly covers up a prettier side. This is the case with Jaap too, figuratively speaking. The therapist thinks that the picture on the plastic bag is quite striking, but he does not discuss it. The bag bears the name of a brand of jeans; against a black background a blond young woman is sitting provocatively with her behind—of course she is wearing a pair of the jeans—towards the viewer.

She looks at you over her bare shoulder, with one arm around an empty pair of pants. A sensuous picture.

Sandra has interpreted the suggestion to carry the stone with her continually as an invitation to take leave of Jaap. She put several things of his into a box, then tore up a shirt that was meant for their baby, and put some other remembrances into the box with them. She put the box into a communal collecting bin.

In the meantime Jaap has once again been admitted by proxy to a psychiatric hospital. Sandra now has the keys to his house (which is also her former home) and she is still carrying the stone. She wants to collect more material and then take leave of everything all at once. The therapist adds that it might be a good idea to do something with the keys to Jaap's house; he is not certain what. Sandra remarks that she is going to move in a few months, and in order to make a new start, she wants to have completed this working through process.

Three weeks later Sandra again comes with the plastic bag and the stone. Not much has happened with it yet, but carrying the stone has roused a lot of thoughts in her. She has become aware that her tie to Jaap consists largely of guilt feelings. Five years ago she had an abortion and the baby had very likely been conceived by another man. On the day of the abortion, Jaap decompensated and had to be admitted to the hospital. Ever since then, he has to be admitted every year around the same time. And every time he leaves the hospital after a few weeks, against medical advice. Sandra thinks that the decompensation and the hospital stay are partly her fault. But she adds to this that her sexual contacts with others were a reaction to similar activities on Jaap's part. He had started with this a year earlier, after the miscarriage. Then, too, he had reacted rather strangely; he had simply left her in the lurch when the cramps came. While he went his merry way, she had to call for help herself. Sandra now feels deeply angry toward Jaap about that.

At a certain point the therapist looks out of the window and says to himself, "How nice it would be if the two of you could bury those two embryos symbolically together—but I don't know if that is like Jaap; I don't know him and I don't know how he would react to something like that." Sandra wonders if it could be discussed with Jaap's doctor. In principle the therapist is willing to get in touch with him, but he feels that it is premature at this point. Sandra, as the most directly concerned, first ought to have every opportunity to find out what would be best; who knows, maybe she will get in touch with Jaap's doctor herself. The therapist calls Sandra's attention to the picture on the plastic bag. To this she says that she has a knack for allowing things to act as symbols. She points out to the therapist the fact that the girl pictured on the bag has her head turned away from the man's pants. "I used to turn away from painful events I had been through. Now I dare to look straight at them, no matter how much it hurts."

The therapist wonders out loud whether it might be a good idea for Sandra to find two small stones—symbolizing the two embryos—and to put them into the bag, too. To think things over and to work it through again, she says she will not decide about this now but will wait until she sees the therapist again three weeks later.

The next time Sandra comes to her appointment without the bag. A lot has happened in the meantime. Two days after the previous session she called Jaap's doctor and told him what had been discussed at the last session. The idea of a leave-taking ritual appealed to him. He said he would talk to Jaap about their conversation. A little later Jaap calls up Sandra. He asks if she will come to see him, because he is moved by what he has heard. In the hospital, Sandra tells the whole story once again. She cries very hard and Jaap, too, is upset. A few days later Jaap is discharged, this time in accordance with the staff's recommendation.

At home he shows Sandra two fruits* (apples) which he picked from a tree on the hospital grounds. He puts them on his desk: "After all those years that you have been worrying about them, I guess it's my turn to do it for a while." A week later Sandra and Jaap, on his initiative, go to a park with the two apples and a spade. Jaap finds a quiet spot and each of them digs a deep hole and puts an apple into the hole the other one dug. Together they cover over the holes. Then they stand still for a while. Sandra cries hard. Jaap envies her this. So much happens to her, while he went through the whole ritual almost numbly: as if he had turned off his feelings. At Sandra's insistence they take another route out of the park. She explains to Jaap: "If we go back the same way, it's like going back to the past, but life goes on . . ."

It becomes clear to Sandra and Jaap that they still care a lot for each other. They decide to give their relationship a chance for about 18 months. Sandra moves into their old house with Jaap. She keeps her own house and will also go ahead with the move to her new house. The therapist asks what she has done or will do with the bag and the stone. "It's at

Translator's note
*An important aspect of the symbolism here is lost in the translation. In the original Dutch both the "embryos" and the "fruits" in the text are called *vruchten* (fruits), *vrucht* being the usual Dutch word for both.

my house. I haven't really thought about what I will do with it. But wait a minute, let me concentrate on it . . . Yes, if things go well between us, I'll write something down about it and I'll put that in the bag too. Then I'll take the bag and the stone to the hospital, because they can keep their psychiatric nonsense . . . If things go badly between us, I'll bury the bag and stone somewhere near my old home, because that was where I fretted over them all these years.''

Sandra and the therapist agree that their talks have reached an end, at least for the time being. Later she will let him know how it went and how things are with her. In parting, she tells him she has lost "that wild blond.'' She feels an inner peace and has acquired a pleasant sort of homeyness.

Follow-up

Sandra and the therapist talk again six months later. She and Jaap have realized that they prefer to live apart after all and Sandra now lives in her new house. She is pleased with it. Right after moving, which Jaap helped her with, she had left his place for her new residence. While packing and clearing up, she once again picked up the stone that symbolized Jaap and looked at it. She put it into a plastic bag and had Jaap (who was not informed about the symbolism) carry it downstairs and put it out with the trash: "Let him carry his own stone.'' After the move, she went back to her old neighborhood again to say a quiet goodbye. After all, it was there that she got better. Then she bought a bunch of flowers at her old flower stand. Contented, she went to her new house.

Her work and her studying are going very well. She says that the picture she had long ago under hypnosis of herself, her house, and her work has now become reality. The house, the furnishings, the office, the orderliness and calm that prevail there, everything looks exactly as she had imagined. She now feels a strong need to develop herself further. She has good friends, but she has also lost several former ones: people who wanted to stay on the old footing. She sees Jaap regularly, but she leads her own life—separate from him.

After the leave-taking ritual with the two apples, Jaap went into therapy. Even though he still has a long way to go, he is now really working on putting things in order. The positive results motivate him strongly to continue. For the first time it is beginning to dawn on him what has happened with him over the past years, and sometimes that is a little too much for him.

Looking back, Sandra is very pleased with the ritual acts she carried out. "It lets you take matters into your own hands, and it gives you the feeling that you have power over your own situation. People used to do what they liked with me, and I couldn't do a thing about it. With the rituals I could do something about it, without needing them and being dependent on them."

Since the leave-taking ritual, she has managed to get rid of one particular problem entirely. She often used to have an inclination to end her life. Later, in difficult situations she would think: "But I can always become seriously ill so that I won't be here any more." The past few years this thought occurred to her less and less often. But only after the execution of the ritual with Jaap did it disappear completely. She has now accepted her age and the fact that she is growing older. Her life does not always go smoothly, but she realizes that if you want to achieve something, you have to make an effort for it and sometimes you must suffer.

Discussion

1. This chapter reported a treatment of a young woman with several problems: unresolved feelings towards her parents and her ex-husband, unresolved grief occasioned by a miscarriage and an abortion, low self-esteem and a negative body image, uncertainties, fears, and difficulties in social contacts.

The therapist regarded the negative body image as a central metaphor for several other problem areas. If it could be improved, then changes ought to take place in the other areas as well. The correction of the body image was not a bad start: this goal was achieved and progress was made in other areas.

2. By directing his initial attention so strongly towards the body image, the therapist overlooked a central affective problem: unresolved grief occasioned by the miscarriage and the abortion (as the client probably indicated with her dream about the twins) and, related to this, unresolved feelings towards her ex-husband. The grief did not come up until the third round of therapy. Then she succeeded in working through it with the aid of a leave-taking ritual.

If we see how, at the end of the therapy, the client herself was able to name this problem explicitly, we can assume that the timing of the ritual was exactly right. But, in the early stages of the therapy, the client had also implicitly indicated something about it; besides, the therapist knew the anamnesis. We keep wondering if the treatment, which was spread over four years, might not have been much shorter if the therapist had paid more attention to this in the early stages.

3. Several chapters mention that a client undergoing a re-grief therapy may be advised to collect symbolic or "linking objects" (Volkan, 1981). The client parts with them in the leave-taking ritual. In her mourning process, it is striking that the client spontaneously tore up and threw away a shirt which was meant for the baby.

One thing we can learn from this example is that it is wise, in the case of unresolved grief, to inquire whether there are such key symbols, and how the client handles them. In this way it can become apparent whether the deceased is being kept alive symbolically and the desirability of leave-taking can be discussed.

4. These symbols or linking objects are condensed symbols. They are affectively loaded and have various implicit meanings. They can also easily take on new meanings or evoke different feelings (cf. chapter 3). We may assume that the fruits which the client and her ex-husband buried in their leave-taking ritual stood for the feelings she had with respect to her unborn babies. But these symbols may also stand for her ambivalent feelings towards her ex-husband: she had been angry at him for leaving her in the lurch during the miscarriage and she had felt guilty about the fact that he had had to be admitted to the hospital after the abortion. Rituals, entities of symbolic actions, not only transform people's subjective experiences, but they also change social relationships.

5. The final remark concerns a basic principle in directive therapy: that the therapist should place the client's problems in a context which is as favorable as possible (cf. Van der Velden et al., 1980). Even though the therapist in this example had overlooked an important problem, the treatment was still successful. This is, in the first place, due to the efforts of the client and in the second place to the fact that the therapist did not stress what might be termed her "pathology." Instead he put her capacities, including her well-developed imagination, in the foreground and helped her to use them for her own benefit.

8

A Ritual for a Young Woman with an Atypical Dissociative Disorder

Kees van der Velden

The treatment described in this chapter involves a young woman whose clinical picture, according to DSM III (APA, 1980) would be termed an "atypical dissociative disorder." The treatment was concluded by means of a ritual bearing resemblances to the other rituals included in this book. Prior to this was a phase of therapy in which she was invited to join in daily life once again by means of an extensive metaphor.

In reducing the patient's uncertainty induced by her behavior and her manner of thought, the therapist employed the psychoanalytical approach. Very likely it would have been quite possible for him to find an orientation on the backgrounds of the patient's difficulties in some other way, but this was the only way familiar to him.

The discussion goes into questions about assessment and diagnosis, the patient-therapist relationship, the therapeutic techniques used, and the utility of the psychoanalytical point of view in this case.

For the sake of clarity, the treatment is presented here in an orderly fashion. It should be pointed out that it did not follow this orderly course. In fact, at the outset, the therapist was only sure of the fact that there was no use in trying to bring about improvement step by step in a congruent manner. He continued to wonder along the way if the strategy he had chosen was correct.

Case description

Summary of previous treatment; assessment

Upon her referral to the mental health center, Claudia Brienen, 24, has undergone two treatments: one short out-patient treatment and a somewhat longer in-patient one. Before the therapist sees Claudia for the first time, he familiarizes himself with the experiences of his predecessors. As is customary, Claudia was referred to the psychiatric out-patient clinic by her physician, who wrote in his referral: "Request treatment for Miss Brienen. She has relational disturbances, and problems at her work in particular. She has a case of unresolved grief resulting from an abortion performed when she was eighteen, with complications (high fever, contractions had to be induced). She lost the remains in the toilet and had to flush them away. She wants to hurt men. This very timid girl clearly exhibits aggression dysregulation."

The psychiatrist who sees Claudia for the first time diagnoses a mood of depression, clouding of consciousness, and hallucinations—that is, with great regularity she sees the lower body of the fetus, a girl, although she knows that these perceptions are in no way real. His conclusion is: a neurotic depression accompanied by dissociative symptoms in a somewhat hysterical young woman. Partly because Claudia indicates that she may never again have pleasure—a vow she made to her "child"—and because she dressed in black and isolates herself from the outside world, he fears suicide.

He sees Claudia eight times in two months, but her condition continually worsens. Finally it is decided to admit her to a hospital. During this time Claudia receives medication (haloperidol) but this does not help. A three-month admission to a psychiatric ward of a general hospital fails to bring about any improvement, despite the psychotherapeutic efforts made on her behalf there. She is discharged unimproved.

The psychiatric ward sees the behavior which the physician considered timid in quite another context: their conclusion is: a serious personality disorder, and it can be inferred from the letter of discharge that a so-called hysterical or histrionic personality is meant. After this, the referral to the mental health center follows. Information from her previous doctors includes the following.

Claudia is the oldest in a family of three children. She is a pretty young woman who used to be a photographic model. She is a typist, but has been sick for quite some time. Her parents live far away; she has a small house in a large city. Her parents, especially her father, are extremely concerned and visit her regularly, and each time they are upset by the condition their daughter is in: poorly nourished, clothed in black, in a house with the blinds drawn, she devotes herself to the images of the headless aborted child. Family members and friends urge her to start to enjoy life again, but without result.

In her first talk with the therapist from the mental health center Claudia makes an important remark: she does not feel guilty about the abortion, but about the fact that she *does not feel guilty* about the abortion, and it is for this reason that she may no longer have any pleasure, she promised her "daughter" this. The only good way of atoning for what she has done would be to die herself. "Pleasure" also stands for sexual contact with men. She is only allowed to humiliate them. This standpoint seems to be so firmly established that it would make no sense to try to get her to see it in a different perspective or to bring her around to other ideas.

Considering the experiences of his predecessors—who worked chiefly in a congruent and direct manner—and the symptomatic presentation of the difficulties, the therapist starts with no other plan than the intention to show a consistently paradoxical reaction until Claudia herself indicates in any way whatsoever that she is able to handle a more congruent approach. Because he also knows that Claudia can remain silent a very long time, generally dodges questions, etc., the therapist decides to take the initiative. The treatment required twenty-one sessions over a year and a half. Between sessions—at the therapist's initiative—several telephone calls took place. Four months later there was one follow-up talk. At Claudia's request there were no subsequent ones, but through her physician the therapist was later able to inform himself somewhat of her condition.

The treatment can be divided into two phases. In the first phase (some sixteen sessions) the emphasis lies on prescribing the complaints and sowing doubt; in the second phase a concrete solution is worked on in a metaphorical way, and a *leave-taking ritual* plays an important role in this. Both phases are described below. The most attention is given to the metaphor which ushered in the conclusion.

Prescribing the complaints and sowing doubt

One should imagine Claudia as a slender woman wrapped in black dresses, shawls, and head scarves, with loose hair hanging to her waist, who sits trembling and smoking in silence with her face turned away. She is pale and does not look well. Instead of waiting to see whether she will indicate what her wishes are, the therapist says approximately the following: "I would like it if we could call each other by our first names. Claudia, I understand that you have something to atone for to your child"—furious glance from Claudia—"and that you want to achieve this atonement by allowing yourself no pleasure any more. By never again entering into a sexual relationship, by humiliating men whenever possible, and perhaps by killing yourself. And apparently when you do permit yourself a short moment of pleasure, 'she' immediately lets you know of 'her' dissent, because right away you are plagued by images of 'her' which remind you of the fact that you went too far. It would seem very sensible to me if, for the coming time, you were to stick to the regimen you have prescribed yourself. Apparently it helps to prevent unwelcome events such as seeing 'her'." Then a cigarette is smoked in silence and a new appointment is made.

The next talk is more or less the same. Claudia again sits trembling and smoking in silence. The therapist does not ask how things have gone, but once again emphasizes the importance of the road she has chosen and proffers the suggestion that she may possibly not be an ordinary woman, but one who wants to go to the very *bottom of her suffering*.

He offers Claudia a cigarette, but she refuses it. Then he asks her for a cigarette, inquires whether she has indeed succeeded in avoiding all pleasure, and when she says that she has, he again indicates that it seems to him the best solution for the time being.

At the next session, a month later, Claudia says that she has had serious complaints again: she saw "her" lower body, again headless, but this time in an adult format, which was very frightening. The therapist sees this as a "sign": apparently she has tried to rush something and "she" warns that things are going too fast. "I think you have been to bed with somebody." It is true. She now starts to make remarks like: "It can't go on like this," "I want to get over it," etc., but the therapist urges her to show some moderation.

At the next session the therapist asks himself out loud how she can be so certain that "she" (who is continually referred to as "she" and "her"—Claudia will not allow any more concrete designation) permits Claudia no pleasure, for "she" has no head and cannot talk. Maybe "she" is really "very nice" and the patient would be better off if she did not become anxious when "she" comes. Perhaps she might try to do something nice back, for instance, by making a friendly remark.

After this session Claudia starts to hallucinate the therapist—also headless. And she indicates she increasingly feels that talking with the therapist is in fact a traitorous act against "her." However complaisant the therapist may be, she still assumes that he has in mind her recovery, and that is counter to "her" intents. The therapist expresses his doubt about this, too: maybe "she" is quite fond of the therapist, more than Claudia suspects, and in any case the therapist is very fond of "her." "There is something very sweet, something original about 'her'," he feels, "but I don't know what gives me that idea." But good, as long as Claudia thinks that "her" intents and those of the therapist are incompatible, Claudia must not rush things and must not cooperate with the therapist any more than she can.

One session later, Claudia has begun to doubt whether it would indeed be "treason" if she were to comply with the therapist, but she is not certain. At the next session Claudia appears to have made peace with "her." The therapist suggests that perhaps they can all work together—"she," Claudia, and he. At any rate, he asks Claudia to give his love to "her" the next time she sees her. This is promised. Apart from this, Claudia is now bothered by pseudo-hallucinations in which she sees terrifying faces. The therapist interprets this as a sign that she is presumably not quite sure of what everything means, but it seems to him quite logical that you think it is very scary when you first hallucinate faces: "You were used to hallucinating people without faces for so long."

There follows a period of increasing complaints: nearly total inactivity, all kinds of hallucinatory perceptions, depression, self-inflicted injuries, excessive drinking, pill-taking, etc. The therapist interprets these crisis-like reactions as normal when you start to doubt about something that has been a steadfast conviction. Claudia has since made clear in a congruent way that she comes from a family where important differences of opinion or painful experiences were not discussed in an open fashion. She has even brought up sexual problems: she cannot enjoy love-making. She is beginning to wonder whether hallucinating has perhaps become a habit. The therapist says it is something that does happen: people who hallucinate from habit.

The metaphoric phase

Because contact with Claudia has become quite rational and he has the impression that Claudia has gained some confidence in him, after sixteen talks the therapist feels it is "enough." The complaints have lasted long enough. But how to convey this conclusion? After all, Claudia is a sensitive person who once before proved to be quite unresponsive to too direct an approach.

He resorts to a metaphor and sets to work as follows: "Claudia, you are a Queen, and I am only a simple commissioner, Johnson. Now I know that there is a certain sentiment among the people, but I don't know if you want to know what that feeling is. You might be insulted and fly into a rage if your commissioner were to tell you about it, but it is also possible that you are appreciative of a commissioner who knows what goes on among the people but who does not dare to express it, because of his timorous respect for the Queen—he is afraid it will cost him his head. What do you want your commissioner to do?" Claudia, laughing: "Commissioner Johnson must tell me what is the matter, and not beat around the bush." Therapist: "Well, the people have not been content for quite some time now. They grumble. The people want a new Queen. You are too old, your views are obsolete. The people want you to abdicate. The situation in the country is bad." Claudia: "Good, then I will abdicate." Therapist: "No, your majesty, it is not that simple. It was not without a reason that you wanted to rule too long. You invested your love and capacities in leading the country and even though you have been aware for quite some time that you have grown too old and that your work no longer amounts to much, you would not have done it if you had not had a special affection for your work, and if it would not make you very sad to give up the throne." Claudia: "Commissioner, you are right, but how should I go about it?"

Commissioner Johnson, or the therapist, gives her the advice of Zeig (1980b) to look for a stone. The stone symbolizes her problem. She will have to carry the stone with her all the time and when she is ready to, she will bury it. She eagerly accepts the therapist's offer of assistance in this. It is agreed that she will come back in a month. When she comes she has a brick with her, wrapped in a black scarf. It turns out that she has sometimes carried the brick and sometimes not, and she is now advised to do this consistently. For the next three months there are occasional telephone calls from which it appears that "everything is still very difficult." For instance, she has had dreams in which she was buried. At one of the last sessions Claudia again shows up with the brick in her purse; she has chopped it to pieces.

She says she is bothered by anxieties, no longer by hallucinations. The therapist asks which anxiety she would like to tell about. This turns out to be a fear of men which, upon closer questioning, cannot solely be called fear. She has the urge to seduce men, to get them into bed, but after intercourse she panics, vomits, and the company must vanish as quickly as possible. Claudia's contempt for men is extensively discussed: "They are only after the outside," etc. The therapist tells her that her tendency to humiliate men will diminish once she meets a man who is stronger than she is: "Now you only associate with men who are push-overs for you."

"They come like roosters and they go like worms," the therapist summarizes the situation, and this remark makes her shriek with laughter. In the meantime several striking changes have taken place. For the first time Claudia is not dressed in black. She is going to go back to work. And she no longer considers it necessary to take the pieces of the brick everywhere with her.

An appointment is made for four months later. At that time Claudia can rightfully be called a different woman. The most important points follow:

—She looks good and has no more complaints.

—The need to humiliate men vanished, she feels, after she and the therapist had laughed about it: 'Why should I keep on doing it?' Not only has the need vanished, but the deed as well.

—She still has the broken brick. It is in her room and "becomes less valuable every day." But she does not want to part with the stone. She does not want to forget it entirely.

—She has played with a baby again, even though she got such a headache that she thought she had lost her head (!).

—She has gone back to work, although in a different department. The personnel manager had asked why she did not want to go back to her old department. Claudia: "Well, you see, if I were to come down with flu or something like that, everybody there would think: There goes Claudia again . . ." Personnel manager: "Yes, but you should be above things like that." Claudia: "You are entirely right. I should, but the point is: I am not." Upon which the man agreed to her transfer.

—She does not want a new appointment: "That just leaves the door ajar, then I can always go back and there is no reason to go back, because I can do it myself."

According to information from Claudia's physician over three years after the conclusion of the treatment, things have continued to go well for her. What ultimately happened to the stone is not known.

Discussion

Some questions might be posed with reference to this treatment which lend themselves to discussion. I will classify them under the following headings: questions concerning assessment and diagnosis, the patient-therapist relationship, the therapeutic techniques used, and the utility of the analytical point of view in this case.

1. *Assessment and diagnosis.* Van Dijck (1980) mentions a category of patients whose symptoms serve to maintain either a family equilibrium or an inner equilibrium (or both). In this case, he sees the symptoms as an adaptive strategy; this is shown, for one thing, by the active resistance on the part of the patient against removal of the complaint. In an earlier version of his chapter he advised the use of family dynamic and/or psychodynamic categories in such cases for an understanding of the problem. (Unfortunately he left out this advice in the definitive version.)

Clearly, Claudia should be reckoned in this category of patients. Progress, decreasing the complaints, would have invalidated her vow to her aborted child and possibly led to her further disintegration. The fact that she had to make this vow has to do with her anger with herself for the absence of guilt feelings and also with her anger with the person who conceived the child and his fellow males, as well as with her parents who belittled the whole issue of abortion at the time. Seen in this way, it was quite sensible of Claudia not to allow herself to be deprived of the complaints, however sympathetic the attempts of previous doctors to do so were.

Several times in the case description missing heads are mentioned: not only is "she" beheaded, but at a certain point the therapist too, who, by the way, brought up the risk of being beheaded in his role as Commissioner Johnson. From an analytical point of view this motive can be related to Claudia's need to humiliate men: both would stem from the castration complex. Apart from the question whether this could now be said to be correct at any other level than the metaphor, it is interesting to note that this idea not only plays an important role in psychoanalysis (see e.g. Freud, 1941), but also in cultural anthropology and mythology (see Sierksma, 1979, van Peursen, 1975, and Ten Berge, 1982).

The only possible diagnosis provided by DSM-III (APA, 1980) on Axis I that fits her condition would seem to be "atypical dissociative disorder." It is much harder to decide what to put down about Claudia on Axis II. Her previous therapists spoke of a "hysterical" or "histrionic personality disorder," but it seems unlikely that a personality can be changed within six months by a paradox, a metaphor, and a ritual.

We were unsuccessful in finding out whether Claudia's personality corresponded to the criteria that DSM III suggests for establishing a histrionic personality disorder. For Claudia and for some other patients, it could not be determined whether their expressions were "exaggerated," whether their reactions should be called "overreactions," whether they were "egocentric," etc. In this respect we tend to agree with Freeman's (1983) conclusion. In a survey of personality disorders, he says that ". . . until the identification of the hysterical personality is more reliable and valid it must remain a suspect term." So Axis II was not used for Claudia.

Surely there is reason to suppose that behind the anger were concealed feelings of grief and helplessness, possibly also in connection with the abortion. Claudia did not avail herself of the opportunity to express them. So whether or not unresolved grief was involved is merely a matter of conjecture.

2. *The patient-therapist relationship.* At the beginning, when he encouraged Claudia to continue along the symptomatic road she had chosen, the therapist defined the relationship as metacomplementary (Haley, 1963). It is usual that after a while the patient starts to offer some opposition, as Claudia did: she cannot go on like this, etc. It is often not sensible to respond immediately to this change in strategy on the part of the patient in a complementary and congruent manner.

In this case an extra-safe way was chosen. When the therapist called himself "Commissioner Johnson" and Claudia "Queen," he avoided all the risks of a more congruent or even confrontal treatment (power struggle, intensification of complaints, etc.). Considering her reaction, his message was not obliterated by his circumspection. The therapist in the role of Commissioner Johnson can be compared to a jester: as long as he disqualifies himself, he may tell the truth, and even the whole truth.

3. *Technical aspects.* No one who was acquainted with the experiences of the previous therapists will be surprised at the paradoxical strategy in the beginning of the treatment. The crisis reactions which followed the 'sowing of doubt' are rather normal. Not only people like Claudia, but also paranoid psychotic people, for instance, run into difficulties when they begin to doubt the amount of truth in their delusions. Even the "sane," for example, people who believe in an ideology or a religion, go through a period of doubt when their convictions are shaken. And if it were only for this reason, the directive principle of short treatments must be seen in its proper perspective, at least for people like Claudia. To thrust someone into a crisis in a short time is easy enough.

To help a person out of it again, to help him find a new orientation, simply takes more time, despite all directive optimism.

I have already remarked on the metaphoric approach above.

Then the question: was the ritual with the stone carried out correctly? Champions of radical leave-taking rituals will perhaps find it not very gratifying that the stone was not buried, but I feel that Claudia did the sensible thing in keeping it. It may be better not to bury or forget important life events. It may be better to let time do its work, to allow the significance of those life events to decrease at a pace that suits the patient. Perhaps one day she will get rid of the stone when she moves, gets engaged, has a baby, perhaps it will be mislaid, or perhaps she will never get rid of it and the pieces will always remind her of an important condition.

The word "condition" indicates that we are not exactly sure what we are talking about. That the stone was a symbol is certain, but *what* the stone was a symbol of is not certain. It might have been a symbol of how much it hurt her to give up her position as "Queen," of the fetus, of the person who caused her to become pregnant, of men in general, of her pregnancy, of herself, of her grief, of her parents, of a future which she may not be able to cope with—and of many other things. In all probability, the stone had different meanings at different times.

4. *The utility of the psychoanalytical point of view*. Claudia's thoughts, feelings, and behavior had a very Freudian ring to them. Her preoccupation with such themes as revenge, castration, guilt, and self-punishment invited a psychoanalytical interpretation. Although he was not analytically trained, the therapist derived support from the fact that he could bring some order into the symptoms, motives, and maneuvers using ideas from Freudian psychology.

The strategy pursued differs in the extreme from what one would expect from a psychoanalytically oriented treatment: the pseudo-hallucinations are seen as a "useful sing," the seriousness of the complaints as a "sign of willingness to go to the very bottom," the worsening of the complaints when doubt arises about the correctness of the self-punishment as a sort of "crisis of faith," retaining the complaints as something "strongly reminiscent of the behavior of a queen," and when Claudia worries about destructive feelings towards men the therapist suggests a positive solution to this in the future.

That even the destructive attitude towards men could be called positive is taught to us by Erickson (Rosen, 1982). He does not speak of a destructive attitude but of superiority, which is shown by the patient's ability to undo an erection.

The Role of the Family Members in a Leave-Taking Ritual: An Example

Jos Ebbers

When prescribing a leave-taking ritual, it is important to find out in advance what the repercussions of the ritual may be on significant persons in the client's environment (cf. Spiegel, 1969). Van der Hart (1983a) reports an example in which this apparently was neglected. The example involved a woman who was to take leave of her ex-husband by means of a ritual. One of the things she had agreed with the therapist was that she would destroy her ex-husband's chair, in which her present boyfriend was not allowed to sit. When she told her boyfriend and her children what she was planning to do, they objected. This made the woman so angry that she attacked the chair with a large knife and cut the upholstery to shreds. The children were bewildered and the boyfriend was so upset that he packed his bags and left that very evening. Later the boyfriend came back and the children showed some understanding for their mother's situation, but obviously the whole incident should have been avoided. Although by definition complications cannot always be foreseen, those which can be foreseen must be taken into account.

Complications can be expected if, aside from the client's problems with the past, for which individual therapy encompassing a leave-taking ritual seems indicated, there are also family or marital troubles. Conflicts between family members or spouses about the present state of affairs can interfere with the execution of the ritual, while the emotions the ritual evokes about the past can put added strain on the family or the relationship.

In our experience, in treating such cases, it is generally preferable to work on ''the past'' and the leave-taking ritual first, and to enlist the cooperation of the family members or the partner in this. Having witnessed a resolution and perhaps having contributed to it may result in a more cooperative attitude on their part in finding a solution to the family or marital problems, for instance, through family therapy.

This was the order used in the example presented below, although for her difficulties in her family situation the client later took part (with success) in group therapy for women with similar problems. The description of this treatment also covers the role of the client's husband in the execution of the ritual, and the manner in which the therapist endeavored to ensure that the husband's role would be facilitative.

The referral

Mr. and Mrs. Mulder (both 39) were referred to a mental health center by their family physician. He has been treating her medicinally for six months for her anxieties and depression, but it has not been helping. During this period she has told him one thing and another about the backgrounds of her complaints. Mrs. Mulder simply dreads the idea of having to tell her story again to a stranger: she is terribly ashamed. The physician therefore mentions in his referral what it is she is ashamed of.

During the first talk, Mrs. Mulder is very tense. It strikes the therapist that her husband tries to cheer her up by saying that everything will probably turn out fine. He immediately thrusts the physician's letter into the therapist's hands. The letter says that it took a lot of effort on the doctor's part to motivate Mrs. Mulder to go to the mental health center. She is terribly ashamed of the fact that she was a prostitute for seven years. She experiences the past as a well-nigh unsupportable burden. He suspects that there are other problems in the family as well, which is why he referred the couple. After the therapist reads this letter out loud, Mrs. Mulder begins to cry. At the same time her husband starts to speak, telling about the difficulties they have had recently, and after a while Mrs. Mulder is able to talk about her difficulties herself.

Mrs. Mulder's complaint is that she feels more and more depressed recently. She also quarrels more and more often with her husband, mostly about housework. Mrs. Mulder feels that she is unfairly treated in the family by being used as a servant. When she is on the street, she is anxious; she is particularly afraid of being recognized by a former client, especially since this actually happened once.

Backgrounds

Mrs. Mulder was the middle child in a family of five children. Her parents often fought, and the general atmosphere was not pleasant. She could not get along at all with her mother, but got on better with her father. He was away often, and she saw him as the victim of her mother's egotistic and domineering personality. At home she often felt lonely. To escape the glum atmosphere and the conflicts with her mother, she got married at nineteen to a boyfriend she had only known for a few months. A year later she had her daughter Lucy and two years after that her son Jack was born. After several miscarriages, another son was born: Adriaan, who turned out to have serious brain damage and had to be admitted to the hospital immediately following the delivery. When the husband, who had not been present at the birth, saw his son for the first time in the hospital he said to her: ''I hope that he dies soon. If he doesn't, then I'll make sure he does.'' Adriaan died when he was thirteen weeks old. Mrs. Mulder went alone to the funeral. Her husband refused to go along; she thought the children were too young for it, and she had not told her parents. During the funeral she felt full of grief, lonely, and deserted by her husband. Memories of the loneliness she used to feel at home came back to her. Her husband's attitude kept on bothering her. Whenever she tried to talk with him about it, it turned into a quarrel and he beat her. The fights and the batterings became more and more frequent. When her father died during this period, she became depressed. Her family was in a bad position financially and materially, and her husband tried to solve these problems by forcing her to become a prostitute. She tells the therapist that during this period she was so incapable of thinking and feeling, that, after having offered resistance a long time, she did what her husband wanted her to do: ''Now I can't comprehend how I could have gone so far.''

After she had been working as a prostitute for seven years, she quit.

For it was then that she met her present husband. He first came to her as a customer. She managed to leave her first husband she filed for a divorce. A long struggle for the children ensued. Finally she was awarded custody of her son; her daughter preferred to remain with her father. After they had lived together a few years, she and her present husband got married.

Mr. Mulder is employed as a manager. He was previously married and has no children of his own. After the divorce he threw himself into his work and became isolated. When he realized this, he started getting out more, and his visits to prostitutes also fell under this heading. It was in this period that he met his present wife.

Assessment

In his first talks with the couple, it strikes the therapist that the female client behaves helplessly. Her husband interprets this behavior to mean that he is expected to stand up for her. For instance, every time the therapist asks Mrs. Mulder a question, the husband answers. In this manner confirms his wife's helpless behavior. But if she comments on what she feels to be an unreasonable division of tasks in the housekeeping, he sometimes makes a biting remark, so it is actually intermittent reinforcement, which increases her symptomatic behavior all the more. She always backs off after such a critical or negative reaction by her husband, according to her, because she is not equal to the fights which might otherwise result. Besides, she says, she is still so afflicted by her past that the occasional tensions between her and her husband seem less important.

Mr. Mulder thinks that his wife ought not to worry so much about the past. He feels her difficulties are more the result of a lack of independence. The paradox here is that he is convinced she will become independent if only she follows his instructions to the letter.

On the other hand, the husband, too, lives in a paradox: for it was he who saved a fallen woman, he took her out of the gutter, he has taken good care of her, and the result is that she has been depressed for six months.

The therapist thinks that the way in which the client undergoes her "past" forms the point of embarkation for the treatment: why doesn't she just do something about the relationship with her husband? Probably because she feels she has no right to. Why should she feel she has no right to? Because, she feels, she has been a "bad woman." Her husband was her salvation from prostitution, but this has put her into a position which gives her no rights, one in which she must be forever *grateful*. To be able to develop a more positive self-image, the client ought to take leave of her past. If she succeeds in this, she will no longer need to be grateful.

Treatment strategy

The therapist suggests to the couple to commence the therapy with unresolved issues from Mrs. Mulder's past. He brings up the idea of a leave-taking ritual. He is willing to assist the client individually with it, but also wishes to have a few talks about it with husband and wife together at the appropriate moment. So it would be individual therapy in the larger framework of marital counseling. Husband and wife agree to this suggestion.

The therapist tells Mr. Mulder that he can greatly contribute to the treatment by relieving his wife as much as possible of the housekeeping tasks. He also makes the rule that Mr. Mulder may only talk with his wife about the therapy if *she* expresses a wish to do so. These are important interventions: if they are complied with, a pathological interaction pattern between husband and wife will be broken, the intermittent reinforcement of the helpless behavior will be eliminated, and the paradoxes in which both of them are trapped will be eliminated.

Since son Jack is likely to notice something about the effects of the therapy on his mother, the couple is advised to inform him of the fact that they have sought help, that his mother still has one thing and another from the past to work through, and further to tell him only what they think necessary. At this stage, the question of what type of help might be offered after the ritual is left open.

In the sessions Mrs. Mulder has alone with the therapist, she also makes it clear to him how much she undergoes her "past" as the most important problem. She is often plagued by memories of painful and sad events and emotions which she is at a loss how to handle. She speaks of a chaos which she would like to make orderly.

Together with the therapist she formulates the following objectives:
1. Drawing a line under her past in prostitution. Memories of this past evoke in her an impotent rage toward her ex-husband.

2. Working through the loss of her son Adriaan. Every year again around his date of birth and date of death she feels overcome by grief. Here, too, she is haunted by memories of her ex-husband's attitude towards their handicapped son and her own impotence.
3. Symbolically telling her dead father about, or submitting to his judgment, her "past." Her father was a person, she says, who would do anything to understand her.
4. Making the relationship with her husband one on equal terms. Compared to what she has been through in the past, Mrs. Mulder is, in general, satisfied with the life she leads with her husband and son. But she is not satisfied about the fact that she is too much the housekeeper in the family.

The therapist thinks that the client can best achieve the first three goals (which refer to the "past") by means of a leave-taking ritual. In order to motivate her to carry it out, which is very demanding emotionally, he makes a suggestive interpretation of her life cycle. In other words, he tells her a *therapeutic myth* which is acceptable to her (cf. Frank, 1973; chapter 2) and on the basis of which she can agree to his plan. He recounts how she fled from her parental home and flung herself into marriage; how much she had to put up with in her first marriage; the loss of Adriaan and the other traumatic events which affected her so much that they still prey on her.

She tried to disregard all this and to put herself at the beck and call of her husband and son, but she is constantly reminded of the failure of this attempt. She still feels the pain it caused her. If she looks this part of her past square in the face by going through these transitons again, but in a symbolic manner, surely this will enable her to relinquish the past. As she so very clearly indicates that she has great difficulty in talking about it, perhaps she might write about it; write until she can draw a line under her past.

This appeals to her. It is especially the idea that she will not need to talk about everything that has happened that stimulates her to set out on this difficult task. She will not need to defend herself continually against someone who asks her all kinds of questions, she remarks. "I want to open this door just to be able to close it again once and for all." The therapist, who has depicted the client solely as a "victim," realizes that she does not see it entirely in this way. It is not really the terrible things that have happened to her that must be worked through, but her guilt feelings, her feeling that she was an accomplice. At the same time, he thinks it is better not to talk about this, but to give the client the opportunity to bring it up while she is writing.

In order to inform Mr. Mulder of what the ritual involves and to ask his cooperation in carrying it out, he is invited for another talk with his wife. The therapist stresses the fact that the ritual will be very demanding on the client, which means that housekeeping may sometimes be too much for her. Mr. Mulder is willing to take over a greater share of the housekeeping tasks while his wife is working on the ritual. This, of course, is in accordance with the client's wish not to be the only one responsible for the housekeeping, but that aspect is not discussed in this session: it would only complicate matters. At her request, the husband and wife together will tell her son Jack something about the ritual.

The therapist makes the following arrangements with the couple: the client will write about her past daily at a fixed time. In general a writing task like this is carried out in a secluded part of the house, which emphasizes the non-routine nature of the task, improves the concentration, and gives the task something in the nature of a "benevolent ordeal" (cf. Haley, 1963; Van der Hart & Ebbers, 1981). But it is the client's wish to carry out the task in the middle of the living room, at her husband's desk. He will clear out all his things so that she can write here. In this way, she says, she can feel the support of his presence while she is writing. As previously agreed, husband and wife will only talk about the therapy, or in this case the ritual, if the client takes the initiative herself.

For her writing, Mrs. Mulder will buy two notebooks, each of them a different color. The first one must be *black*, she feels. In this one she wants to write down her experiences in her first marriage, which caused her much grief and distress. She particularly wants to go into the prostitution, the death of her child, and the beatings. The second notebook must be *green*. This one is intended for working through her guilt feelings. Here she wants to account for herself to her father and to ask his compassion for the mistakes she has made in her life. She is convinced that her father would understand her if only she dared to look things in the face. Mrs. Mulder and the therapist agree that he will not read the notebooks: Mrs. Mulder suspects that this would make her feel inhibited in writing.

The therapist prepares the couple for the crises which may occur in the coming months: violent emotions, perhaps deeper depression, and suicidal tendencies. He urges the client to call him when things get difficult. Reference is made to the fact that Mrs. Mulder will have to carry out a leave-taking ceremony with the notebooks when she is finished writing ("such an important task can't simply be put aside"), but no further details are discussed.

The ritual

At the next session a week later the client says that the talk with Jack went well. He thought it all a little strange, but if it was good for his mother, he had no objections. He was not told what was going to come up in the ritual.

Mrs. Mulder experiences the first weeks she spends in writing as a hell. The amazement that she can recollect things so vividly soon gives way to the fury which she feels mounting inside towards her ex-husband. Sometimes it makes her feel anxious, and then her husband has to stimulate her to go on writing. The supportive role of her husband had not been mentioned in their agreements with the therapist, but the client is glad of his help, and the therapist later expresses his appreciation of it.

What happened in this "black period," as she calls it, when her ex-husband forced her into prostitution and he started to batter her, is the hardest for her. Re-experiencing how she tried to keep her torn family together makes her feel quite numb. At other times she is overcome by surges of regret. She also starts to recall many emotionally charged situations at her parents' home. The most important seems to be the unjustified anger of her mother toward her, and the understanding that her father asked her to have for her mother when she complained to him about it.

Too many things come back in a short time. For this reason she first comes to see the therapist twice a week, and he helps her to order the material. Together they find out what from the black notebook, in the form of new insights, can go into the green one, and thus symbolically be submitted for her father's approval. To support her, the therapist also stresses the fact that, thanks to her sacrifices and her not imposing her difficulties on her children, they still had a reasonably good time of it. She was a good mother for them, even under the hardest circumstances.

In this way she learns to accept what has happened, including the fact that she gave in to her ex-husband and went into prostitution. She can see things in perspective, she can deal with her feelings better and better, and she less frequently needs to call upon the therapist. It is also a big help that her husband keeps to his part of the agreement. He no longer needs to encourage her to go on writing. Once in a while her son Jack asks her what it is she is doing. She tells him about her unresolved grief for the death of Adriaan and her father, and that she wants to write something about it every day. She says she will tell him more about her difficulties when everything is over and done with.

After a few months Mrs. Mulder has filled several notebooks, and she has worked through a great deal of the grief for her dead son and her father; she has also unloosed herself from her guilt feelings about the prostitution. She has said everything she had to say. To involve her husband in the planning and the execution of the leave-taking ceremony, he is once again invited.

In talking about the plans for the leave-taking ceremony, it becomes clear to Mrs. Mulder that she wants to carry it out in two steps. First she wants to take leave of the experiences described in the black notebooks: the period in which she was a prostitute and the time she was living with her ex-husband. After she has concluded this, she wants to part with the green notebooks and then go and visit the graves of her father and her son Adriaan. Together with her husband and the therapist, she fixes the day on which she intends to accomplish all this. Her husband will accompany her during the ritual and be of as much support as possible to her. How he will do that and what other part he may have in the procedures is not discussed in the talks with the therapist. He believes that husband and wife will handle it well by themselves.

Mrs. Mulder also wants to involve her son in the leave-taking ceremony and the subsequent family reunion. The first phase—taking leave of the prostitution—is not suitable for this. The second phase is; Jack already knows something about his mother's writing about the death of Adriaan and her father. The client wants to invite him to be present at this ceremony on the day itself.

The leave-taking ceremony

After 20 talks with the therapist, which took place over some five months, the concluding ceremony is carried out.

The first step. On the agreed day, Mr. and Mrs. Mulder get up at five o'clock to carry out the first part of the definitive leave-taking undisturbed. They let their son Jack sleep: they want to involve him in the second phase. The prostitution period is symbolized by a large packet of condoms that Mrs. Mulder still had around. Mr. Mulder will carry this, at his wife's request. Mrs. Mulder takes the black notebook, a plastic garbage bag, and a rock. The meaning of the symbol and the fact that he was the one to carry it were not discussed.

In silence they first walk past the house where Mrs. Mulder's ex-husband and daughter live. While they stand still in front of it for a minute, the client sees several images pass before her eyes, images which she has described in the past months, and once again she feels she is growing angry. They go on walking to the neighborhood where Mrs. Mulder worked as a prostitute. Again she grows angry, but then she realizes that this life was her only possibility to continue taking care of her children. She also feels some pride at the fact that she was able to keep hidden from her children the offensive deeds of her ex-husband. She no longer feels the anxiety which she so often felt.

While her husband watches at a distance, Mrs. Mulder takes the black notebook and tears it to pieces. She puts the pieces into the plastic bag, puts in the packet of condoms and the rock, and closes the bag. Opposite the house where she used to work, she throws the bag into the water. Later she says that, at that moment, she physically felt that she was actually casting a heavy burden from her shoulders. This was not only due to the weight of the stone; it was also as if the anger disappeared from her body. After the bag sinks, she cries. Her husband comes to her and she allows herself to be comforted by him.

When they come home, they make breakfast. They wake up Jack, who has not noticed their absence, but who now sees that his mother has been crying. Mrs. Mulder tells him that today is the day she wants to go somewhere and burn the notebooks in which she has written about her father and about Adriaan. She is convinced, she adds, in order to reassure Jack, that by doing this, she is making a new start in life. She does not mention what happened earlier that morning. She asks Jack to wait for the two of them to come back home, so that they can all three go out and have a nice day. Jack thinks this is a good idea, because he was beginning to have enough of the long faces.

The second step. The burning of the green notebooks takes place in a secluded place in a wood. The couple drives to the woods by car and then they walk in silence to the spot. Mrs. Mulder makes the fire and puts the pages in one at a time. While she is doing this, memories of her father and her son come back to her. She has brought along a special tool to gather the ashes: the spoon which was intended for Adriaan. Using this spoon, she scrapes some ashes together and puts them into a plastic bag. She spreads the remainder of the ashes over an open space. With her husband she then drives to the cemetery where her father and her son are buried. Later she says that this difficult trip was necessary for her. With the spoon, she makes a hole in the ground above the grave of her father, and she fills this hole with some of the ashes from the green notebooks. A little later she does the same at the grave of her son. She and her husband stand a while by the graves and she feels sad. On the way home she notices that her sadness is diminishing. She gives the spoon a special place in her bedroom.

The reunion. Back home, the client feels fatigued and contented. She suggests that the three of them go to a restaurant near the sea. She tells Jack about the rituals in the woods and at the cemetery. She also feels it is necessary to inform him about her past, but she does not think the time is ripe. After their meal they take a long walk on the beach. There is a strong wind. She feels as if the wind takes with it the last "black thoughts." The walk is thus experienced as a cleansing rite.

The group therapy

A few weeks after the ritual Mrs. Mulder feels capable of telling her son about her past as a prostitute. She does not tell him that she was forced into it, nor that she met her present husband in this way. Jack is rather abashed by her story. He retreats to his room. Few words are exchanged in the week that follows. Then Mrs. Mulder once again talks about it. This time, Jack seems to be able to adjust to the knowledge, and their relationship returns to its former basis.

Although things are going much better for the client—she is cheerful, she takes initiatives, she is no longer troubled by anxiety—the relationship with her husband is still not what she would like it to be. Three weeks after the ritual she mentions this to the therapist. She becomes irritated with her husband, particularly when she is busy with the housekeeping and he is sitting reading a book or newspaper. She does feel that housekeeping is her task, but the way things are she feels she is the family slave. When she discusses this with her husband, he takes over a larger share of the housekeeping, but after a while, the same thing begins all over again.

This problem could perhaps be solved by marital counselling; Mr. Mulder's cooperation in the previous phase of therapy seems to point in this direction. But the therapist has also seen good results from a colleague's group therapy for women with similar problems. He puts the question to the client: which possibility appeals to her more?

Mrs. Mulder is taken aback by the idea of group therapy, but she decides to try it. She takes part in the group for four months. By sharing experiences with the other women, she feels strengthened. She has never been through anything like this before. The examples she encounters in the group inspire her to start taking a more distinct stand towards her husband and her son. Not only does she make arrangements with them about the division of tasks at home, but she also makes sure they keep their part of the bargain. She no longer feels inclined to do it herself.

Toward the end of her participation in the group, she tells about her period as a prostitute. The group does not show reproval; on the contrary, her confession brings unbosomings from the other women. She feels this is the most important event in the group.

After this, at Mrs. Mulder's request, the therapist has a few more individual talks with her. As soon as she indicates she can manage on her own, the therapy is terminated.

An appointment a year later

A year later, Mrs. Mulder calls and asks if she can come to talk about the death of her mother. An appointment is made. When she comes a week later, she says that she regrets having phoned: "I was alone at home and had just heard that my mother had died, and I guess I reacted impulsively. I spent a few days at her bedside, but I wasn't really prepared for her death. Later, when I told my husband about my appointment with you, he got mad because he felt he was being overlooked. And actually I agree with him, because we get along much better now than we used to and we don't need a therapist any more."

The progress made in therapy had been maintained over the past year. The climate in the family is an open one, and she is satisfied with the division of tasks. Mrs. Mulder again has contact with her daughter, who now lives on her own. She told her about the therapy and about her "past," and her daughter reacted well to this.

In the intervening year Mrs. Mulder had visited her mother again, because she wanted to do something with her before it was too late. She did not talk about the past. It turned into a sort of kaffeeklatsch, implying that the link between the two of them was restored. Mrs. Mulder is glad that she now has memories of a good relationship with her mother. She has no contact with her ex-husband. She still notices that she sometimes reproaches him, but it does not tyrannize her. She has told her son and daughter very little about his distasteful role in the past, so that they can continue to see their father without inhibition. Mrs. Mulder now has a part-time job as a nurse. She greatly enjoys not being so financially dependent on her husband.

Discussion

1. The cumbersome past the client had to take leave of in this example was not the only problem for which she sought help. There were also tensions in the marriage, involving the unequal division of tasks in the housekeeping and Mrs. Mulder's incapacity to change this. The first task of the therapist here was the question of *which* problem to start with. The client indicated she preferred to start out with the past rather than the present. However, this was not the only reason for choosing this order. The therapist's prime consideration was that the client felt guilty about her past as a prostitute. She felt she owed a debt of gratitude to her husband, since he had gotten her out. If she could really see her past as behind her, she would no longer need to be grateful and she would be able to tackle the present difficulties in her relationship.

Apart from the specific issue in this case (the guilt feelings about the prostitution), it probably would have been a good idea to start with the *past* anyway. Current family and marital problems are difficult to solve if they are contaminated by unresolved problems from the past (cf. Solomon, 1973). If the other family members or the spouse are capable of lending the person in question the necessary support in the leave-taking ritual, this is often a good foundation for solving family or marital problems. But it is no guarantee of the outcome of such therapy. It would be naïve to assume that such problems can always be solved without disrupting the existing relationship: in a similar case, the best solution turned out to be a divorce.

2. The second task of the therapist was to decide *who* should be involved in the various phases of treatment. In the first phase, which revolved around reorganizing material for the leave-taking ritual, the stress lay on individual support to Mrs. Mulder. But the role her husband could have in it—taking over her housekeeping tasks, for instance, which was also an important symbolic gesture—and the knowledge which the son would need to have about the ritual were not neglected. In this way, a sort of collaboration developed between husband and wife in which he supported her in her difficult task. The husband and son were involved

in the ceremony itself to different degrees. It is quite likely that many complications were avoided because of the husband's cooperative attitude. Had his role been ignored, an important source of help might have been left unutilized.

In the second phase, about the marital difficulties, the client preferred group therapy for women with similar problems to marital counselling. As it turned out, the group was not a bad choice. The examples the client encountered in the group enabled her to transcend the paradox her husband gave her ("become independent by following my instructions").

3. An important aspect of rituals is that there is no communication *about* the social relationships involved. They are brought to expression in action (Van der Hart, 1983a, p. 14). This aspect played a role in the leave-taking ritual described here. The most outstanding examples of this are: writing at her husband's desk in the middle of the living room, and taking leave of the packet of condoms he had once bought and which he had to carry to the site of the ritual. What this expressed about the relationship between husband and wife was not discussed, but it was telling in itself.

It should be mentioned that the symbols in this example are condensed symbols which have more than one meaning. The meaning which the therapist ascribed to them was only one of several possibilities. It may not be necessary that all the levels of meaning of the symbols and symbolic actions are made explicit by the participants to themselves.

4. Chapter 2 discussed how the Navajo principles of "making prestations" and "removing ugly conditions" play a large role in leave-taking rituals. The example described here shows how physically the "removal of ugly conditions" can be experienced. During the first step of the leave-taking ceremony, when the client threw the bag containing the shredded black notebooks, the packet of condoms and the rock into the water, she said she felt that she was physically casting off a heavy load; it was as if the anger disappeared from her body. Jan, in the example in chapter 4, realized after his symbols had disappeared into the waves, that his tenseness and his uneasiness had disappeared as well. He also showed something of the identification with a (to him) positive power: the mighty sea whose power seemed to surge into him. After the package that she and her husband had dropped into the water had finally sunk, Debbie (chapter 10), too, had the feeling that a burden had been removed from her shoulders and she felt like she was almost floating in the air.

All these examples mention the symbolism of casting off a heavy load. In the leave-taking rituals which consisted of burning and burying the key symbols, "removing ugly conditions" was not experienced in the same way: there it was more a feeling of emptiness that predominated. Entirely aside from the client's freedom of choice, it may be worth examining whether there are indications for either form. And perhaps better forms can be designed for the principle of "identification with the positive powers."

10

A Burial at Sea

George A. Sargent

Therapeutic leave-taking rituals are usually performed in order to part with a deceased person or an ex-spouse or ex-lover (cf. Selvini Palazzoli et al., 1974, 1979; Van der Hart, 1983a). But there are other cases in which such rituals can be utilized as well. One of these is a situation frequently encountered in marital therapy: after some initial progress, the partners arrive at an impasse stemming from the fact that they keep on feeling resentful and hostile because of injustices done to them. A suitable leave-taking ritual can transcend such an impasse. The ritual enables the couple to take leave of a painful and agonizing past and to redefine their relationship in a positive way.

This chapter describes the therapy of a couple with two children, who had gotten married when they were both very young. They ran into just such an impasse. A ritual helped the husband and wife leave their painful past behind them and celebrate their new relationship. The ritual helped them weave into their new relationship the positive changes which had taken place earlier in the therapy. The couple, Debbie and Jim, have read the report of their therapy and commented on it. Their reactions in retrospect are an essential part of this story, because, after all, it is primarily about their experiences, and not the therapist's. Their comments show in what perspective they see the ritual in the process of change.

The referral

Jim and Debbie had been married for eleven years when they were referred by their family physician for marital counselling. They were on the verge of breaking up because, for the second time in a few years, he was having an affair with another woman. Jim, a 32-year-old Navy nurse, had a mild flirtation with a patient on the ward where he worked. But it gradually evolved into an emotional and sexual relationship, and it had been going on for nearly a year when Jim "confessed" the affair to his wife. After being discharged from the hospital, his girl friend came back regularly for follow-up treatment. After each visit to the doctor, she always sought out Jim. It looked like the visits to the doctor had become her alibi for continuing her relationship with him.

At the first session, Jim, a tall, blond, and lean young man, gave the impression he was bewildered by his own behavior and the resulting chaos in his marriage. Debbie, a very competent and extremely strict young woman from a strait-laced Boston family, was depressed. She was reserved and bitter, hurt and very much on her guard. Both husband and wife said they wanted to save their marriage, but Debbie declared she was not sure if she could ever learn to trust Jim again. She doubted whether he would be capable of moderation in his relationships with other women. As a matter of fact, he had his doubts about this as well.

The fact that Debbie threatened to divorce him had brought Jim to the decision to go into therapy. He presented his own personality as the problem. He wanted to understand why he could not suppress his romantic interest in other women and he wanted to understand why he remained involved in the relationship he had at the outset of therapy. By presenting the problem like this, Jim denied any responsibility for the choices which had gotten him into difficulties and had so hurt his wife. While saying that he was to blame, he was also saying that he could not really be held accountable for his behavior (cf. Haley, 1963). Debbie sat quietly tearful or angrily stoic while Jim continued to heap the blame on himself. He clung to his implicit view of therapy: only if he had some insight into the reasons why he kept on looking for other relationships would he be able to stop.

Whenever Debbie did say anything, it was about her constant thoughts of leaving Jim. How could she ever trust him again? Jim had promised her the last time that he would never have another affair, and she had trusted him. Debbie's conduct was maternal, stern, and responsible. While Jim did not like her taking on the mother role, he continued to act like an irresponsible child.

The treatment

The therapy first focused on getting Jim to take responsibility for his own behavior. He began to realize that he was looking elsewhere for what he wanted from his marriage instead of confronting Debbie with his discontentment. With the therapist's help, he began to discover how and when he had learned to avoid confrontations with people who were close to him. He turned his attention to the relationships in his family of origin. Some Gestalt work with an empty chair (cf. Kempler, 1974) helped him see how he had given up his own power and self-esteem to his parents. As he became more aware of this and learned to act differently, his self-assurance and self-respect increased.

During the next four sessions, Jim made several important decisions. His use of language changed. It showed that he was starting to take more responsibility for his behavior. "I can't stop" became "I won't stop" and then "I will stop." He put an end to the affair he was having, making it perfectly clear to his girl friend that he wanted to make his marriage succeed. Jim also started to take more responsibility for money matters. Instead of letting Debbie manage their checkbook and making her be the one who had to say "no" to his urge to spend money, he started to take this responsibility himself and to say "no" to himself. In other areas, too, he changed in much the same direction. He became keenly aware of how much his marriage meant to him, and he made genuine efforts for what he and Debbie called their "new relationship." And Debbie managed to give up her incessant thoughts of leaving.

Then the therapy reached an impasse. Debbie's response to the changes Jim was going through was positive, but she could not rid herself of her resentment, even though she badly wanted to. She had waited a long time for many of these changes in Jim, and intellectually she appreciated them very much. But emotionally she was left cold and incapable of accepting the changes that had taken place. Both of them said they were "stuck." The therapy came to a standstill.

The preparation for the ritual

Reading about the use of rituals in therapy had made me an enthusiast. At the eleventh session, it suddenly struck me that Debbie and Jim referred to their "old" relationship—the one prior to therapy—as "dead." They called their present relationship "new." When I realized this, I suggested to them that their inability to make any further progress might be resolved with a fitting ritual to mourn the death of their old relationship and to celebrate the birth of the new one.

They reacted positively. It was as if I had said exactly the right thing, had found the right words for something they, too, felt but could not express. I discussed with them why it might be a good idea to design and carry out a fitting ritual, and we talked about how, in our society, rituals help people to make transitions in traditional ways, especially at times of stress and loss. At such times it is really too difficult to invent one's behavior from moment to moment. Performing ritualized behaviors helps us to define our experiences. Especially when its direction and sequence are carefully prescribed beforehand, action can help us through the transition or crisis. I took the example of the death of a relative or a good friend to remind us of the structure and symbolism attendant on leave-taking rituals. I asked Debbie and Jim to think over the idea of designing a burial rite for their old relationship; perhaps later we could devise a ritual to celebrate their new, more committed and more satisfying relationship.

Our talk of a leave-taking ritual for their old relationship brought to light that Debbie and Jim had never really made a choice for their "first marriage." They had gone together in high school, and had simply stayed together and gotten married. They had not considered other alternatives; in fact they had scarcely considered their personal needs. The commitment of marriage had only been words to them. But now they were much more aware of their responsibility.

"We want to be together now, even knowing each other's faults," they said, "but somehow our old marriage has got to be laid to rest." It was remarkable how readily Debbie and Jim adapted their words to the metaphor of loss and leave-taking, and how clear the cause of their impasse became to the therapist once their metaphor was understood.

They were not given greatly detailed instructions on how the ritual was to be conducted. "Certain words need to be said," I explained, "as in almost all rituals, but the words should be the ones you mutually decide are appropriate. Symbols should be involved, ones that stand for your old relationship, but you know best what they are. You must, however, be willing to say goodbye to them forever. You may like to bury them or burn them. You may want to mark their place of rest so you can return to honor your old relationship from time to time. Perhaps not. What is most important is that you two design the essentials and carry out the ritual with a sense of ceremony." With these suggestions, the session came to an end. We were all three enthusiastic about the possibilities it contained. The next time they would tell how the ritual had gone.

The ritual

The next time Debbie and Jim came in, they looked different. Debbie looked less serious. She walked with a lighter step, smiled at me very warmly and held my gaze easily as they sat down. Jim looked very pleased with himself.

They needed no encouragement to report on their assignment. They said that, after the last session, they had decided to have a burial at sea. "We had a picture of ourselves taken on our wedding day," said Jim. "We put that in a sack along with a special wedding gift each of us had given to the other." (Debbie had given Jim an engraved cigarette lighter, he had given her a ceramic ballerina music box that played "Here comes the bride.")

"It was hard to think about giving those gifts up forever," said Debbie, "but it was strange, we both knew we had to do it. Those were the right symbols."

Jim: "I put a heavy rock in the sack, too, and we walked out to the very end of the pier. After saying some things about how nice and how awful our old relationship had been, we threw the bag as far out into the ocean as we could."

"It had been raining," said Debbie, "the surface was rough and the water was murky."

"The scary thing was that the bag didn't sink right away," said Jim. "What would we have done if it hadn't sunk, even with the big rock inside?"

"That's right," laughed Debbie, "we got really quiet until it finally began to go under. What a relief! When I turned around after it sank, I felt as though twenty-five pounds had been lifted from my shoulders. As we walked back down the pier I felt I was almost floating."

"I wasn't floating," said Jim thoughtfully. "That was the longest aisle I ever walked down. It felt good, though, I felt good. And Debbie was whistling."

"Yes," Debbie put in, "and I didn't even realize that I was until we were about halfway back to the shoreline. I was whistling the *1812 Overture*." When I later asked Debbie whether this particular tune had any special meaning for her, she thought briefly and said, "Oh, of course. That's the song that Arthur Fiedler always plays at the end of the evening when he conducts the Boston Pops Orchestra. It's the finale."

"What did you do after the burial ceremony?" I asked.

"Well, we went out to a delicious dinner, and went home and made mad, passionate love," said Jim, smiling across at his wife. "It felt like a funeral and a wedding on the same day."

"That's right," said Debbie, "and we had a good laugh when we told my parents we had just been to a funeral and a wedding when they telephoned the next day. They didn't understand what we were talking about, of course, but I think they realized how happy we sounded."

I was struck by how poetically and spontaneously Debbie and Jim had devised and performed their transitional rituals. The way they gave expression to the metaphor of burying the past was consistent and beautiful. The symbols they had chosen seemed perfect for the occasion. And they had spontaneously made up their own reunion ritual. Sharing a meal and making love are often key symbols in traditional reunion rituals (cf. Van der Hart, 1983a).

Debbie and Jim had broken a month's impasse in the space of a week. Changes again started to take place in how they got along with themselves and with each other. Debbie grew more spontaneous and less rigid; she lost her bitterness. Jim, now that he felt his responsibility in the marriage had been acknowledged and appreciated, started to work directly on matters concerning his relationship to his parents.

A few months later Jim and Debbie announced that they were ready to think about winding up therapy. They asked only for a few check-up sessions every six weeks. "We will keep working on our individual and relationship growth," they said, "but we need to do it ourselves if we can. We think we can."

The therapy was concluded after 21 sessions. Things were going well with Debbie and Jim. They had integrated many of the changes which had taken place in therapy.

Follow-up

Three months after the therapy was ended, a follow-up talk took place. Debbie and Jim said that things were going well and that they were still working on improving their relationship. If they have a difference of opinion, they listen to each other and they solve the problem together. For Jim, the most important phase in therapy was the time when he took it upon himself to change some bad habits. He no longer flirts with every woman he meets, he takes more responsibility, and he gets along better with the children. He has also developed new interests. Debbie found a job she liked; for the first time, she didn't need to work only to make ends meet. Both of them feel their relationship has become much more mature and they find more emotional satisfaction in it.

When asked about their recollection of the ritual, they replied that they had not felt it was thrust upon them; it was an idea and it was entirely up to them to make a decision on it. They had done that right after the therapy session. At first they had wanted to bury the sack with the symbols of their old relationship in the ground, but they had given up that idea: Debbie did not want to know where it was. "I wanted it at a place where it just wouldn't come back. I didn't want to come back and know it was there, walk by it, have somebody crying. It had to really be gone." They had thought of burning and other ways, but they always found a reason not to do it. Debbie: "It was almost like we were trying to get rid of a body."

The idea of a burial at sea appealed very much to both of them. Jim: "We thought of different places in the ocean, we thought about the harbor, we thought about the pier, various places, but for some reason we just decided on the pier. The pier may have had another impact on us that we didn't see outright, and that is that it was on the pier that we had our first heated discussion. (To Debbie) Do you remember that, you came down and I was fishing there that day? We got into a conversation, I blurted something out, and that's how it developed from there."

Debbie: "That's when the talk came up: 'Are we going to see George to work it out or just to ease apart without too many hard feelings?' You said, 'Break up without the hard feelings,' and then I said, 'Well, that's it, I'm leaving.' The pier did not hold good memories at first."

Debbie and Jim tried to throw the package into the sea without anyone noticing what they were doing. Jim: "They must have thought we were tossing a body overboard. It wasn't an easy feeling. Then of course it wouldn't sink, because we had put it in a plastic bag. It just floated and floated."

Debbie: "It had a rock in it. It was like, Oh God, it's like it's not going to allow us to bury it. It was sort of odd, a sickening feeling in my stomach."

Jim: "I can't understand why we put it in a plastic bag. It's like we wanted to keep it dry or something, but that wouldn't make sense. Of course we had so much to tell about it after we did it. We said, 'Oh my goodness, what happens if it gets washed up on the shore? Some poor fisherman is going to drop his line down there and think he has got a big one and come up with this package.' "

After telling their recollections of the ritual, Debbie and Jim read the foregoing report of the treatment. Jim remarked that they had not thrown the package into the ocean as far as possible, but that they had just dropped it in the water. Debbie did not think that she came from such a strait-laced family, while Jim did. Both of them felt the report was accurate ("yes, that's it") but it missed something of the hard work and the struggle they had put into the sessions, especially before the ritual. On paper the therapy just seemed to flow, while in reality a lot of hard work was involved. They felt the ritual to be an event laden with emotions, an event which got them going again when they came to a standstill and gave new significance to their relationship.

Discussion

1. Contrary to the experience of Selvini Palazzoli et al., it was not necessary to prescribe the ritual in great detail. In fact, with Debbie and Jim, it seems to have been extremely important that this was not done. Because of their creative contributions to it, the ritual very likely took on a more personalized and deeper meaning. Had I insisted on the stricter form I initially envisioned, the ritual might never have been performed.

The differences between the approach described here and that of Selvini Palazzoli et al. may have to do with the fact that she and her colleagues generally work with seriously disturbed families. They have even remarked that their approach can run into difficulties precisely with less troubled families. Van der Hart and Defares (1978) discussed a typology of families in which the most disturbed are characterized by an unspoken agreement not to acknowledge problems. These families have a rigid structure, poor problem-solving skills, incongruent communication patterns, an inability to metacommunicate (the family members are not capable of looking critically at their own communication), and serious psychiatric symptoms in one or more of the members. Van der Hart and Defares call them type B families. Because of their unspoken conspiracy against change, it is extremely difficult to help this type of family using a direct and congruent approach.

Debbie and Jim represent a more flexible type of family called type A. These families are characterized by more congruent communications, some ability to metacommunicate, and better developed problem-solving skills: the family members are capable of recognizing problems and taking the responsibility for their solution. Thanks to its more flexible structure, this type of family is more open to a direct therapeutic approach. The family members are in mental or physical distress and gladly accept the help offered them.

The ritual prescribed to Debbie and Jim which they performed so creatively was, in my view, a direct intervention. It could be effective even in the broad outline form given by the therapist because they were a type A couple. They were capable of acting on suggestions for homework rather than sabotaging them. Perhaps rituals for type B families must be set down specifically and in great detail by the therapist.

2. The ritual described here is unique, as are all therapeutic rituals. Its form and content were precisely suited to the clients and their situation. But the type of problem the ritual was intended to solve was not unique. There are many other troublesome situations in which past events continue to distress the partners. In all such cases, designing and carrying out this type of ritual can well be worthwhile. Seltzer and Seltzer (1983) give a good example of such a ritual for a couple with sexual difficulties. Their problems had started in a period when the husband was away from home a lot and there was a great deal of friction between him and his wife. Although they now spent more time together and their attitude was much more positive, the persistent idea of the "bad sex" had them so much in its grip that any overtures they made just fizzled out. Here, too, the myth (about where the "bad sex" came from) was obsolete, but it was still particularly powerful.

At one of the sessions the therapist asked the husband and wife to arrange a funeral for their "bad sex." While their daughter spent the night somewhere else, they were to prepare their favorite meal and have some good wine on hand. They were to sit down in front of the fireplace with pencil and paper. On each piece of paper they would write down a word representing an aspect of their "bad sex." Then they would read each paper out loud, throw it into the fire, and watch it go up in smoke. After this "funeral" ("cremation" would be a better word) they were to have a "fiesta" and enjoy the food and drink.

At the following session, they said that the funeral, which had lasted two hours, had caused them a lot of sorrow, and that it gave both of them the feeling that they had had enough of their "bad sex." Although the ritual had been a big exertion, they still felt restored by it. During the fiesta they had made plans for a trip abroad, and their sexual relations afterwards had been quite satisfying. It was no longer a topic of discussion at later sessions.

3. The transition that Debbie and Jim carried out was based on the

metaphor of loss and leave-taking. Their old marriage was dead and had to be buried. The birth of their new, more satisfying relationship had to be celebrated. The example of Seltzer and Seltzer (1983) also makes reference to a metaphor: how the "bad sex" went up in smoke.

According to Van der Hart (1981) an effective metaphor is capable of emotionally moving those involved and of providing them with an outline, a program to help them reorganize their lives. The ritual based on this metaphor helps them to take some essential steps. Fernandez (1977, p. 101) expresses this as follows: ". . . metaphors provide organizing images which ritual action puts into effect. This ritualization of metaphor enables the persons participating in ritual to undergo apt integrations and transformations in their experience."

PART III
REFLECTIONS

Exposure and Leave-Taking Rituals

Maarten Dormaar

As therapeutic methods and techniques increase in number, it becomes more and more important to know on what grounds one is to choose a particular mode of intervention. In strategic or directive therapy, the therapist's interest focuses on the answer to the question: "What will be effective for this problem, with this client, in this situation?" (Van der Velden & van Dijck, 1977).

The purpose of this article is to compare two different approaches to emotional problems encountered in working through difficult situations. This will be illustrated by a case description. The concept of working through is here taken to refer to a process in which vehement emotions attending a traumatic event abate to such a degree that other experiences and courses of conduct can be resumed without impediment (Rachman, 1980). If the process of working through is somehow improper or inadequate, emotions from the past will continue to exert an adverse influence on the individual's present functioning. This chapter is not concerned with treatment of ordinary emotional working-through processes, for these need not be treated as a rule. Rather, it has to do with the distress of clients who were unable to cope with their emotions adequately.

Many publications on difficulties with working through specifically treat *mourning*. Van der Hart (1983a) calls mourning a problem involved in transitions. Ramsay and Happée (1977) likewise relate grief and bereavement to all kinds of changes in life; they speak of mourning behavior and grief when the loss involves the death of a parent, spouse, or child, for instance. But "what we have to say about the mourning process is equally true of other types of loss" (Ramsay, 1979).

Van der Hart (1983a) considers it the task of the therapist to ease the client's passage through a transition into the next phase of life. To this end he employs therapeutic rituals. A significant loss, such as the death of a partner or relative, is regarded as a "radical transition" from the phase preceding the loss to that following it. As in other transitions or important changes in life, this may generate tensions in those affected. The approach advocated by Ramsay (1979) involves exposure to the stimuli and emotions relating to the deceased until extinction of the grief-linked emotional responses has been achieved. Van der Hart describes transitional rituals as symbolic actions which, in a more or less defined manner, facilitate abandonment of the previous phase and acceptance of the new one. In the following case, the method of exposure, using a technique derived from Gestalt therapy, was initially chosen for treatment. Subsequently a ritual was prescribed for the client. Both approaches contributed to a successful outcome. The discussion will compare and contrast the two methods of treatment.

Case description

Mrs. Jaarsma, the client, is a widow. She is 61 and has a neat, well-groomed appearance. Her behavior is very tense and formal. She has lived alone since the last of her four children left the house some six years before. Her relationship with all four is excellent; she speaks of them with warmth and admiration and says there is no friction in the relationship. All but one of the children live far from her, and she only sees them on such occasions as birthdays and holidays; however, they do keep in touch by telephone. Her husband died suddenly ten years ago. She thinks she coped quite well during the first few years, and until a few months ago her memories of him did not make her cry. Now they do. Her mother, well into her eighties, lives in a home for the elderly in a small neighboring town. The client is an only child and feels highly ambivalent towards her mother; she loves and appreciates her mother's spunk, but she feels blackmailed by all her complaining about the physical infirmities and the loneliness of old age. Mrs. Jaarsma thinks that her mother takes up too much of her time. Mother phones every day between five and six to hear how her daughter is doing and to drop subtle hints that the daughter's love for her old and sick mother leaves much to be desired. Her mother also feels that her daughter's visits are not frequent and long enough; her acquaintances in the home are loved, respected, and admired much more by their children and grandchildren. This pattern of complaining and hinting has been in existence since the death of the client's husband, who was very good at protecting his wife from her mother's claims. But her reactions are never adequate, and she alternately feels angry and guilty.

Before getting married, she had an interesting job; later, she worked as a volunteer for a long time. She quit her volunteer work two years after her husband's death because she felt too unstable. She had several somatic complaints which are still bothering her now. She also felt anxious and depressed. Her youngest son was the last one to get married, a few months before her first contact with the therapist. Since then things have grown even more difficult, for her relationship with her mother, the only relative she sees very often, has become more oppressive. Complaints that had been troubling her to some extent have become worse: headaches, retching, dizziness, panicking if she has to wait somewhere, in a store or when traveling, for instance. She has been attended by her family physician for high blood pressure for years.

Before her husband died, when the children were still at home, she had many social contacts, wide and varied interests, and many hobbies. These past years the contacts and activities have greatly diminished because she did not feel up to it. She has become gloomy: "As far as I am concerned, my life may come to an end, only I am too much of a coward to get out. I feel left behind in an empty nest. I don't know myself any more, I used to be very active and cheerful."

Her mood is subject to daily fluctuations; her appetite is poor and she suffers from sleeping disorders. There are other depressive complaints and symptoms: she is irresolute, bad-tempered, continually fatigued.

Assessment

The client's primary complaint is the frustrating relationship with her mother. The acuteness of the problem very likely has to do with the recent marriage of her youngest son: the marriage definitely put an end to her role as a mother, and she does not feel capable of dealing with the one remaining relationship, that between her mother and herself, of which her mother is in such firm control.

It looks like her primary problem—lack of freedom from her mother—is linked to a more central one: inability to cope with the transition from the mother-with-children status to that of a woman on her own (the "empty nest"). Her social isolation and her subassertive attitude towards her mother aggravate the depressive feelings provoked by this inability; she once again starts to miss her husband because it was he who shielded her from her mother's presumptuousness. The mental state of the client reflects an agitated depressive syndrome with vital symptoms.

Treatment

The client's primary objective is to increase her freedom from her mother, but a broader goal would be for her to feel free and happy as a widow living alone. As her motivation largely relates to the goal she has set herself, this is made the focal point of treatment; the therapist expects that the second objective will come up along the way. To accomplish her purpose, the client may have to make it clear to her mother that she is not the self-sacrificing daughter the mother wants and that she does not want to receive so many phone calls from her. Seeing that Mrs. Jaarsma does not want to run the risk of a breach in the relationship with her mother, it is likely to prove very difficult to get her to adopt this assertive attitude. A more indirect manner of helping her free herself from the pressures exerted by her mother will have to be considered (cf. Van der Velden & Habekotté, 1980). The problem is further complicated by her mother's deafness: the client cannot call her mother because she does not hear the telephone ringing. For the calls she dials herself, the mother places a special amplifier on the receiver.

Owing to a tight schedule, the therapist is obliged to postpone an appointment for the commencement of treatment with the client by a few months. Mrs. Jaarsma is to consult her family physician for an antidepressant during the waiting period. Three months later, one of the children phones the therapist to say that his mother is not doing very well. Shortly after that a second talk takes place in which Mrs. Jaarsma mentions that her mother died suddenly four weeks ago. This event has brought about a great change in her life, in the problems she is facing, and, of course, in the therapy. On the one hand her mother's death brings relief, on the other it rekindles her feelings of guilt, now because of the fact that she feels relieved. There is a lot of unvented rage at her mother as well as self-reproach. She is highly perturbed by the fact that she allowed herself to be dominated by her mother for so many years. She believes she would never subject her own children to anything like this, and that she has let go of them as she should. She is proud that it is usually the children who ask her to drop by or to contact them. The therapist indicates he thinks they should wait and see how she handles the situation. But Mrs. Jaarsma feels quite at loose ends, even though her vital depressive symptoms have decreased as a result of the medication. She wants the treatment to go ahead as planned to aid her in working through the confused emotions about her mother. She is afraid that she cannot cope on her own. The therapist decides to go along with her, and the client agrees to the proposed strategy: exposure to the painful emotions, so that they can abate.

At the second session an empty chair dialogue with the mother takes place as part of the exposure technique. Despite her initial trouble in talking to her mother like this, the client ultimately manages very reasonably to express her feelings, which are mainly aggressive. The third session two weeks later shows she is feeling much better. Her mood has improved suddenly and dramatically; on occasion she has even noticed herself whistling. For the first time, a checkup by her physician has shown a substantial drop in her blood pressure, which means that this medication can be reduced. In consultation with her doctor, she is also going to reduce the dosage of the antidepressant and then give it up entirely. Moreover, she has found the energy to make the necessary arrangements to divide her mother's estate.

This initial success of the treatment has a stimulating effect on both client and therapist. Her complaints have improved and this is proof to both of them that the strategy chosen is the right one. But she found it rather embarrassing and not at all like her to have to express her emotions about her relationship with her mother in front of the much younger therapist. The therapist feels he should respect her sentiments, and he suggests a different procedure with which the same goal can be reached. Now that the exposure session has shown her how her complaints are determined by her feelings towards her mother, the therapist thinks she will be able to accomplish a great deal on her own. They decide that she is to write a "continuous letter" (Rubinstein in: Van der Hart, 1983a, p. 121). The daily telephone hour (from five to six)—which, understandably, still reminds her of her former relationship with her mother—is to be her writing time. She will write while sitting in her mother's chair, which she took over from the estate. At this stage it is not yet decided what is to be done with the letter eventually, although they agree that something is to happen once it is finished.

The next two sessions are utilized to bring to the forefront significant experiences and episodes in her past contacts with her mother and her feelings about them. This will give more substance to her letter and will help her to put the "complete message" (Kempler, 1974) down on paper. Old grievances about her mother's reaction to her daughter's deceased husband must be brought up and discussed as well. She never managed to talk about this when her mother was still alive. Now she can also write to her about what a burden it is to go on without her husband, she can tell her mother how much she reproached her for never having wanted to listen to this.

During the next session, the sixth, positive feelings for her mother are also discussed. Client and therapist agree that the letter will now be completed. They consider what should be done with it once it is finished and jointly conceive the following leave-taking ritual: Mrs. Jaarsma will burn the letter and then fix a very fine dinner and treat herself to a bottle of good wine. During this session the client mentions a reunion with former colleagues of hers which she would love to attend. Both client and therapist think it would be nice if she could manage to take leave of her past before the reunion. After the leave-taking ritual she is to phone the therapist for a final appointment.

The seventh and last session takes place six weeks later. She carried out the leave-taking ritual as agreed. The letter, which had become quite a tome, she burned; she felt very solemn while she watched the flames consuming the paper and was surprised that she did not think: "What a waste of all that work of writing." The dinner was quiet and pleasant. She put some candles on the table to make it more festive. The next day she went to the reunion by train. She felt free and cheerful and immensely enjoyed seeing her one-time colleagues again. She was surprised but proud that she did not panic in the train, not for a single moment. After the reunion she went to see a newly-born grandchild and then went home, contented and quite at ease.

She truly feels she has mastered the situation and is ready for new experiences and for contacts with friends and with her children. The therapist knows that Mrs. Jaarsma is fond of gardening and, by way of a parting gift, he presents her with a cutting of a plant from his own garden which she had greatly admired. During a follow-up phone talk four months later, she turns out to be doing "well to very well". She says: "I am now much more aware than before I came to you that my own personal life is significant. I used to think that I should always help anybody who asked for it. Now it is much easier for me to turn down my children's requests if they disrupt my own plans."

Discussion

1. *Therapy or not?* It would have been a reason in itself to defer further treatment when, at the second session, the client's mother had died. This would have been a good point to see how Mrs. Jaarsma would cope with this loss on her own. But she urged that the treatment be continued because her complaints persisted and because she felt at loose ends. I feel that in the event of mourning and other working-through problems, it is not so much the period of time that has elapsed but the symptomatology which is decisive in the question of whether or not treatment should follow. Another important argument in favor of treatment was that it was her inability to cope with her status as an older, independent woman rather than her frustrating relationship with her mother that was at the nucleus of her difficulties. There was no reason to expect that the client would handle this problem better now that her mother had died.

2. *Treatment.* This treatment of working-through problems consisted of a one-session exposure treatment and a subsequent, ritualized writing of a leave-taking letter combined with a leave-taking and a reunion ritual (Van der Hart, 1983a). The burning of the letter, the fine dinner as a woman on her own, and the resumption of social contacts (her reunion and her visit to her grandchild) in this new role are their expression.

We might ask ourselves if we should speak of a *grudge* rather than *mourning*. In my view, this can justly be called mourning: the client is assisted in coping with a significant loss. The death of the client's mother, with whom she had such an intensive relationship for so many years, may certainly be regarded as a tremendous loss, however negative the relationship may have been to the client, and especially during the last few years. Once the mourning problem had been dealt with, the client turned out to be quite capable of completing the transition to the stage of a woman on her own.

3. *Similarities and differences*. The ritualized writing can be regarded as a form of exposure implemented by the client herself. The intention of the letter was to elicit any emotions thus far avoided and to induce any provocative stimuli before the client would decide that it was complete. Mrs. Jaarsma used the letter to take leave of her mother while incorporating certain memories of her husband in the process. In this sense, the therapeutic ritual shows an affinity with the procedure advocated by Ramsay.

On the other hand, De Tempe (chapter 13) demonstrates that the manner in which Ramsay effects a mourning therapy resembles a therapeutic ritual. This is not so surprising, since every psychotherapy can be described as a ritual event (Van der Hart, 1983a, p. xvi).

But alongside these analogies there are differences. A ritual calls for greater creativity on the part of the therapist, but he will find it to be less strenuous and time-consuming than the exposure technique (which, I feel, also encompasses the imaginary confrontation (Burger, 1978) and the primal scream therapy (Janov, 1970)). A Ramsay therapy, as outlined by him and confirmed by my own experience, is often highly exacting and tiring: the therapist must cut off gently but firmly any avoidance maneuver on the part of the client. The duration of a session can hardly be predicted, for it should be ended only after some degree of extinction of the emotions evoked during the session has been achieved. This can create great difficulties in scheduling appointments with clients.

In my opinion, the most eloquent element of a ritual is that the client *independently* performs a series of actions that have far-reaching emotional and cognitive consequences. Going through a mourning process or another working-through problem often involves eliminating a relationship of *dependence*, and a ritual gives fitting expression to this.

However, there are some clients for whom a ritual is not appropriate. There are those who are unaffected by rituals. To them, rituals are empty, childish, merely idle show. It is also difficult to introduce rituals to clients in the very midst of the negation phase of the working through process. An example is a client who, when the question comes up of her difficulty in mourning her husband's death (which took place four years ago), turns out never to have come to terms with the death of her father, who has been dead for forty years. It is most likely that this demonstrates her strong inclination to avoid performing the real "work" of mourning. By such denials, clients avoid experiencing and expressing their emotions attending traumatic events and they often generate phobic and somatic complaints (see also Ramsay, 1979, p. 12). Clients who persist in their denial are not ready for transition (Van der Hart, 1983a, p. 133), nor can they be motivated to perform the ritual properly. They skip parts of their emotional experience or leave it out entirely, they do not address the deceased or the person they miss directly, they "forget" to write or to be ritually engaged in other ways. This is understandable: the ritual confronts them with strong emotions, which is exactly what they are trying to escape or against which they are putting up such fierce resistance—there lies the reason for their phobic and somatic complaints. Their complaints seem to be aggravated by the writing and this often induces them to stop, so they never feel the relief of having said everything that was on their mind. An exposure technique properly monitored by the therapist provides a better opportunity to check the tendency to avoidance and to see to it that during the session the client is continually confronted with the stimuli and emotions he or she so fears. For those who are quite unaffected by ritual, something can be done to overcome this, but with strong avoidance and, hence, denial, the use of therapeutic rituals would seem to be counterindicated.

4. *The choice between the two approaches*. When equally favorable therapeutic results can be achieved using either technique, I think the therapeutic ritual is to be preferred. Here it is the client who performs the work, while the therapist attends to the context, to the transfer of the "complete message," and aids the client in appropriately terminating one phase of life, thus facilitating the transition to the next.

In the case of a recent loss, the following should also be considered: as a rule, traditional mourning rituals are performed shortly after a death. This means such rituals resemble what Averill (1968) terms "mourning": the mourning behavior defined by social conventions and customs.

Seen in this light, a therapeutic mourning ritual might be regarded as a substitute for incomplete or inadequate conventional mourning. Ramsay (1979, p. 14) states that only in exceptional circumstances is "flooding" advisable if one year has not yet passed since the loss. Clients with more open and accepted mourning difficulties are more easily motivated for the use of a ritual. Processes which have somehow gotten bogged down and are thus usually characterized by avoidance and denial can better be approached using an exposure method guided by the therapist. If a ritual approach is nevertheless favored, the preparatory phase (see p. 16) and, more in particular, motivating the client for this approach, will take a lot of time and energy.

The client whose treatment was reported in this article was sensitive to the meaning of rituals. This was evident from the description she gave of certain habits and activities that she, her husband, and their children enjoyed (celebrating certain events, giving presents) and from her favorite writers (Tagore, for instance). Furthermore, she had not yet had time to disengage herself from her mother's death and from her confused feelings about it. If the confusion had become prolonged, the client might have come to avoid the working-through process altogether.

A combination of the two approaches does have the advantage that the direct confrontation inherent in the exposure method sets in motion the process of working through. The way is paved for a smooth start to a ritual. The two approaches were similarly combined in the case described here, although we can say in retrospect that it was not strictly necessary since the empty chair dialogue went quite effortlessly.

Further experience with the combined approach has shown that a leave-taking ritual is generally performed with great conviction after a few exposure sessions the directness of which serves to loosen the process. These sessions are quite strenuous for both client and therapist and it is rewarding for them if they can continue treatment after this and conclude it with a leave-taking ritual. This does the most justice to the client's pace and his or her manner of self-expression.

Adaptive Defense Mechanisms in Post-Traumatic Stress Disorders and Leave-Taking Rituals

Berthold P. R. Gersons

In psychotherapy, leave-taking rituals are primarily used to deal with, and get into perspective, traumatic experiences which have not yet been worked through. The trauma often centers on the death of a loved one, a separation or a divorce, but it may also involve a painful experience such as a dismissal from one's job, rape, battering, or degradation. Putting these experiences definitively into the past by means of a leave-taking ritual starts by once again evoking the often half-sublimated or forgotten memories and images. The emotions aroused by the traumatic event are reexperienced, sometimes more vehemently than at first. After this catharsis, generally a festive conclusion to the ritual follows. Such an ending indicates that the unpleasant experience now occupies a less painful place in the person's past.

Although the term "leave-taking ritual" refers to a parting with persons or events, what it primarily achieves is that a particular traumatic experience is ascribed a new and less disturbing connotative significance. This is clearly exemplified in the treatment by Milton H. Erickson of the farmer's wife cited in chapter 1. After many difficulties, this woman had finally succeeded in becoming pregnant. Six months after it was born, this so intensely desired baby died suddenly. The farmer's wife reacted to this by going into a depression and she expressed suicidal wishes.

Erickson told her to plant a eucalyptus tree, which she was to name Cynthia after her dead baby. The tree would grow quickly. When she was old, he assured her, the tree would be so big that she would be able to rest in its shade. This symbolic transformation made the death of her beloved baby somewhat bearable for the farmer's wife. She could retain the ties with her dead baby in a positive manner, through sublimation. And thus the traumatic event occupied a less painful position in her life. Planting the tree enabled her to take leave of her baby more overtly than before. In this way she could keep up the enduring ties symbolically.

This chapter attempts to clarify from a psychodynamic point of view how a therapeutic leave-taking ritual works. Attention will be paid chiefly to the use of repetition in the ritual as a means of working through psychic traumas. The ritual offers an opportunity to deal with the traumatic experience more gradually. Using a ritual, catharsis can take place bit by bit, and the person need not be inundated by emotions.

First, recognizing the *symptomatology of unworked through traumas* will be discussed. Then we will turn our attention to the *transition theory*, because it provides a frame of reference to explain the process of working through in several phases. Working through takes place step by step by means of a defensive process: often an individual tries not to allow his ambivalent feelings to enter into his conscious experience because of their tumultuousness and incompatibility. Several strategies can be employed to this end, and these will be described in terms of defense mechanisms. Putting up too rigid a defense will cause stagnation in the working-through process. In such a case, a leave-taking ritual will be of help in relaxing the defense. This is made possible by the strategic use of defense mechanisms in the ritual. For this reason, the effect of various defense mechanisms in the process of grief and mourning will be described. The next section will give a psychodynamic explanation of the therapeutic effect of leave-taking rituals, based on these considerations.

In the example of Cynthia, for instance, we might safely assume that the therapist did his best to encourage his client's sublimating her desires and wishes which were bound up with the baby and which could no longer be satisfied now that she was dead. The woman could no longer nurse her baby, but she could water the tree. Here we might even wonder to what extent watering takes the place of crying. The feeling of powerlessness in the face of death is lessened by the positive activity aimed at growth and life. As we will see, a leave-taking ritual provides an alternative manner of working through a traumatic experience alongside the verbal one on analytic lines. Especially when anxiety and resistance run high, a leave-taking ritual is sometimes the only therapeutic option.

Symptoms of unresolved traumas

Larger and smaller disasters occur in everyone's life which upset their equilibrium. This book shows a few examples, such as Marjan in chapter 2 who lost her husband and little girl in a traffic accident. Quite often people are able to cope with such occurrences thanks to the help of others, such as family and friends. But sometimes the trauma was so serious, the circumstances so dramatic, or support from the environment so sorely inadequate that a person simply cannot get over it. Such a person becomes fixated on the trauma: the traumatic experience continues to pursue him, and the idea of leading a normal life again seems heaven on earth to him.

In this case we speak of a *traumatic neurosis* which, according to Fenichel (1945, p. 118) is characterized by the following symptoms: (a) blocking of or decrease in various ego functions, (b) spells of uncontrollable emotions, especially of anxiety and frequently of rage, occasionally even convulsive attacks, (c) sleeplessness or severe disturbances of sleep with typical dreams in which the trauma is experienced again and again; also mental repetitions, during the day, of the traumatic situation in whole or in part in the form of fantasies, thoughts, or feelings, (d) psychoneurotic secondary complications. By category (d) Fenichel means symptoms accompanying the development of a character neurosis. An example would be the man described in chapter 2 who had been admitted to a psychiatric institution because of his constant preoccupation with the adultery he had committed 40 years earlier. For this man, an overly strict conscience was probably a great impediment to working through the event.

With such people, the trauma reveals a neurotic personality structure which had hitherto been concealed. This interpretation has led therapists to wonder to what extent the symptoms of a traumatic neurosis result from a predisposition in the personality—the "neurosis"—and to what extent from the trauma (Horowitz, 1976, p. 28). Horowitz avoids a choice between personality and other grounds as etiological factors by speaking of a *stress response syndrome*. The symptoms are interpreted as a form of reaction to the stressful experience. The experience itself is the result of interaction between the seriousness of the trauma and a person's personality.

The Diagnostic and Statistical Manual of Mental Disorders (Third Edition) (APA, 1980, p. 238), borrowing in part from Horowitz, speaks of a *post-traumatic stress disorder* (PTS), which can be subdivided into an *acute* syndrome and a *chronic* or *delayed* syndrome. The syndrome is chronic if the symptoms are still in existence more than six months after the trauma, delayed if the symptoms only manifest themselves after six months or later.

This manual lays down the following diagnostic criteria for the post-traumatic stress disorder:

A. Existence of a recognizable stressor that would evoke significant symptoms of distress in almost everyone.
B. Re-experiencing of the trauma as evidenced by at least one of the following:
   (1) recurrent and intrusive recollections of the event,
   (2) recurrent dreams of the event,
   (3) sudden acting or feeling as if the traumatic event were reoccur-ring, because of an association with an environmental or idea-tional stimulus.
C. Numbing of responsiveness to or reduced involvement with the ex-ternal world, beginning some time after the trauma, as shown by at least one of the following:
   (1) markedly diminished interest in one or more significant activities,
   (2) feeling of detachment or estrangement from others,
   (3) constricted affect.
D. At least two of the following symptoms that were not present before the trauma:
   (1) hyperalertness or exaggerated startle response,
   (2) sleep disturbance,
   (3) guilt about surviving when others have not, or about behavior required for survival,
   (4) memory impairment or trouble concentrating,
   (5) avoidance of activities that arouse recollection of the traumatic event,
   (6) intensification of symptoms by exposure to events that symbolize or resemble the traumatic event.

Persons suffering from PTS may or may not be aware of the rela-tionship of their complaints to the traumatic experience. Those who are aware of it can be more easily convinced of the necessity of working through the trauma than those who are not. In particular, people whose symptoms did not appear until quite some time after the traumatic event will less readily recognize the relationship between the trauma and their complaints. As a rule, the first category will be more open to the suggestion of dealing with and working through the traumatic event by means of a leave-taking ritual. Although they are aware of the relationship between their complaints and the event, they cannot cope without the help of a therapist.

If a leave-taking ritual is to be considered for persons in the second category, then the therapist will have to take time to make clear to them the causal relationship between the trauma and their complaints. In other words, the preparatory phase for the ritual (cf. chapter 2) will last much longer. For such clients, the possibility of getting rid of the complaints by performing a ritual cannot be raised until a much later stage.

Transition theory

No matter what it is, a traumatic event immediately leads to extreme changes in a person's life. One minute you are at work or at school. The next minute, after taking a bad tumble, for instance, you can wind up in a hospital with a terribly painful broken bone. Suddenly you are preoccupied with the pain and the medical attention. Will everything turn out all right? How long will it take? The future suddenly looks drastically different. You will not be able to go to work or to school for a while. Plans for activities such as sports will have to be postponed.

This example shows how suddenly a drastic event sets into motion a succession of changes. The previous section discussed the symptomatology which may occur in this process when it comes to a standstill. Now we will turn our attention to the process itself.

The process has been analyzed in studies of the effects of crises and disasters. These studies have become known as crisis theory or transition theory (Parad, 1965; Parad et al., 1976). They showed that the process following a crisis follows a certain course. The course is determined by the need to make a transition from the situation as it was before the crisis to the period after it is over (Bain, 1978; Golan, 1980; Tyhurst, 1957; Weiss, 1976). The division into phases greatly resembles the description by Van Gennep (1909), who speaks of *rites de passage*, transitional rituals through which the process of necessary changes can take place.

The transitional period starts with the *impact phase*, as Tyhurst calls it. In this phase a person's attention is entirely fixed on the stress-evoking event. All action is also exclusively oriented to the event. The concentration of thought and action can be so extreme that even pain is not felt. The dissociation of pain sensations and the action-oriented cognitions serve a protective purpose and enable a person to cope with the crisis situation. The stricken individual is not swept away with emotions during the necessary action. A policeman told how he did not feel the violent pain from a bullet wound which had pierced his arm until he was forced to stop chasing a car because gunfire had flattened one of his tires. As we will see later on, dissociation is also employed in leave-taking rituals.

Once the danger has been averted or, for instance, the death has been established of someone dear who had been near death for some time, the *recoil phase* sets in. Characteristic of this phase is the fact that the traumatic event is no longer causing stress because the actual event is over. But the person is still entirely wrapped up in what has just taken place. This is why many of them have a staring look on their face (Janis et al., 1969). External stimuli do not get through to people in this state. In such cases these people will have to be removed from the scene, generally with the assistance of others. In the recoil phase, the need to recount the event repeatedly is felt either immediately or gradually. Then the powerful emotions receive expression in suppressed sobs, loud screams, weeping, striking, or kicking things to vent one's rage at the feeling of powerlessness, alternated by deep grief.

After this first catharsis comes the *post-traumatic phase*, in which the event and its consequences can be worked through and slowly eroded over the years. In everyday language, it is particularly the recoil phase with its powerful emotions that is referred to as the "crisis." Such a crisis never lasts long: a person cannot continually express such vehement emotions. As the crisis nears its end, the transition is marked to a new situation, the post-traumatic phase, in which working through can take place more gradually.

A remarkable phenomenon in a period of transition is the changed time experience. During the impact phase, the person is absorbed by the *present*. In the recoil phase, too, he or she has attention only for what has just happened. In the subsequent post-traumatic phase the mood often turns into one of depression. The person is still so preoccupied with the traumatic event that he or she has no interest whatsoever in the future. Loewald (1972) calls this fragmentation of time experience. The complementary relationship between past, present, and future has ceased to exist. It is striking that a person with a serious depression experiences time as a slow torment. Present and future become terms with no content. Especially after a deeply traumatic experience with far-reaching consequences, people seem to go through life facing the past, with their back to the future. After the trauma, so it seems to people who went through such an intense experience, nothing takes place of any importance. The memories of the traumatic event stand in sharp contrast to this. Its every detail is recalled with extreme precision, as if it had happened yesterday instead of months or years ago. People in this situation are stuck in the recoil phase.

A leave-taking ritual can help to get them out of this rut. This is done by relating the ritual to the point in time where these people still live in their thoughts, which is generally immediately after the trauma. They are asked to write a letter about it. The ritual of the ''continuous letter'' plays a role in setting in motion again the process of working through and change.

Adaptive defense mechanisms in resolving grief

Where the transition theory provides a framework in which the process of working through and resolving a trauma can be explained by means of empirical observation, psychoanalytic theory offers an interpretative framework. One does not acquire any insight into the therapeutic effect of leave-taking rituals simply by discovering that there is a relationship between the type of reaction to a trauma and a person's personality which leads to the formation of symptoms. Symptoms reflect the subconscious strategies which are used to avoid having to feel powerful or contradictory feelings, or to open the door to them little by little. Since it is safe to assume that leave-taking rituals will tie in closely with existing symptoms as strategies of getting rid of them, the next step is to describe the psychoanalytic framework used in interpreting them.

''The process of mourning (trauerarbeit) taken in its analytical sense means to us the individual's effort to accept a fact in the external world (the loss of the cathected object) and to effect corresponding changes in the inner world (withdrawal of libido from the lost object, identification with the lost object)'' (A. Freud, 1960, p. 58). Here Anna Freud is telling us very distinctly that a discrepancy can arise between the facts of the external world and a person's emotional experiencing of them in the inner world after a trauma. And the more traumatic a person feels the event to be (the death of a dear companion, for instance), the longer and the more dramatic will be the emotional process which is necessary to let go of the loved one. Bowlby (1980) gives an extensive description of the letting go as a defensive process.

In order to understand mourning and how symptoms originate, we must first be aware that a person who is in mourning is defending himself emotionally, inwardly, against what has unquestionably happened. The pain and grief are so powerful that these feelings can only be admitted little by little. Adaptive defense mechanisms are used to determine the pace at which such vehement emotions enter into one's conscious experience.

The reason for a person's defense against such feelings can be their great vehemence, but it might also be their inadmissibility. It is very hard to allow oneself to feel rage towards a person who is dead (S. Freud, 1953). The defense can be used to prevent contradictory feelings from becoming conscious. This implies that adaptive defense mechanisms serve both to sublimate feelings and fantasies (the defensive process, Bowlby, 1980, pp. 44 ff.), and to ensure that the working through process can take place gradually. In this case, it can be regarded as an adaptive process.

The most familiar defense mechanism is *denial*, which Bowlby (1980) prefers to call "disbelief." Denial can lead to absurd situations, including near-delusions—think of the surviving partner who behaves as if his or her spouse were not dead. Denial can also take the less extreme form of false perceptions. For a minute, the person thought he or she heard the familiar sound of the deceased, caught a glimpse of him or her "standing" somewhere. The yearning to be with the person who has died probably plays a role here. False perceptions often arouse a great deal of anxiety. Denial is the prelude to feelings that are unleashed when the surviving person gradually comes to realize that the wish the dead companion will come back to life will not come true. This realization becomes more and more difficult to avoid and it gives the survivor a feeling of powerlessness. The survivor becomes aware of how dependent he or she feels, emotionally and materially, on the deceased. The defense mechanism of *turning into the opposite* helps to avoid the feeling of dependence. The reversal becomes apparent in the survivor's blaming himself for what has taken place. "If only I had done such and such, then it would not have happened." It is not the survivor who is dependent on the deceased person, but the deceased was dependent on the survivor, so this fantasy goes. The death took place entirely by chance, out of sheer negligence. In this fantasy, one also imagines himself to be powerful rather than powerless. Here we can recognize the defense mechanism of *turning passivity into activity.* Sometimes the feeling of powerlessness is combatted using the defense mechanism of *displacement.* This occurs, for instance, when the doctor is blamed for the death of the loved one while there is actually no reason at all to do so. It is not the survivor who is powerless, but the doctor is reproached for having no power. This maneuver also enables the person to express his rage at his own powerlessness by displacing it. His anger is in fact directed towards the deceased person for the very reason that he has died. This feeling is displaced and vented on the doctor. Shifting the focus of one's feelings also has the advantage that it enables one to overcome one's feeling of passiveness by dropping one doctor and consulting another, for instance. Such a manner of conduct is called *acting out.* In this way a person is ensured that he need not undergo his feelings in relation to their actual cause, but that he may express them in action involving others. A familiar example in connection with mourning is falling madly in love with someone else very soon. These feelings of loneliness, of being left in the lurch, of powerlessness and grief do not need to be experienced.

Feelings can also be warded off by *intellectualization* and by *undoing* (undoing the event of the feelings associated with it). "I just don't understand why I couldn't cry at the funeral. It was like nothing really came through to me." This is a typical complaint of people who subconsciously undo the event of the emotion. They feel strangely unreal. We call this depersonalization. Sometimes people are not aware of this themselves, but others who knew them before the loss notice it.

A defense mechanism which helps to make ambivalent feelings more bearable is *dissociation* (uncoupling the conflicting feelings). It is very difficult to combine the feelings of wanting the deceased person back and the anger towards him or her at being left behind. A person who vents his anger on the doctor will find it easier to express only positive feelings toward the deceased.

An example will illustrate the complex effect of defense mechanisms the object of which is adaptation. After the death of her husband, a woman had conceived the idea that she was being watched and followed. She regarded this as undeserved punishment. Why she should be punished like this she could not explain. She often also told what a good man her husband had been. He had been a church elder and had often been away in the evening to help others. This woman had never been able to feel her deep anger towards her husband who helped others but who so often left her in the lurch. His death meant he had left her behind quite finally, and her symptoms enabled her to cling to her conviction that her husband had been very good to her. She was unaware of her rage toward her husband, but she was equally unaware of the fact that she felt it was bad of her to feel this. This was probably the reason why she had to be punished.

Another striking aspect was that she constantly told her family and friends delusive stories about how much she was being punished. The result of this continuously repeated behavior was that those who had to listen to her grew more and more irritated and thus listened less and less. Her anger, which had remained unconscious, seemed to be expressed in the reactions of those closest to her. For this woman, repetition of her behavior did not lead to a resolution of her difficult emotions. Psychoanalytic therapies and leave-taking rituals use the repetitive urge to deal with such emotions productively.

Apparently, the often agonizing re-experiencing of the trauma reflects the inner need to allow sublimated feelings to penetrate conscious experience. Often it is only after a lengthy and intense catharsis of the event that a person comes to inner peace. After this, the traumatic experience is no longer relived again and again. So we can say that defense mechanisms are used to allow the process of adapting to the new situation to take place gradually.

But in the interaction between personality and trauma, these same defense mechanisms can be used to excess, thus precluding all or part of the working through process. In such instances we might speak of unsuccessful or pathological mourning, which manifests itself to the person in question or to the environment in the form of troublesome symptoms.

The therapeutic effect of leave-taking rituals

Based on the above discussion of how symptoms arise after a trauma, we may make the following statements:
1. the stress response symdrome can be regarded as an unsuccessful transition which has become mired down;
2. defense mechanisms are used to allow difficult and conflicting emotions to penetrate to conscious experience only gradually or to ward them off indefinitely.

At a conscious level, a person is still suffering from the traumatic event, but the suffering is easier to endure than difficult emotions and ambivalent feelings.

The performance of a leave-taking ritual once again sets this fixated configuration in motion. This is done first of all by setting the transition in motion. It must be noted that the therapist does this at a conscious level. Together the therapist and the client reach the conclusion that the complaints are related to certain unresolved traumatic experiences, and therefore a definite leave must be taken of these experiences. This will only be possible, the therapist explains to the client, if the experiences are vividly called to mind once again. In this way the therapist imme-diately makes a distinction between present and past. The client is in no way urged simply to forget the event. On the contrary: he or she is urged to relive the traumatic past once more in the imagination for as long as need be. In other words, the client is encouraged to go back to the recoil phase, in which feelings were extremely powerful. The leave-taking ritual serves to arrive at a resolution of this phase. By writing a continuous letter, by burning clothes, by throwing into the water stones to which a meaning has been attached, the person enters into a trance in which the vehement emotions are released. It is *as if* a person goes through the event once again, but the support afforded by the leave-taking ritual enables him to experience the powerful and confusing emotions more freely (cf. Fromm & Eisen, 1982).

The question now is how a leave-taking ritual makes it possible to express feelings which have always been fended off and avoided. In a psychoanalytic therapy, the attempt is made to decrease the resistance against sublimated feelings by developing a transference relationship with the therapist. In working with leave-taking rituals, the therapist makes no explicit use of transference; *spontaneous transference* (Glover, 1955, p. 122) results. The client trusts the therapist and takes his or her advice as if it came from a kind and protective parent. In a leave-taking ritual, the therapist makes no explicit reference to feelings of transference. They will be left undiscussed whenever possible, allowing the therapist to take a concrete approach to the client, to assign him or her tasks and to offer support and assistance in carrying out the ritual. The number of sessions is generally limited as well. The client is urged to be active outside of the sessions, for instance by writing a continuous leave-taking letter. Apart from one of spontaneous transference, the relationship between therapist and client can therefore also be defined as a *working alliance* (Greenson, 1974, p. 192). Here the client and the therapist maintain a reasonable and goal-oriented working relationship. In analytic therapies, a transference neurosis will develop alongside the *working alliance*.

A therapist who uses a leave-taking ritual in psychotherapy will try to confine himself to building up a working alliance. In a leave-taking ritual, the difficult emotions are shifted to objects rather than to the therapist. In this way a transference to objects is created. We know that small children also make use of objects such as dolls or blankets to help them bear certain difficulties, such as the absence of their mother when they are put to bed. Such objects can be a source of comfort. Winnicott (1953) calls them *transitional objects* which enable children to learn to accept separation from the mother. Similarly, the eucalyptus tree Cynthia offered the farmer's wife comfort as a substitute for her dead baby (see p. 6).

Volkan (1981; cf. chapter 3) refers to such objects as *linking objects*. By this he means objects that serve to maintain the link with the deceased. In a leave-taking ritual, certain objects are selected as linking objects. In the example of the farmer's wife, the linking object is kept. Here it stands for the positive feelings, which are transferred to the object.

Objects can also serve to express negative feelings. In chapter 3, Van der Hart describes a woman who tosses her engagement ring into the water, rather than the fiancé whom she is mad at. The ritual burning of letters or clothes (such as Marjan in chapter 2 who does this after burying paintings representing her late husband and child) has significance both as a conclusion to the final phase of the ritual and probably, too, as an expression of the negative feelings which may now be felt. Small children also show how transitional objects can be used to express anger towards father or mother. The doll is flung downstairs furiously. At the bottom it is picked up again and cuddled by the child. Evidently, objects can alternately reflect positive and negative feelings.

Using objects to achieve a separation of the positive and negative transference feelings also implies that no ambivalence need be felt, because the feelings can now be experienced separately, in time as well. It is remarkable that in many of the examples in this book we encounter no negative feelings toward the therapist; they are expressed toward objects. By burying or burning objects it is possible to relinquish these feelings for once and for all.

The use of objects also implies that we are dealing with the defense mechanisms of *displacement* and *projection*. In the example of Marjan, the two paintings represent her late husband Johan and daughter Marijke. The paintings seem to stand for the positive feelings. When she later buries the paintings and also throws away some objects which remind her of them, the negative feelings seem to have taken over. We call this *splitting* or *dissociation* of the feelings. Another important aspect is that

Marjan (in this example) is no longer passive, a mere victim of what happens to her, but that she may now repeat everything herself, in a figurative sense. At the hospital where her husband and son died, *now* she herself throws things into the water. She makes the paintings and she buries them. She burns her own clothes. Here we see the positive effects of the defense mechanism of *turning passivity into activity*. The active performance of the ritual helps to diminish feelings of powerlessness.

If we review the list of adaptive defense mechanisms used in leave-taking rituals, we see there is no mention of mechanisms such as denial and intellectualization. Such defense mechanisms result in the sublimation of any and every emotion. Obviously they can have no place in a ritual which is used precisely to allow feelings to have expression.

Splitting is not generally regarded as an adaptive defense mechanism (Kernberg, 1976, p. 46). Kernberg defines it as follows: "Splitting consists in dissociating or actively maintaining apart identification systems with opposite valences (conflicting identification systems) without regard to access to consciousness or to perceptual or motor control." And so it is remarkable that this defense mechanism can be called "adaptive" in its applications in leave-taking rituals, where non-living objects are split and where a symbolic meaning is attached to them.

Discussion

1. Leave-taking rituals help in making the defense of feelings involved in a traumatic experience less rigid and therefore less obstructive. They do not try to interpret the defense and the sublimated feelings. They make positive use of the adaptive effects of defense mechanisms in order to resolve the traumatic experience as well as possible. In this sense, the ritual can be seen as a reorganization of the defensive process.

As many of the examples in this book have shown, the ritual may be part of a lengthier psychotherapy. In chapter 2, Marjan and Theo's therapy commences with a leave-taking ritual to enable Marjan to work through the death of her first husband and her child. Marital therapy for the two of them can take place only after this is completed. Chapter 7 describes Sandra's therapy, where the leave-taking ritual is used to conclude therapy. In other examples (for instance, chapter 10: Debbie and Jim's therapy) the leave-taking ritual is used to get a therapy moving again which had come to a standstill. From these examples it is evident that therapy may consist of no more than the performance of a leave-taking ritual. In other cases is may be used to reach a preliminary therapeutic goal, or a therapy may even be successfully concluded by a ritual.

2. Leave-taking rituals would seem to be indicated primarily in cases where it is likely to prove extremely difficult to get rid of denial, undoing and intellectualization in an analytic therapy so that emotions can be felt. If necessary, after the ritual more extensive psychotherapy can be provided. But in any subsequent analytically-based therapy, the point of transference will not be an easy topic when it started with a leave-taking ritual.

Very strong resistance against letting go of a traumatic experience is the most important indication for the use of leave-taking rituals. In such cases, this approach will be more effective and also more efficient when measured in the length of time needed as compared to other approaches. One limitation lies in the receptiveness of the client to this type of therapy. Several examples in this book have shown that a religious background is helpful in accepting the ritual as therapy.

3. Although both a leave-taking ritual and an analytic therapy can enable a client to lead a happier life without the complaints he or she had, there are still differences between them. Both will lead to greater awareness of the fact that the expression of feelings is very important for mental health. But in a leave-taking ritual the client does not really reflect on his own behavior and personality, except perhaps while writing a continuous letter. In this case, a person is less aware of how and why he wards off ambivalent feelings. The reason for this is because the transference relationship with the therapist is not used as a means of obtaining insight into one's own motivation. A person with a neurotic personality who undergoes a successful psychoanalytic psychotherapy will be less vulnerable to future traumatic experiences, thanks to better self-insight.*

4. No cases have been described in which leave-taking rituals seem to be contraindicated. The method which leaves it to the client to decide whether the idea of a leave-taking ritual appeals to him of course provides an important safeguard against incorrect indications. When people are

---

*Editor's note: The author's clinical impression is stated here. Note that he does not compare therapeutic leave-taking rituals with psychoanalytical grief therapy of short duration, but with a lengthy psychoanalytical psychotherapy. If the results show differences in vulnerability, it is quite possible that the length of the therapy is the decisive factor rather than insight. But whatever the results, to my knowledge no study has yet been made of the question whether psychoanalytical psychotherapy leads to less vulnerability to future traumatic experiences than other forms of therapy.

easily swayed and easy prey to their own feelings and impulses, it is better to be cautious with the use of leave-taking rituals. Here we might think of persons who express or conduct themselves in a suicidal manner. People with an extremely negative self-image, such as in melancholia, or those who tend to this, will have a hard time benefiting by a leave-taking ritual. Those who have a great deal of trouble in distinguishing fact from fantasy, such as psychotics and persons with a borderline structure, only risk becoming more confused by a leave-taking ritual. Empirical research will be needed to define more closely the indications for leave-taking rituals than can be done on the basis of the first, nevertheless hope-giving, examples.

5. Transition theory and the defense mechanism frame of reference provide a means of explaining the therapeutic effects of leave-taking rituals. Based on this knowledge, it is possible in theory to construct leave-taking rituals in accordance with a person's own situation. The examples in this book do not make it clear how the therapists arrived at the specific form for each ritual, apart from the order given by Van der Hart in chapter 2. The discussion of rituals from the point of view of defense mechanisms shows that turning passivity into activity and dissociation are the chief characteristics of the leave-taking rituals used here.

Grief Therapy from an Anthropological Point of View

Jolanthe de Tempe

In memoriam Joost Drost

In western countries, mourning is considered to be a primarily mental process of working through very personal feelings. In some non-western death rituals, on the other hand, social rules so strongly prescribe the behavior of survivors, including the expression of certain emotions, that they seem to leave hardly any leeway for personal experience.

In the 1920s, the anthropologist Malinowski (1929) described rituals and modes of conduct of the Trobriand Islanders in Melanesia after a death. Two remarkable customs were the following. A deceased man's widow and children were not considered to be his relatives; they were not among the most bereaved and were not considered to feel any real grief. Yet they and their own relatives were the ones who mourned most openly and loudly; the deceased's own kin bore their grief, which was felt to be much more sincere, in worthy silence. Another even more exotic custom required that the sons of a deceased man remove the bones from the body and cleanse them with their own mouths; some of the bones were then made into jewelry and useful objects. Malinowski found it difficult to understand these customs; perplexed, he looked for what he felt were "natural" expressions of grief at a person's death, but largely in vain.

Marielou Creyghton (1974), who cites Malinowski's story, interprets these customs in terms of their therapeutic effects on the individual survivors and on the community. The prescribed actions turn potentially dangerous feelings into less harmful ones, and potential social chaos into new social relationships. Creyghton suggests that some western mourning customs might well have the same function, and she concludes: ". . . now that an interest is developing in non-western techniques for mental health, it is to be expected that anthropologists and social psychologists will concern themselves with this question."

I am only too glad to accept this advice. The first version of this chapter was written for presentation at a social ritual in which I felt more than merely professional involvement. It was a ritual gathering of sociologists and anthropologists at a conference on death and birth. I have a degree in cultural anthopology and I am a trained family therapist, and have always felt that these two professions cover a good deal of common ground. But their social networks, at least in the Netherlands, are entirely separate. I have long looked for an opportunity to integrate these two facets of my identity.

Others have crossed the border between psychotherapy and anthropology as well. Van der Hart (1978, 1983a; and ch. 1, 2, and 3), has studied non-western healing and transitional rituals to set down guidelines for the design of rituals in western psychotherapeutic practice.

The issue at hand

The link between my own identity and a ritual gathering of colleagues foreshadows the main theme of this chapter. It is my premise that rituals and feelings are intricately interwoven, and only seldom are they in direct opposition. Although westerners would let themselves believe they have somehow outgrown this, they have not; their actions are often not in accordance with the widespread dislike of ritual. This dislike results from the great gap we tend to feel between private life and the community, between mental and physical aspects and social aspects, between the interior and the exterior, each with their own sciences and professions. This imaginary gap is a result of developments in social reality (see e.g. Elias, 1969; De Swaan et al., 1979).

Malinowski, in his reaction to the death rituals of the Trobriand Islanders, shows something of the western prejudice towards the relationship between personal feelings and social rituals. The example of the Trobriand Islanders brings up many questions: How universally human are the rules of individual mourning as described by western psychologists? How much correspondence with them do culturally prescribed rituals show? Do they assist the mourning process? If they do, then why are they so scarce in western countries—or do they only seem to be scarce?

First I will briefly go into mourning theory and therapy as developed by psychologists and psychiatrists. Interest arose in this subject quite recently and suddenly. In explanation of this, I look to the disappearance of widespread and general social rules and rituals of mourning among certain groups of people in western countries. Psychotherapists presented themselves as furnishers of new rules and rituals in the ensuing vacuum.

This suggests that a basic assumption of the theory that mourning is separate from a social and cultural context is untenable. A look at anthropological research of mourning in many other cultures shows that we cannot yet draw very clear conclusions as to whether or not there is a universally human and systematic mourning process. This comparing of cultures, however, once again points up the lack of large public mourning rituals in the western world. The lack is a large public rituals, not of mourning rituals in general; they have simply become less tangible in western countries, they take place in various closed circles and are left more to personal taste than they used to be. The fact that in psychological theory mourning is reduced to grief, its emotional and personal aspect, is the result of a historically developed task division between "public life" and "private life." Private life more and more has become the domain of personal relationships, emotional ties, and individual identity. Mourning became part of this private life at a comparatively late date.

It became the function of psychotherapy to assist people with problems in this private life. In this it can be likened to what clergymen traditionally did, or shamans and other ritual leaders, albeit that psychotherapy is not a public event and has but a limited reach. Using an analysis of a grief therapy, I will attempt to show that it is entirely appropriate to regard such therapy as a transitional ritual, even though the participants may not see it as such.

The psychological theory of mourning and grief

The world over, the loss of a significant person or thing leads to a disruption in the normal course of affairs for a shorter or longer period of time, both interpersonally and intrapersonally. Ultimately a modus vivendi is found in the new situation. During the period of transition, people think and feel things differently. The death of a person is generally less predictable than many other kinds of transitions in life, and the effects are frequently hard to keep under control.

People in different social positions and in different societies differ, too, in the way in which they handle the disruption and make the transition back to normal life. The Balinese do not cry after a person's death. In other places, entire dramas are acted out. And the pressure on people to return to normal life also varies. For instance, we tend to view it more leniently when an elderly woman continues to mourn her husband than when a young widow with children does the same, while in the second case the transition is much more fundamental.

Mourning was discovered on a large scale in the 1960s, first as a topic of research and theorizing, and later as the domain of a special form of therapy which was primarily developed in the Netherlands by the behavioral therapist Ramsay. The therapy is based on theories quite generally accepted in psychology and it has been described quite precisely. I will briefly discuss its theoretical basis.

The theory commonly distinguishes between mourning and grief. The former comprises social and cultural customs, the latter psychological and physiological reactions of an individual to a loss. The latter is also the domain of the psychologist. A basic assumption of the psychological theory of mourning is that physiological reactions form a fairly standard pattern. Relatively independent of social and cultural customs. This distinction is apparently borrowed from the "nature-nurture" debates in various fields of human behavior, debates which largely turned out to be fruitless. But whether or not grief is universally human, theorizing and research, primarily among widows, have yielded approximately the following model (see i.a. Ramsey, 1975, 1977, 1979; Ramsay & Happée, 1976; Bowlby, 1980; Parkes, 1975; Vrolijk, 1980).

Considerable changes in behavior occur in persons who have lost someone close to them as a result of death or in another way. Some typical symptoms are: a withdrawal from social contact, sleeping and eating disturbances, fatigue and other physical complaints, hallucinations, and vehement emotions such as grief, anger, guilt. Grief seems to have several phases: numbness, denial, with confused and changing emotions, and then acceptance, adaptation to the new situation. Initially it was also tried to fit the various emotions into the phase model, but they were not so predictable. Ramsay prefers to call the emotions "components" of the mourning process, thus leaving open the question of their occurrence, their order and intensity.

A second point on which the model has gradually been expanded is the length of time a mourning process takes. This has turned out to be highly variable and longer than was initially thought. Periods of over a year are now considered quite normal, and people who have lost some-one very close to them often need more (cf. Worden, 1982). (In this connection, it is worthy of note that the traditionally prescribed mourning period in the Netherlands was one and a half years.)

The psychological model of mourning also serves to indicate and to account for "pathological mourning processes." These are cases in which something went awry, making psychotherapeutic help necessary.

All authors assume that the majority of the phases, the various emotions and behaviors described in the literature must have taken place before a person can permanently get over the loss. If not, some part of the mourning process will become chronic, or sooner or later other dis-turbances, such as phobias, depressions, and psychomatic complaints, will occur.

Our knowledge of the causes of "pathological" mourning processes is still fragmentary. Factors which might account for differences in mourning processes are primarily found at the social level (emotional and social relationship to the deceased, social position of the mourner, re-actions of the environment). From the psychological literature (e.g. Bowlby, 1980; Parkes, 1975), we know, for instance, that an unexpected death or one by suicide, a very young death, an ambivalent relationship with the deceased, and not in the last place an environment which is intolerant of deviant behavior by the mourner, increase the chance of a complicated and lengthy mourning process. Little can be said with cer-tainty about a relationship between the mourning process and personality traits. But, despite the decisive role played by social factors, the dis-tinction between mourning as a psychophysiological process and as a social process is still employed.

In the model of a "normal" mourning process and in grief therapy, we find the familiar western ideas of repression and catharsis (although they are sometimes called by different names, such as the behavioral therapeutic terms of avoidance and extinction). Put quite simply, this is the theory that people tend to stash away "somewhere" their unpleasant or confusing feelings; if the imaginary cupboard becomes too full, the feelings will commit sabotage. To prevent this happening, they must be faced and expressed in time. The exact requirements for their expression are not clearly defined, and in fact form one of the most important points of contention between the various psychotherapeutic schools. How long may it take? Must it be accomplished alone, or with others? In words, in emotional outbursts, or in other actions?

Ramsay's method is to confront the client with the painful facts in order to evoke the feelings which were thus far avoided and then to extinguish them. He does place some restrictions on the client's actions, but he does not set the requirement that feelings should be put into words, as does psychoanalysis, for instance.

But no matter how vague the theory may be about what mourning precisely involves, in therapeutic practice, expressing and working through grief are subject to fairly strict rules, although not all of them are explicitly formulated. This justifies the comparison between therapies and rituals which I will later discuss more extensively. Mourning is not a sort of natural occurrence taking place in an individual; it is a social process according to social rules—in grief therapy as well.

The increased interest in the subject of mourning

The history of the psychological theory of mourning and grief is intriguing. Two general lines in it are the increased interest in the topic and the shift in the norms. Aside from the classic publications by Freud (1917/1957) and Lindemann (1944, published in Dutch as late as 1970), theory formation on the subject of mourning had more or less come to a standstill. Its fairly sudden popularity in the 1960s was not limited to psychological and psychiatrical professions. Interest arose in a series of related topics having to do with death, and it also spread to groups with social ties to these professions (Wouters & Ten Kroode, 1980).

We can see the distinction between grief and mourning as an attempt to justify the introduction of the subject into the field of psychology. It led to a fairly rigid model of the mourning process; when this turned out to be untenable, it was expanded. In recent years, the model has been expanded on at least two points: the amount of time allotted for a normal mourning process has been increased, and the idea of a predictable succession of emotions has been relinquished. One drawback to these changes is that the model has become vaguer. However, they also have the advantage that the term "pathological mourning process" is employed with greater caution, although it has not been discarded.

In the contemporary literature on mourning, tolerance for differences has increased: people are allowed to mourn, it is even compulsory, but within certain bounds. The way in which Raapis Dingman (1975) treats the concept of a pathological mourning process is typical of the present state of affairs. After holding forth on the arbitrariness of the distinction between healthy and pathological, in conclusion he cites the following statement by Freud (1957, p. 244) which is quite ambiguous in this context: "It is only because we know so well to explain it (mourning) that this attitude does not seem to us pathological." Having thus excused himself, he proceeds to employ these concepts (albeit in quotation marks) without further ado.

The increased interest in mourning in psychological theory and in psychotherapeutic practice; establishing rules for "healthy mourning," then expanding them but not relinquishing them—how can we account for these developments?

De Swaan et al. (1979), Brinkgreve and Korzec (1978) Brinkgreve et al. (1979) have shown how psychotherapy was only gradually able to acquire a social position in the Netherlands, and then at the expense of church influence. Over the past forty years, the development of this profession has gone hand in hand with the creation of a potential circle of clients among groups with a similar social status, educational level, and field of interest as the psychotherapists, groups that came to see their problems as "mental" and "personal," for which the aid of an expert could be called in.

Along with industrialization, division of labor, and the greater influence of the state, social networks became looser, the influence of the churches decreased, and the gap between public and private life widened. Conventions, rituals, and knowledge in the realm of private life disappeared. Psychotherapists took on more importance as specialized furnishers of norms and models when things got out of hand in the private life. Mourning theory and therapy are fairly late offshoots of these developments. Although death and mourning have been receding into the realm of private life for centuries, the process has certainly not yet reached its conclusion (Ariès, 1974; Fortuin, 1980).

In this context—the creation of a new concept in a new field—it is easier to understand why the term "pathological" was employed without sufficient theoretical and empirical foundation: it is a polemic term whose purpose is to justify the introduction of the new topic into psychology and particularly into psychotherapy the new topic. Pathological mourning processes are simply mourning processes requiring psychotherapeutic treatment.

Mourning in non-western cultures

The information about mourning processes western studies have yielded indicate that it is premature to consider the similarities in human behavior more important than the differences, and even more premature to assume that the similarities are the expression of a natural occurrence in individuals, comparatively isolated from social circumstances.

Rosenblatt et al. (1976) set out to establish the similarities and differences between mourning processes among various cultures in the world. One of their intentions was to investigate the universal validity of the psychological theory of mourning. They analyzed 78 ethnographical studies for their research.

The data show that most societies have something resembling mourning behavior that is different from other day-to-day behavior, *and* that this behavior shows extreme variation both among societies and among people in one society. The western mourning described by psychologists, when compared with that of other cultures, is not very exceptional, but neither is it representative for humanity. Rosenblatt et al. state that the psychological model of the mourning process turns out to be reasonably tenable. But from the great variation in the data we would be equally justified in drawing the conclusion that little evidence is offered of a universally human pattern of mourning, comparatively independent of cultural and societal circumstances.

Here are some examples of similarities and differences. The length of the socially acceptable mourning period varies per society, with the social position of the mourner, and with the relationship to the deceased. On the average, widows mourn for over a year, much longer than do widowers or adult children who have lost a parent. The length of the mourning period goes together with the extent to which a person was dependent on the deceased in daily life and for social status.

Many societies have more than one ritual after a person's death. A series of rituals, sometimes spread out over a year or more and involving more people than the direct survivors, allows both the transition of the deceased to the realm of the dead and the transition of the others back to normal life to take place gradually. In such societies, unlike ours, the deceased person continues to occupy a recognized place in social life for a while after his death, and the primary task of the mourners is towards him, rather than towards themselves or the social environment, as it is for us. The mourning period is often officially concluded with a final ritual. It seems safe to say that deviant behavior beyond the socially accepted period is rarer in societies with final rituals (even if the mourning period is not very long) than in societies without them (Rosenblatt et al., 1976, p. 90 ff.; cf. Van der Hart, ch. 2).

The expression of feelings which psychology associates with grief occurs quite generally in the rest of the world, but with great variation. Some forms this can take are crying, aggressive behavior, attempts at self-mutilation (we would consider this pathological), anxieties, avoiding things which call the deceased to mind, and apparitions of the deceased (what we would call hallucinations and what we would surely consider to border on the pathological, especially if the person believed in their realness).

In quite a few societies, survivors abuse themselves or others physically or verbally more than we do. It can be standard practice, for instance, to blame one or more persons for the death, or to inflict injuries on oneself. If differences in emotional behavior are sex-linked, then the men are generally aggressive, while the women weep and practice self-mutilation. Aggressive behavior and self-mutilation generally occur side by side.

Aggressive behavior occurs less frequently in societies that assign an important place to ritual specialists. Rosenblatt et al. (1976, p. 33) define ritual specialists as persons whose task it is to organize the behavior of others in ceremonies such as transitional and healing rituals (our psychotherapists also fall under this definition). The reason for the relationship between aggression and ritual specialization is not clear-cut, the authors feel. Perhaps the specialists assist in converting aggression into something less harmful, perhaps they give names to the confused feelings of the survivors in such a way that aggression is excluded.

But the societies that produce ritual specialists (and in general, they are more highly developed, with higher levels of economic production, political centralization, and social complexity) also have many other means of controlling aggressive behavior, such as professional keepers of the peace (for instance, police and law courts), and methods of child-rearing that curb such behavior at a very early age. Elias (1969) showed how westerners, over the past centuries, have had to acquire greater and greater control of their impulses, in particular the aggressive and violent ones. The need for such control was part of people's increasing interdependence due to the formation of large economic and political unities, where the state monopolizes the right to physical violence. It is no wonder that aggression is a "dangerous" emotion, both for laymen and for psychotherapists. We will see in the example of a grief therapy that aggression plays a rather striking but ambiguous role there as well.

Modern western mourning

The emergence of specialized psychological knowledge about mourning is only one example of a much larger division of labor in the field of death and mourning and in the realm of private life. The individual mourning process is not a natural occurrence but indirectly influenced by the social surroundings; it is the result of a social structure that distributes the burden of relationships in general and the burden of the loss of relationships in particular very unfairly.

In western countries, there is a high degree of professional specialization in death. Rosenblatt et al (1976) mention doctors, nurses, undertakers, and clergymen as examples. Our general knowledge, our rules and rituals for death and mourning can only be called poor. The only social activity which can be compared to non-western death rituals in that it is public, obligatory, and standardized, is the funeral or cremation. Many societies not only have such a ritual immediately after a person's death, but they have one or more subsequent rituals as well. This lack of openness about death and mourning in western countries is comparatively recent. And among those who are not members of a church, even the last remaining public ritual, the burial, more and more often takes place in a closed circle and is not officially announced beforehand (Fortuin, 1980).

Our specialists in the field of death are so specialized with respect to one another and to laymen that they no longer take part in the same large and public rituals. The transitional crisis has been split up into numerous specialized and closed rituals that differ greatly in the extent to which they are governed by fixed rules. Perhaps we can better call them rites, because they are less comprehensive than what we understand by the word "ritual."

The care and treatment of the dying and the dead is in the hands of special personnel; the greater part of this work takes place behind closed doors and only a small part is public, such as the lying in state and the funeral. The hasty removel of the body from the daily surroundings, for motives of hygiene, gives dying something unreal. Due to the lack of ritual actions with respect to the body, the possessions of the deceased acquire special significance. They readily become the object of self-made rituals, such as devoutly keeping the room of the deceased intact.

After the funeral (unless there happens to be a requiem mass), the public and standardized transitional rituals are completed. The rest of the transition to daily life with one less participant is subject to a high degree of division of labor corresponding to the division of labor in relationships in general.

In western countries, emotional needs and relationships have largely been delegated to private life: the family, the circle of close relatives, friends, and neighbors—and primarily to the women among them, specialists *par excellence* in emotions. It is a logical result that the more emotional aspects involved in working through a person's death also fall to this personal network. Not until this point can we speak of mourning processes (and of possible pathology). This private life—and again chiefly the women—is psychotherapy's field of operation.

The behavior prescribed for mourning may have become less strict (survivors, for instance, no longer need to wear black to distinguish themselves), but mourning has become much more exclusively the task of only one segment of the network of the deceased; it has become a task that must largely be carried out individually, while all eyes are watching. Birth, marriage, and death, traditionally the great transitions of life, assembled entire networks; even those who had no place in the rest of their life for religion continued to fall back upon church rituals for these events. But the death rate dropped, social networks became secular and looser (so that the members no longer know one another), and this means that the transfer of conventions and general knowledge about transitional problems in life takes place more slowly, if at all. With a little luck, a survivor will find a few people with a good deal of experience in the field of death and mourning in his own network. The situation in itself makes the mourner unsure of himself, not to mention the effect of people around him who either do not know how to behave, or who make contradictory demands.

It has often been suggested that western societies suffer from a collective denial of death. Considering the lack of widely applied rules of behavior in this field, it would seem more plausible and simpler to attribute this attitude to factual ignorance of death (cf. Rosenblatt et al., 1976, p. 115). In situations where both parties are unsure of themselves, situations for which no one has learned any rules, the easiest course is to act as if nothing has happened. This pushes the transition even deeper into private life.

But it is not correct to say that no more transitional rituals take place in this private life. Individuals and small groups of mourners, such as families, tend to create personal rituals (ranging from covert to overt) when there are no established cultural models. Simple examples are commemorating birth dates or dates of death. A fairly self-evident field inviting ritual formation is the possessions of the deceased. Some people leave everything as it was, others clear it out as quickly as possible, others clear it up a little at a time. Such actions are not only expressions of feelings through symbolic objects, they also help to shape these feelings and thus to hasten or delay the transition to normal life.

To recapitulate: in western countries, the most dangerous and least easily regulated side of the problems of transition after a person's death, working through it emotionally, is left to individuals, at best a fairly loose network of family and friends, all of whom have but few cultural models at their disposal for the solution of their problems. In this respect, mourning has followed the same course taken by family life and child-rearing, for instance. On the one hand, more and more practical aspects of child-rearing are taken over from the family by special organizations, or placed under their supervision. But at the same time higher and more exacting demands are made of the family, primarily of the woman in it, in the realm of emotional relationships: a combination of high-flown cultural ideals and few, or contradictory, rules. And psychology made no small contribution to the propagation of these ideals. A while later, psychotherapy came on the scene to put the cases where it had gotten completely out of hand back on the right track. Then came the do-it-yourself handbooks to prevent such occurrences. Women run more risk than men of becoming emotionally disturbed and winding up in psychotherapy (Tennov, 1976). The woman's role is the one with the most high-flown ideals and vague tasks in the field of private life.

In the literature, the mourning processes of young mothers and young widows are known for their difficulty and complexity. Women also have the highest chance of reactive depressions and other forms of abnormal mourning (Bowlby, 1980; Parkes, 1975). In mourning, too, the situation has arisen of high-flown ideals and few or contradictory rules. Mothers who continue to mourn a dead child break one rule—relinquishing the deceased—by taking another—being a good mother—too literally. When should they stop, without risking being considered heartless?

Psychotherapists are starting to provide in the need for individual or group mourning prescriptions and rituals, although it is still the exception and not the rule.

Psychotherapists and transitional rituals

With the disappearance of religious rituals, western countries were left with few concrete guidelines for the transition after death and bereavement. The emergence of special grief theories and therapies can be seen in the same context as psychotherapy in the preceding section: they have filled the vacuum left by the churches and the social surroundings. Grief therapy can be seen as a social ritual that structures and completes this transition, even though it generally takes place between no more than two persons and neither the therapist nor the client need regard their activities as a mourning ritual. At least one of the reasons for the re- markable effectiveness of such relatively short therapies is their function as a concluding ritual.

This view of the function of psychotherapy implies a certain cor- respondence with religious rituals. There is another correspondence: that with non-western ritual specialists such as shamans and medicine men. This comparison has often been made, but it was understandably rather painful for a profession that was just beginning to emerge from rivalry with the church. Many psychiatrists and even many anthropologists re- garded shamans as hysterical, as paranoid schizophrenics, and generally as madmen; but there was always a school that recognized the shaman as a colleague, although at a more primitive, pre-scientific level. Lewis (1971; cf. also Torrey, 1972; and Van der Hart, Ch. 2), gives a summary of these viewpoints, but goes even further: he calls shamans more com- plete healers than western psychiatrists, because they approach the com- plaints from several angles at once—mentally, physically, and socially.

Gradually, psychotherapists are coming to realize that there may be something to learn from these primitive colleagues. But they were able to take a humble stand only when psychotherapy itself had acquired a respectable social status.

Interest in non-western healing methods is especially linked to the advent of therapeutic approaches that broke with several traditions in psychotherapy. These new approaches required the therapist to be active; they no longer focused on emotional insight personality changes in the client, but on changes in symptoms, behavior, and environment, in as short a time as possible. Behavioral and family therapists were the pi- oneers in this field in the fifties and sixties. Parts of these two schools coalesced with established psychiatry. The remainder is not averse to comparisons between their work and that of shamans or even of western prayer healers (e.g. Fisch, 1973).

This comparison goes more than skin-deep. A change in how the problems of clients were viewed preceded this change in how the tasks of the therapist were viewed. Advocates of these approaches see the symptoms of illness and disturbance as a link in the structure and interaction of the social surroundings to which the person belongs. Any problems in this interaction often result from an unsuccessful or incomplete transition to another stage of life, a transition made necessary by altered circumstances such as children leaving home, or demanded by the wider social environment.

Directive therapists try to influence the symptoms of the "patient" by bringing about changes in interaction. They sometimes begin with the "patient" himself, but they frequently call together other members of the network, varying from spouses, children, or other members of the household and the extended family, and representatives of official organizations that have some connection with the "patient," to entire social networks of some forty people (Speck & Attneave, 1973). These methods managed to achieve wonderful "cures" in fairly short periods of time, cures of "individual" disturbances which had received treatment for many years in vain and which had been given up as chronic, such as cases of adolescent schizophrenia, anorexia nervosa, or psychosomatic illness.

There is very little systematic knowledge about problems of transition resulting from a person's death. The work of Van der Hart (1983a and ch. 1, 2, and 3) is a milestone in this area. He recommends the transitional and healing rituals as described by anthropologists highly as a field of study to western therapists. As far as I have been able to ascertain, the guidelines he gives in these studies for the design of grief therapies and the work of Ramsay and his associates are the first extensive western codifications of such rituals.

Van der Hart (1983a, p. 33) defines a ritual as follows: a series of actions which must be performed according to fixed rules, which may or may not be performed in combination with words, and which has several meanings. For one thing, rituals symbolize both relationships and personal feelings as well as changes in them. Transitional rites often have three phases: isolation from day-to-day life, the preparation of the ritual in no man's land, and the reunion. In the second phase, normal social rules have been suspended and the participants have quite a lot of leeway in how they choose to act; after this, the rules once again become strict, and the emotional meaning has been altered by the actions in such a way that it can be integrated into the new social identity.

Anthropologists often distinguish a social function (confirming or altering relationships) and an individual function (expressing personal feelings) in rituals. But in the view of Van der Hart, the psychological and the social effects of rituals cannot be divorced. An effective ritual influences the individual performers precisely because it is much more than the expression of existing feelings: it also creates and transforms feelings. This corresponds to Creyghton's (1974) interpretation of the Trobriand mourning rituals.

The view that I have elaborated here is quite different from the view of the founder of grief therapy in the Netherlands, the behavioral therapist Ramsay. He himself regards this form of therapy as a process which takes place primarily at the level of the individual expression of feelings. The mourning process was never completed, because the client began avoiding painful things and thoughts that were related to the deceased. The therapist once again presents these ideas and objects, and continues to do so until the painful feelings are extinguished. Only then can the client once more turn to other things. The order is sometimes different in rituals: because a person must perform certain actions, the emotions change, often without their needing to be expressed. But Ramsay's own therapy is a more complex series of interactions than he suggests, and it exhibits ritual characteristics.

The following description is based on a content analysis (Van der Zee, 1978) of one of Ramsay's grief therapies and a short film which shows most of the highlights. It is my intention to show that it is useful to regard this therapy as a transitional ritual in which the therapist accompanies the client to no man's land and back, but without this being the conscious purpose, and to make the radical metamorphosis the client undergoes more readily comprehensible. The quotations are borrowed from Ramsay (1975).

A *modern western mourning ritual*

Two and a half years ago Ramsay's client lost her mother and her 12-year-old daughter in a fire in the mother's trailer. She had had very close and intense ties with the two of them; she felt more at home in the world of female family members than she did with her husband and son. After the accident, she had tried to adopt another child, and had been treated by doctors, psychiatrists, and even a prayer healer. When her son turned twelve, she again went into a depression. She is afraid that something will happen to him, too. She still cannot really grasp the fact that her daughter will never come back, and, at the urging of her husband and son, she avoids places and things which remind her of the dead. The avoidance of painful situations and the assistance of others in doing so has always been characteristic of her life. It is in this condition that she is referred to Ramsay.

In general lines, the therapy goes as follows (to simplify matters, I will put the number of each session in parentheses). After an initial talk (1) in which the client hears what she will and will not have to do, and what to expect, the therapist (2) asks her to call her daughter to mind, to describe what she sees and remembers, and then to tell the child or herself that it is all irrevocably past. The client fails to respond to most of the instructions, and goes on talking about the past in story form. Again and again, the therapist pursues her with new instructions, or with statements that the loss is irretrievable. He points out her "avoidance behavior" to her and promises her that, once she has taken leave of her dead, they will be returned to her in a more gratifying way.

The nex time (3) the client cannot manage to address and take leave of her dead mother. She finally does this later (4), after a great deal of urging. In saying goodbye, she thanks her mother. For the first time in a long time, she has talked with her husband about her mother and daughter. When, at the third session, she tells the therapist of her guilt feelings towards her son, whom she feels she neglects, he quickly drops the subject; the therapy is limited to her relationship with the dead.

The next time (5) she says that taking leave of her mother has done her good, but that she is not yet able to do so with her daughter. The therapist brings the conversation around to the guilt she and her husband might have in the fire, but she scarcely responds to these attempts to induce her to make self-accusations or to express aggression towards her husband. He ultimately leaves it at that.

The next day (6) the client says that she has been really happy for the first time since the accident. The therapist now confronts her with photographs of the dead. Only after a great deal of inducement can she look at them. She must take leave of her mother again, but now with the picture in front of her, and in angry words. She flatly refuses the latter; finally she takes leave, after a fashion, of the person in the picture, but not in the very direct way the therapist asks for. The mourning of the mother is considered to have been concluded.

After this (7) things settle down somewhat. The therapist asks the client to do or to imagine doing some things she otherwise avoids, such as lighting a fire. The situations he suggests are just too difficult, she feels, so she is allowed to choose something herself. Despite this, the next time (8) she says she is completely exhausted and did not really want to come; but, at his encouragement, she manages to express with great difficulty a little of the anger she feels towards the therapist. At this session, the instructions again become more difficult. She must now do the same thing with her daughter's picture as she did with her mother's: speak to the picture, tell the girl how much pain she has caused her, and take leave of her. She tries to address the picture but cannot; when she finally does, she merely repeats the therapist's words. After a short break (9), with the continual prodding of the therapist, she complies with the instruction to take leave of her daughter, but without expressing any negative feelings towards her.

On the next day (10), the sixth day of therapy, the client has undergone a complete metamorphosis. Thinking about the dead is no longer painful. She has been shopping and bought all kinds of things. Others, too, say that she has changed. She looks cheerful at this session and listens quietly to music that used to be laden with emotions and was therefore taboo. The therapist suggests winding up the therapy. At a final session (11) two days afterward, he gives her some information and advice for later.

At first glance, the client's feelings, her grief and her resistance, her inability to accept the death of her child and her mother, seem to be predominant. But, even though the role of the therapist is not always in the foreground, he carefully sets the stage for what does happen. Out of the total number of sentences spoken, he speaks 38% or over a third, and his share increases in the course of the therapy. It is also apparent from *what* he says that he leads the proceedings: the number of questions and descriptions of situations and persons decreases, while the number of instructions to perform certain actions and the confrontations with painful things increase (Van der Zee, 1978, p. 64–78). And, although the client often shows resistance and he even gives in to this several times, he continues to urge and prod, and she ultimately makes the most important confrontations and carries out the most important instructions. The entire course of events is in accordance with Van der Hart's (1983a) definition of a ritual, which is in this case a transitional ritual.

First, there is the frame in which it takes place: "this is a grief therapy." The client is exempted from the demands of day-to-day life. The problem is defined as her personal problem. She is alone with the therapist, and the task they are to perform has been set down in advance. She must change, and in order to do so, must do certain things that were impossible for her in daily life, things that present dangers to her, and the therapist is there to make sure she gets through it unscathed, as long as she accepts his role as leader of the proceedings. Other business, other subjects are out of bounds, even her son. The therapy is the no man's land between two phases in life: between her role as a mother and daughter and her responsibility towards those who are alive. This frame determines everything the two of them do; the frame itself, and thus their relationship, is not a matter of discussion. If she cries, it has nothing to do with the therapist, but shows her grief for her dead; if she shows resistance, it is resistance against the fact that they are dead. What the therapist does is all on her behalf and towards the conclusion of the mourning process.

The therapy has a complex structure. Three themes are treated: the relationship to the mother, to the daughter, and to places and things that have to do with the dead. Here I will restrict my comments to the main theme: the daughter.

In reference to the relationship to her dead daughter, the same thing is repeated over and over again, but there are two important turning points in these repetitions. It can be compared to a drama that begins with the daughter's life and ends with her burial by the client. The dynamics in this drama are not the product of the chronological order of events. With every sentence, each time the therapist and client interact, the story is reformulated, but each time there are small changes.

Twice a new act begins because the story of life and death has just been formulated differently: it is at once a repetition and a closer approach to the final result. The three acts of the drama are the beginning, middle, and end of the trip through no man's land, and each is rehearsed a few times before the actual performance. In the first act, the daughter is called up in her imagination: again and again, the therapist pronounces her dead in a set formula. In the second act, the girl takes the form of a photograph, and again the therapist pronounces her dead, this time in a somewhat altered formula: "You will never see her again." The third act begins when he tells the client to send them away (in the form of the photograph) herself.

Each of these acts continually alternates between freedom and restriction for the client, between going back to how things were and going ahead. The therapist generally pleads in favor of the new identity, the client acts as defendant of the old one.

The transition to the third act of the play is very dramatic. It is a trap. The therapist has just evoked her old identity and, as soon as she goes along with him in it, he makes a frontal attack. He asks, "And she is with you?"

Emphatically, now with a tender and nearly contented tone in her voice, the client answers, "Always."

"Then send her away," he says immediately.

The differences between the three acts are primarily the work of the therapist. The most important differences are:

—The symbolism becomes more and more tangible. First the girl is present in the third person and in the past tense, then in the imagination (and must be addressed), then in a photograph. The general pronouncement "She is dead" becomes "You will never see her again" and then "Send her away."

—The pronouncements are more and more often replaced by instructions. In this way, the client's task is defined more and more precisely, but she retains a certain freedom of choice in the manner in which she carries out a task. It is sufficient at first that she let the pronouncement "she is dead" sink in, and that she show some sort of reaction to it. Then she has to look at the picture, talk to it. Then she must take leave of it, in certain prescribed terms.

—The behavior required of her becomes more active, more in keeping with her new identity. Having to send her daughter to her death, and with harsh words at that, is entirely incompatible with her old identity as the loving mother of this child.

—The client is drawn into a greater and greater social vacuum. First she may talk with the therapist *about* the dead, then she must resort to a monologue to them, and finally she must even send away her passive conversational partner. Not until she has done that may she "return"; the therapist is again available as a normal conversant, and she may leave the therapy.

—Her struggle against the therapist is converted into a struggle against the dead, not only as described above but in other ways as well. Her crying, her declarations that she cannot at the beginning of the therapy are ambiguous in their meaning: they could equally well be aimed at the therapist or at the death of her mother and daughter. And it is exactly when her resistance to the therapy as a whole becomes very obvious (although it again takes the form of "I cannot") that the therapist hands her the picture of her daughter, so that she can tell of her grief and resistance to it. Finally she herself takes over an earlier role of Ramsay and defines the conflict as one between her old and her new identity: "I don't want to, but I've got to. I can't grieve all the time for you . . . I don't want you dead" (therapist: "She is dead."). "I won't have you dead, but he says she is dead . . . I am trying to accept it, but it's so hard." Ramsay suggests a fairly aggressive formulation: "Tell her she has caused you so much pain." But the client prefers to send the dead away in a milder fashion.

The role played by aggression in this therapy is particularly interesting, considering the restrictions our society places on it in general and, too, in mourning, and especially for women. This client's behavioral repertoire allows for hardly any direct expression of aggression, neither towards the dead nor towards others in her environment, and she stubbornly rejects the therapist's suggestions in that direction. In difficult situations she goes into a depression, she cries, she tries to run away, or she attempts suicide: violence turned on herself. Rosenblatt et al. (1976, p. 39) suggest that, in societies where little aggression enters into mourning, ritual specialists (including psychotherapists) assume an active role in the restriction of such behavior. At first glance, their premise seems to be in disagreement with what takes place in this therapy. The therapist asks the client for more expressions of aggression than she is capable of: toward her husband, her mother, her daughter, and toward him, the therapist. But these expressions of aggression have a particular focus, in a context in which physical violence and suicide are prohibited, and they are not obligatory. Only one form of aggression is very urgently needed, because the success of the therapy is conditional on it: sending away the dead with a last message of "you have caused me so much pain."

The therapist does more than merely show the client painful things from the past in order for the feelings to be extinguished. He offers her rules of conduct, and stages several rehearsals for discarding the old identity and building up a new one. Direct pressure is not the only way in which he exerts his influence; he also uses temptation. But the most important role in the client's improvement might well be played by the subtle and complex structure of the therapy as a whole. The client is given a variety of instructions, all of which have several unspoken symbolic implications and create a change in identity and feelings. When she has carried out all the prescribed actions—and only then—there is no way back. She has become a different person with different feelings.

Conclusion

Above I have treated expressions of grief and mourning as well as mourning theory and therapy as products of social and historical construction. This is not to say that I dispute the sincerity of western expressions of grief and mourning, that I doubt the usefulness of grief therapy or the validity of the theory of mourning and grief for the groups that have been studied. Placing activities or ideas in their social context does not imply criticism or censure. But viewing grief as a social product necessarily has some consequences for the validity of the theory of mourning and grief and for the therapy based on it. I would like to mention a few of those consequences.

First, there are good reasons to assume that the theory of mourning and grief as it has been developed so far will not be universally valid. It looks like social conditions play a decisive role in the course of a mourning process. This means that the social and cultural aspect of mourning which the distinction between "grief" and "mourning" has removed from the theory will have to be put back in, and it will have to have priority in further study. And until more is known about the effects of social factors on mourning processes, the use of the term 'pathological mourning process' can better be dispensed with. There is not yet sufficient scientific basis for its use, and inherent in the term is a risk of stigmatization.

This brings us to a second consequence of the fact that grief is socially and historically determined. Any theory, scientific ones included, has an impact on daily life (cf. Meeuwisse & Van der Ploeg, 1979, on the "hostage syndrome"). Mourning theory and therapy not only satisfy a social need, but they also help to create this need. They give us something to go on, but at the same time they give new norms to determine what people brand as abnormal, pathological, and dangerous in themselves and in others. And it is perhaps even more difficult to defy demands made in the name of your own "normal mourning process" than it is social conventions or religious duties.

Culture, Leave-Taking Rituals and the Psychotherapist

Wencke J. and Michael R. Seltzer

Our understanding of psychotherapeutic rituals in general and leave-taking rituals in particular is still very much in its infancy. In this chapter, we will deviate from the general outlines of the case histories presented thus far. Here, rather than a concern with individual clients performing leave-taking rites prescribed for them by individual therapists, our focus will be on leave-taking rituals in the disengagement of the cultures borne by families and hospital staff. Rather than describing scenarios where therapists act and clients are acted upon, our description is of a reversal of this pattern. Our presentation describes leave-taking rituals initiated, staged, and directed by families at the conclusion of their engagement in the anorexic treatment program of the Pediatrics Clinic of the National Hospital of Norway (see Seltzer, 1984 for a more detailed description of the pre-leavetaking stages in this program).

Our primary focus is on the events in the clients' exit from therapy. In all of the cases thus far described, exiting was an event which took place *after* various leave-taking rites had been prescribed by therapists and performed by clients. Here we wish to draw attention to families' exits from therapy, and the role played by leave-taking rituals during these particularly vulnerable times in the healing process. There are two compelling reasons why the focus is on exiting.

First, there exists in the literature of therapy a very obvious imbalance in descriptions of the beginnings and conclusions of therapeutic encounters. In much of the writing about therapeutic stages, processes, and interventions, there is little to be found about the process of leave-taking of therapy itself. This is somewhat remarkable since all experienced therapists know that the termination of a therapeutic involvement can be just as critical and crucial as initial interviews and meetings with individual clients and client systems. Nonetheless, only a very few therapists in recent years have devoted attention to leave-taking from therapy (Rabkin, 1977; Kramer, 1981; Van der Hart, 1983a). The following is meant as one small attempt to help redress this imbalance and add to our understanding of the exiting process.

Secondly, and perhaps even more importantly, our focus on the role of leave-taking rituals at the end of therapy is aimed at redressing another imbalance. As we have already seen in this book and others (e.g., Selvini Palazzoli et al., 1978; Van der Hart, 1983a), rituals can be powerful instruments of therapeutic *engagement*. Here, our goal is a description and discussion of rituals as instruments of *disengagement* from therapy. Since we describe rituals of leave-taking from therapy with families who have been hospitalized, our attention will be directed to the breaking apart of two, if not more, behavior systems or cultures. We emphasize that the family taking leave of the hospital treatment situation is but one set of actors among several. They are involved in a highly complicated process whereby the once intimately intertwined and interconnected cultural systems borne by several groups are being unraveled.

We attempt to describe how rites of leave-taking operate as instruments of *cultural* disengagement. We then turn to a discussion of what our experiences with these processes may tell us about leave-taking rituals in psychotherapy as well as the more generalized role of ritual in the conduct of human affairs. Though our point of departure deviates from the others in this book, and our focus is on groups rather than individuals, we believe that our presentation may underscore the similarities in what may well be different levels of leave-taking rituals in psychotherapy. Since the role of leave-taking rituals in psychotherapy is a relatively uncharted domain of the human condition, the mode for its scientific exploration must be multifaceted. By adding our understanding of the leave-taking ritual involved in the disengagement of cultures borne by the two groups—both providing and receiving therapy—to what has already been presented by our co-contributors, we hope to further expand our knowledge of a little-known area of human behavior.

Culture and Psychotherapy

Family therapy, as we have described elsewhere (Seltzer and Seltzer, 1983), differs from individual therapy. It is the combining of two behavior systems; that of the family and of the therapist or co-therapists. When family therapy takes place in a large hospital setting, as in the case of a recently developed program for treating anorexia nervosa in the Pediatrics Clinic of the National Hospital of Norway, it involves the incorporating of a number of behavior systems or cultures (Seltzer, 1983, 1984).

By culture, we mean the system of learned and patterned behavior shared by members of different groups. Every culture consists of unique patterns of actions, thoughts, and feelings. These, in turn, can be further reduced into identifiable subsystems, existing on both a material and ideational plane.

On the material plane are found the observable patterns of behavior exhibited by a culture's bearers.* In operation, these are most clearly represented by rituals: the particular procedures for action and reaction adhered to—in varying degrees—by those bearing the culture. The ideational plane of any culture is the locus of the nonmaterial, and thus unobservable, beliefs and affects shared wholly or in part by its bearers. It is on this plane that cognitions on a continuum from unconscious to conscious and affects associated with rituals are found in such forms as myths and thematic beliefs.

Seen in this light, all of us are bearers of the cultures of the groups to which we belong. Indeed, nearly all of us are bearers of a number of cultures: the culture of the families in which we are raised, of the families we form through marriage, of the occupational groups we work in, and of the countries to which we owe allegiance, as well as the ethnic and religious cultures of the groups with which we identify.

Usually, cultural systems possess enough flexibility to allow their bearers to change in response to alterations in their environment. The ideologies and actions of culture bearers generally appear to be connected in ways conducive to change. In most cultural systems, there exists a dialectic between material practice and ideational reflection upon this practice, which appears to promote change. Through processes akin to

---

Editor's note:
*The term "culture bearers" is an anthropological one. Where sociologists or social psychologists would talk about the members of a group, anthropologists refer more to the culture, i.e. learned and shared behavior patterns, borne by the members of that group.

what systems theorists describe as "feedback" and "looping," the bearers of a cultural system can adapt their actions and ideologies to changed circumstances in their environment.

History, however, reveals that this is not always the case. For many reasons, some natural (such as drought or famine) and others man-made, some cultural systems lose this dialectic fluidity and their bearers become inflexible and stagnate. Ideational and material planes seem frozen at various points along their shared interface, and the social relationships assume a repetitive and death-like non-dynamic character. When this occurs in large-scale cultural systems, such as states or chiefdoms, anthropologists describe this condition as "cultural involution" (Kroeber, 1944; Geertz, 1963). When it is found in small-scale cultural systems, such as families, psychotherapists refer to it as a "dead" or "locked" relationship.

In most instances, the bearers of such locked systems possess enough inventiveness and problem-solving abilities to "thaw" the culture, thus restoring the dynamic interplay between action and ideology. Sometimes, however, outside intervention is necessary. In large-scale systems, this is often provided by leaders of "revitalization movements" (Wallace, 1961), "revivalistic movements" (Linton, 1961), and "revolutionary movements" (Leggett, 1974). In small-scale systems, such as that of the hunting band, this is provided by a shaman. In the smaller-scale system of the family, as we have indicated elsewhere (Seltzer & Seltzer, 1983), this is provided in Euro-American contexts by family therapists operating in the role of change inducement specialists.

Though they differ in appearance, the core of all such exercises in cultural change involves the ritualized manipulation of symbolic material by the agent of change. The successful agent provides culture bearers with a new frame of reference (Lévi-Strauss, 1949) and a "reformulated mazeway" (Wallace, 1961). This is a synthesized culture now borne by a group who have experienced a transformation of previously stalemated relations between material behavior (the signifying) and ideational behavior (the signified). Change has occurred, and the relations between these planes are again operating dialectically and adaptively.

Applying this understanding of culture and cultural change sheds a somewhat different light on what has been presented thus far in this book. In one sense, the cultures of the families of the clients described by our co-contributors all appeared to add to the problem which had brought them to therapy. Although not all the family biographical data is sufficient to be conclusive, there are enough signs to indicate that each client arrived at therapy as the repository of some of the frozen elements of her or his own family culture. In other words, the ideologies and material practices of the family cultures borne by Debbie, Jim, Jan, Sandra, and the other clients described earlier were sources of much of the pain and stagnation they experienced prior to therapy. In another sense, each of the therapists operated as agents of cultural change. Though different in terms of their own educational backgrounds and professional identities, they engaged with ritualistic tools the ideational and material systems of their clients. Through the use of these sequential material procedures loaded with meaning, the therapists forced a dialectic between action and ideology in the systems borne by their clients. By employing objects invested with meaning in these rituals, the therapists probably did much more than simply endow matter, such as letters and personal artifacts, with meaning. Tactically, they made it impossible for clients to resist engagement. Thus, clients wishing to deal with their "bad" feelings at the ideational level were forced, by ritual, to deal with the concrete condensations of these feelings at the material level. Through such ritualized linking of idea and feeling with matter, the therapists were able to penetrate and then engage their clients' behavior systems. They were then in the position to guide clients from their frozen states into a more dynamic future. Thus, Debbie and Jim abandoned their dead relationship which largely revolved around the family roles assigned them in earlier periods of their lives. Sandra ceased attempting to fulfil paternal expectations; Jan stopped worshipping at the shrine of his dead spouse. And the other clients similarly took leave of individuals, situations, and identities from their pasts. In this respect, it does not seem too farfetched to suggest that these clients left therapy with new, synthesized and revitalized systems of behavior.

The evidence presented so far by our co-contributors underscores the role of leave-taking rituals as instruments for system engagement and system change at the individual level. This parallels much of our own experience with the use of ritual as an instrument of cultural engagement and change in psychotherapeutic work with families (Seltzer & Seltzer, 1983; Seltzer, 1983). In the following, however, we attempt to describe the role of leave-taking rituals as instruments of disengagement, rather than of engagement, in psychotherapy. In order to provide a fuller understanding of this role, it will be necessary to describe briefly some features of the treatment program for anorexic families as provided by this author and a small multi-disciplinary team in the Pediatrics Clinic of the National Hospital of Norway.

Leave-taking from an anorexic treatment program: a Norwegian example

Experience with the anorexic families leaving the treatment program of the Pediatrics Clinic of the National Hospital of Norway during the past three years indicates that feelings of anxiety, apprehension, and uncertainty run high among both families and staff. One factor undoubtedly contributing to this is the complex character of anorexia nervosa. Typically, the culture of the anorexic family is strong, deceptive, and highly resistant to change (see, for example, Minuchin et al., 1978; Selvini Palazzoli, 1974). Considerable therapeutic skill and effort are required to break through the often extremely deceptive defenses of such a family. This necessitates a high degree of engagement on the part of the therapist and therapeutic team. Once these cultures are engaged and transformed, the process of *disengagement* from them requires similar efforts.

In addition to the complexities involved in disengagement, there are other factors contributing to the difficulties involved in the process of discharging anorexic families from treatment in the hospital. Some are apparently directly related to the design and evolution of the treatment program. This is a multisystemic effort by an interdisciplinary team consisting of a family therapist and a co-therapist, a ward physician, two contact nurses, and a hospital dietician. The treatment program involves the whole family of the primary patient in therapy, and family members are housed in the hospital for a short in-patient period ranging from one to three weeks. Without exception, the treatment period in the hospital is an extremely tense and intense time since the primary patient invariably arrives at the hospital in critical condition, both physically and psychologically. During this time, the treatment team invests a great deal of hard work, considerable time, and often great personal courage in daily encounters with the family (see Seltzer, 1983, 1984 for a detailed account).

As the time for discharge approaches, the engagement-disengagement process becomes an obvious problem in the interaction between family, team, and other hospital staff. At this point it is common for staff members to express concern that the family may not make it on its own. Such concern may be real enough, but it may also partly be a reflection of the staff's own feelings of being abandoned. One staff member summarized these kinds of feelings about a family's impending discharge by lamenting, "After all the work and involvement we have put in, they take off, just like that!"

Similar feelings of not being ready and of incompleteness in relation to the family are expressed by staff in various ways at this time. This may have to do with the fact that the staff has only differentially experienced some, but not all, aspects of the treatment program. Unlike the family therapist and co-therapist, who, in the course of therapy sessions, have had opportunities to work through and follow the very complex relationships exhibited by anorexic families, many staff members have had much more limited contact with the family.

The family, too, contributes to the difficulties involved in the discharge process. This may be due in part to the "release anxiety" phenomenon: the reoccurrence of previously abandoned symptoms by patients or patient systems immediately prior to discharge. Although some contend this is the patient's reaction to his own fears and apprehensions about re-entering the non-institutional world (e.g., Goffman, 1961), there is reason to believe that it may also be an expression by the family of the anorexic of loyalty to and/or dependence on staff members. The peculiarity of symptoms recurring as soon as plans for discharge are discussed may express, on the part of the family, a deeply sensitive and protective reaction toward those staff members who are perceived as not being ready to "let go" of the family, and who implicitly still depend on the family as a symptom-preserving unit. At the same time, however, more peripheral staff seem to generate the opposite reaction: the desire to be rid of the family as soon as possible. Their perceptions appear to cast the families in roles of patients who are overly demanding and emotionally draining for their co-workers in the treatment program. For a variety of reasons which we hypothesize have to do with the staff's engagement/disengagement in relation to the family, some of them exhibit feelings of frustration toward members of the treatment team as the time for discharge of the anorexic family draws near. The team, it should be noted, has the executive role in the treatment program, and is hence the unit which proposes the discharge.

A final factor contributing to the "multisystemic anxiety," apprehension, and frustration surrounding the anorexic family's leave-taking concerns the relative newness of the treatment program. As already mentioned, the program has been in existence for only four years. Moreover, it is nontraditional in that it is a psychiatrically directed program in the setting of a conventional somatic hospital. At its inception and during the early stages of its evolution, the program did not include any sort of leave-taking procedures for families discharged from the hospital. During this period, this vacuum was partially filled, by default, through the hospital's standardized discharge procedures required for all patients. But it soon became apparent that this procedure, involving essentially only the signing of papers, was a far from adequate solution to all the problems generated by the discharge of anorexic families from the hospital.

The hospital ritual

After experiencing some of the problems involved in discharging the first families treated in the program, the treatment team initiated a leave-taking rite in an attempt to deal with the anxieties of the family and staff. From its inception this hospital ritual was intended as a set of procedures aimed at helping the family and hospital staff to become culturally disentangled from one another.

In practice, the ritual was enacted to attain certain well-defined goals. Among these were structured opportunities to reduce the anxieties of the family and staff members, instill a sense of responsibility for decision making in all systems, and afford a ceremonial exchange of farewells and good wishes. In addition, the importance of the attendance of all members of the treatment systems involved was emphasized. The entire family was likewise asked to be present. The staff were required to schedule their work and appointments so as not to interfere with the hour alloted for the leave-taking rite. This, incidentally, is no small undertaking in a busy hospital.

Generally, the ritual proceeds along the following lines. At the prescribed time all participants arrive and are seated in separate chairs in a circle in the meeting room. The family therapist welcomes everyone to the meeting, stresses its importance, and then summarizes the common history shared by all participants from the very first day the family was admitted to the hospital. The therapist concludes this historical review at the present—the day when the family is scheduled to leave. This formal opening ends with the therapist announcing that it is important for each participant to mark a spot in the meeting by saying and sharing whatever thoughts or feelings she/he may have about the past, present, and future. Typically, this announcement triggers remembrances of past events familiar to all. Usually, at this point, the family will indicate how difficult the hospitalization period was for them. They generally add that the stay, despite its hardships, may have been helpful. This then leads to a history of intersystemic conflicts which took place during hospitalization, particularly at the beginning when the primary patient's life was threatened, and staff and family members were afraid. These conflicts, however, are invariably described in the past tense.

Following this, the members of the treatment team designate the areas of the post-hospitalization treatment plan they wish the family to continue to practice. This leads to a general discussion of how this can best be accomplished. The dietician may have a diet plan which she reviews with the primary patient in the presence of all; the ward physician may read a letter aloud she/he is sending to the nurse or physician in the family's home community about monitoring the primary patient's weight in the coming months; and the nurses may ask the family to send a note to the ward to let them know how the family is doing. Finally, the family therapist and co-therapist share with the participants the scheduling for the family's return to the hospital for follow-up outpatient therapy sessions. The family comments on the plans, asks questions, and then makes various request for "assistance" from the health facilities in the home community.

This leads to a discussion of how it will feel for the family to return home after such a long time away, and what kinds of plans they may have for their homecoming. The plans often deal with apprehensions of the family as well as their return to school, work, and community activities. This "viewing out" away from the hospital produces a mood of euphoria. Then all participants wish each other well and shake hands all around. The meeting ends, and the participants depart. The family returns to "their" room in the hospital. There they gather their possessions, call for transportation, and leave.

However the contact between the family and the therapists does not stop here. The family continues therapy on an outpatient basis. This working relationship between the therapist and the family is formally concluded when the therapists make a final visit to the home of the family. As therapy nears conclusion, a meeting at the family's home is scheduled. This generally involves considerable planning since the distance between the National Hospital in Oslo and the home is often great. (The hospital serves a country the length of which is equivalent to the distance between Oslo and Rome.)

The Home Ritual

Before describing a leave-taking ritual involving family and therapists in the family home, it is important to point out that the general aspects of this particular ritual have been found in nearly all of the homes visited thus far in the treatment program. It is also important to emphasize that these home rituals, unlike the hospital leave-taking rites, are neither the product nor the design of the therapists. Each of the leave-taking rituals experienced by the therapists is planned and staged by families having no knowledge of how closely their rituals resemble those of other families. Each family designs its own unique leave-taking ritual to deal with its disengagement from the therapists. This occurs independently and may be understood as each family's attempt to supplement the hospital ritual with procedures more appropriate to their own needs at this time.

One typical example of such a home ritual is that of a family living on an island far out in the ocean along the Norwegian coast. After the necessary travel arrangements had been made, the therapists boarded a passenger boat and travelled two hours in rough seas to the port nearest the family home. Both therapists became seasick on the voyage and were pale and queasy when met by the mother and youngest family member. On the drive to the family's house, both mother and child took considerable pleasure in pointing out to the therapists all the places which had significance for the family. Several had been touched upon in the course of therapy, and some were sites of previously discussed and therapeutically relevant themes in therapy.

As in other "sight seeing" preludes to home visits, the places and persons pointed out to the therapists by the family corresponded in a curious way to the mental images formed in the course of therapy. Throughout the tour, it was a great source of pleasure for the mother and child when the therapists recognized these "sights" spontaneously.

The car tour ended at the family home, where the father and previously anorexic daughter stood on the doorstep and welcomed the therapists. After a lengthy round of handshaking and small talk, the therapists were conducted on a tour of the household. The children, in particular, showed off their rooms and possessions; these were often symbolic condensations of each child's particular identity and position in the family. The rooms were meticulously clean and the entire interior of the house was festively decorated with flowers, the best tablecloths were used, etc.

After the tour, the therapists were invited to sit down with the family for coffee and party sandwiches. While all were eating, it was pointed out that the previously anorexic daughter helped to prepare, serve, and *eat* the foods on the table. There was a rather gay and frivolous atmosphere at the table during this time, which reflected the mood of the ceremonies in other homes visited by the therapists at the conclusion of treatment.

When all participants had eaten their fill and were no longer hungry, the atmosphere became even more relaxed. At this point, several previously sensitive topics in therapy were brought up or mentioned in passing. The children in the family used this occasion to point out to the therapists the location of a metaphor which had been a focus in therapy. During the hospitalization period, they had expressed a feeling that the family was like a "bomb" ready to explode. They led the therapists to a spot on the living room floor under which they had felt this bomb was located. Using the past tense throughout, the children assembled everyone around this spot to show where they believed this explosive device had been located.

As in all other home visits, the beginning of the end of the visit was signaled by the arrival at the home, almost on cue, of several members of the extended families. Grandparents, aunts, uncles, and other relatives arrived en masse to meet the therapists. Although this meeting was essentially one of lengthy handshaking and small talk, the therapists viewed it as an inspection of them conducted by the extended family. (Curiously, many of the anorexic families included in the treatment program lived next to one or both families of origin—often on the same plot of land.) Following this inspection, the therapists left the family and returned to the port for their departure to the mainland.

Discussion

On the surface, the meetings in the hospital and the home appear to be little more than social gatherings. But when we begin to look beyond the appearances, some very definite and complex patterns begin to emerge.

First, these are very clearly cultural phenomena in the sense we have indicated earlier: They are not simply the coming together of groups of individuals in situations differing only in their degree of formality and informality. They are cultural in the sense that the participants in these encounters exhibit very distinct learned and shared patterns of behavior. Each encounter has a clearly defined beginning and end: in the hospital this is demarcated by the therapist who directs the start and finish of the encounter, while in the home this is accomplished by the family. At the material level, these patterns are represented in the spatial and temporal procedures which guide the participants in relation to each other as well as to their material environments. In the hospital, this is found in the ordered gathering and dispersal of the participants, the spatial arrangements and the ordering of events at this encounter. In the home a similar pattern is found, although here there is an emphasis on the activities of eating and the location and identification of objects and places. At the ideational level, these patterns are represented by the meanings attached by the participants to procedures, persons, objects, and places.

One way of arriving at an understanding of the interplay of these levels, and hence a grasp of their therapeutic significance, is to examine the most basic differences between these two leave-taking rituals. In both, individual groups depart from each other. In the hospital, the family leaves the hospital staff, and in the home the therapists leave the family. The primary contrast between the two, however, concerns which group directs the leave-taking procedures. In the hospital it is accomplished by the therapeutic team, in the home by the family. Basically, defining the leave-taking situation is done by the group upon whose territory the ritual occurs.

The hospital ritual, as indicated, was implemented primarily by the therapeutic team to deal with the different forms of anxiety exhibited by both the family and hospital staff. The underlying rationale for this ritual was based on a scientific understanding of ritual. A number of scholars have amassed considerable evidence for the role of ritual in alleviating and reducing anxiety among humans at both the individual level (e.g., Freud, 1907) and the group level (Malinowski, 1978; Homans, 1941); and these findings played a major role in planning the hospital ritual. In addition, the cultural perspective of the treatment program (see Seltzer, 1983) suggested strongly that the separation of family from hospital staff was a process very much akin to the disentanglement of cultures involved in migration. It, too, is a process of cultural disengagement involving considerable anxiety and pain, with virtually no prescribed rituals to help those who are going through disengagement with their problems (see e.g., Sluzki, 1979). It was against the backdrop of general knowledge about ritual and anxiety and the practical problems of disentangling family from staff that the hospital leave-taking ritual was instituted.

The home rituals of the families, in contrast to those of the hospital, did not appear to be influenced in any way by scientific reasoning. Rather, they appeared in almost identical forms in independent families as the families' response to their own fears and anxieties associated with the final disengagement of themselves from those conducting therapy. In one sense the leave-taking rites of each family underscored the primary lesson to be learned by students of human behavior who focus on ritual—that, when traditional rituals are weak or non-existent, people will invent them in an attempt to deal with the fears and anxieties they experience.

Moreover, an examination of the contrasts seems to suggest that both the hospital and the home leave-taking rituals must be considered as one. The independent invention of the home leave-taking rite by each family may be understood as an attempt to take care of issues left unresolved or not dealt with effectively by the hospital ritual. This suggests, then, that each of these leave-taking rituals is not simply an independent phenomenon occurring at different times and places; rather, that these two procedures are part of a much larger whole—a leave-taking ritual complex. Seen in this light, the differences that exist within this whole become even more marked: socially, spatially, and temporally. At the beginning of the leave-taking ritual complex, the power and authority to direct ritual procedures is endowed in the therapeutic team by the other participants. The therapists orchestrate the ritual and conduct its movements from beginning to end. As conductors, they lead and the other participants follow. The status or ranking system of the hospital is clearcut: the therapists are the superiors of the family. At the other end of this complex, in the home of the family, the system is reversed. It is the therapists, rather than the family, who are directed and assisted. Here the family acts and the therapists are acted upon. In its own territory, the family is the superior of the therapists. There is, however, one point in the transformation of systems where both are social equals. This occurs on those occasions in all home rituals where meals, cakes, cookies, and other snacks are consumed by the participants. Sociologically, the spatial arrangements of these eating activities are of considerable importance. Commensalism, or the sharing of food at one table, has long been used by sociological students of class and status (e.g., Weber, 1979) as an indicator of social equality. Masters do not normally dine with their slaves or servants, nor do officers in military and maritime organizations dine with their subordinates. Indeed, the design of a military base and a ship almost always include separate dining and drinking facilities to prevent commensalism. So the meeting of family and therapists at a common dining table may be seen as an act symbolically underscoring the equivalent ranking of both systems. By joining the family at their table and at their invitation, the therapists become in this sense their social equals. This, too, represents a marked contrast to the eating patterns of both sets of actors during the hospitalization period. There it was often observed that even though members of families and the treatment team used the hospital cafeteria at the same time, they rarely shared the same tables.

The consumption of food during family rituals provides contrasts to earlier times in the history of the participants in other respects as well. In any anorexic treatment program, the intake of food is a particularly emotionally loaded issue. As contrasted to the emotional and conflict-ridden atmosphere during treatment, the festive atmosphere during the home ritual may be understood as an indication of the end of the family's troubles as well as a beginning of a new phase of family life and development. (In this respect, it is interesting to note that Minuchin and his associates utilize a family dining session at the *beginning* of therapy with anorexic families to expose the discrepancies in the decision-making and other practices of these families (Rosman et al., 1975).)

Another contrast which underscores the transformation of things into their opposites is provided in the leave-taking ritual complex by the "inspection" of the therapists by the extended family. Prior to this inspection, the therapists may very well have assumed mythical and omnipotent proportions in their eyes. During the family's hospital stay, the therapists have taken on what the extended family, particularly the grandparental generation, might construe as a parenting role. At a distant place in an unfamiliar setting, the therapists have carried out a mysterious process called therapy with the anorexic family. Thus, prior to this inspection there may well be some jealousy and anger on the part of the extended family toward these somewhat magical individuals who have intruded into the most intimate history and functions of the family. So the inspection of the therapists by the extended family appears to do several things. First, it deflates the mystified status of the therapists by revealing them as ordinary individuals. Secondly, it may reassure the extended family of the "normalization" of their relatives who were involved in a mysterious process which is now coming to an end, as defined by the final home visit. Thirdly, it may reassure the extended family that their relatives have finally come home from a distant and strange place where other individuals, rather than kin, had assumed the role of healers.

In this respect, the transformation of the therapists from superior and mystical beings into ordinary social equals which occurs in the dining and inspection processes of the home visit parallels, in certain ways, the symbolic events of more formalized degradation rituals. The therapists, like priests defrocked and officers drummed out of the corps, lose their status. They are, in effect, demoted and leave the ritual complex stripped of much of the power and authority they possessed in the hospital. The therapists are, of course, still the same individuals. What they have lost is the symbolic meanings attached to them by the family.

This relates directly to what is perhaps the most fascinating aspect of the home ritual as the final part of the whole ritual. What may not be altogether explicit in this complex, beginning in the hospital and ending in the home, is that the disengagement of the cultural systems finalized in the home, involves a surrender on the part of the therapists. In other words, in order for leave-taking and disengagement to occur, the therapists must surrender their ritualistic tools. These instruments, once absolutely necessary for engaging, penetrating, and stimulating change in the family system, are in a sense handed over to the family in the leave-taking finale. The ritualistic tools, such as rites demoting the sacred and mystical to the commonplace, remain more or less the same. Yet, in the home rituals, the rituals have been surrendered and have become incorporated into the culture of the system once under therapy.

It is sometimes said that the therapist must fail if the family is to succeed. The evidence provided by the home rituals of previously anorexic families suggests that one way of "failing" on the part of the therapist is through the surrender of rituals to the family. By doing this and by relinquishing what were once necessary tools of engagement, penetration, and change, the therapists supply the bearers of the once-engaged family with proof of their new status as a functioning and fully disengaged independent group.

The transfer of rituals from the therapists to the family is one of the key processes occurring in the ritual complex. Paralleling this is the process whereby the therapists themselves are also transformed in terms of status, power, and other related attributes. In the home ritual, for example, the therapists are changed from the helpers to those helped; from guides to followers; and from those with knowledge to those who are ignorant. Certainly most of these transformations are at least partially related to a spatial transformation occurring in this complex. The hospital ritual, together with the hospitalization phase of the treatment program, takes place on the home territory of the therapists. Here, families are strangers in unknown surroundings. In the home ritual, the therapists are strangers in territory familiar to the family. The roles of the two systems become spatially reversed. In this reversal, much of the knowledge and authority of the therapeutic system is lost and reappears as attributes of the family system.

The spatial dimension of the transformation of systems into their opposites is also paralleled by processes involving a temporal dimension. In the first minutes of the hospital ritual, the participants are involved in the past as the therapist recounts the intersystemic history of the treatment program. In the closing moments of the home ritual, prior to the extended family's inspection and the departure of the therapists from the home, the talk at the dining table invariably includes discussions of the family's future and the pre-hospitalization past when the therapists did not exist for the family. There is, then, in this ritual complex a very clear shift in the temporal frame of reference, beginning in story form when the systems were engaged and ending in story form when the systems are disengaged.

Operating along this time dimension, the ritual complex appears to function as both a transporter and transformer of states. Clearly, it involves the participants in a reframing of time perspectives from past to future. In this respect, the patterning of the whole aids this reframing through the processes of preparation, reorganization, and finalization already described by Onno van der Hart in this book. Though differing in their purposes, the preparations of both the home and hospital rituals appear to aim toward a future of system disengagement. Similarly, the reorganization of the familiar into new patterns in both the hospital meeting room and the family home also appear to reinforce this movement from past toward future. Thus, both the dining arrangement in the home and the seating arrangement in the hospital reorganize and add new meaning to the individuals and objects involved. There is, for example, a very marked egalitarian character to the arrangements of both; each participant is allowed to have her/his say, and the power of one set of actors over another, once vital to the treatment, is more or less equally shared—especially at the dining table. There is a well-defined pattern of cleansing and purification involved in the hospital and the home. In the hospital this is provided by the opportunities for each participant to clear the air of past grievances, frustrations, and conflicts—real or imagined. Similarly, the rigorous housecleaning undertaken, which produces an exceptionally clean home with an immaculate dining area, underscores the symbolic (and hygienic) removal of the old from the arena in which the ritual is carried out.

In short, many of the individuals and objects symbolizing attachment to the past are reorganized in the hospital and home to allow for detachment and make way for the future. Symbolically, the concluding concrete acts between the bearers of the cultural systems in both locales may underscore the finalization of system disengagement. The handshaking between staff and family in the hospital and between the bearers of therapeutic culture and family culture in the home are material manifestations of disengagement. These highly ritualized farewells customary in everyday life allow the different groups to touch and then pull away from one another.

Time and its transformation through rituals also occur in a somewhat different manner in these as well as the other leave-takings described in this book. Conceptually, one way of understanding this is to divide time into categories: objective or chronologic time and subjective or experiential time. The former is designated in named units or measures such as minutes, hours, days, weeks, months, years, etc. In formal and non-personal encounters with the world around us, objective time is the unit through which almost all communication occurs. On the other hand, the time of our personal and intimate lives is highly subjective. Sometimes these two temporal categories coincide. Often, however, they do not. We know, for example, that temporal experiences of subjects in induced altered states of consciousness, such as hypnotic trances and sensory deprivation experiments, become seriously distorted in relation to objective time. We also know that more "meaning" may be attached to a time during one phase of life than during other phases. Thus elderly and institutionalized individuals often expand the times in their lives when they were more active and life had more meaning for them. In this way, they appear to "live" in this expanded past, in clear discrepancy with objective time which is constantly moving forward. Objective time cannot be stopped in its march forward, while experiential or subjective time can be halted.

When life for individuals or intimate familial groups becomes lodged in past niches of subjective time, this can be characterized in many instances as pathological. It is pathological primarily because natural human development is prevented by this frozen temporal state. The case of Jan, described earlier by Jos Ebbers, illustrates this very well. Unable to accept the death of his wife, he created a mental picture of her which was mythical and static. Since he viewed her as myth, Jan could not be objective or rational, and time became locked for him. Ultimately, the seriously distorted relationship between subjective and objective time for Jan was corrected by a leave-taking ritual combining matter and idea in a particular way. This therapeutically prescribed rite transformed the relationship and brought Jan's subjective time into alignment with the objective time ordering communication in the world about him.

Many therapists are well acquainted with similar pathological time distortions exhibited by suicidal clients. During periods of crisis—especially when feelings of self-worth are low—it is not uncommon for individuals to attempt to preserve time by threatening to or by actually killing themselves. Carl Whitaker (1975) has dealt with this by asking clients to produce imaginary accounts of their funerals. Under his direction, the preparation and finalization of the funeral leave-taking rite is mostly ideational. It is material in the sense that the thought is transformed into words, and thus shared with others, and becomes conscious in its shared meaning. Whitaker is thorough, and the client is required to include in the funeral account answers to such questions as to who would be present, who would be most grief-stricken, who would be least grief-stricken, how the ceremony would be performed (in detail) and how life would continue for all participants after the funeral. Similarly, other therapists deal with the suicidal fantasies of clients by asking them future-directed questions about their lives in two, five, or ten years and about the roles to be played in the future by those nearest them.

The common denominator underlying such therapeutic interventions and those described throughout this book is the unfreezing or thawing of the relationship between subjective and objective time. In all these cases, the rituals (imagined in the case of Whitaker, but actualized in the cases presented here) force these frozen constellations into contact with reality, where exposure eventually melts them. In some instances this forcing has an ideational emphasis, as in the cases of families in the hospital told to fantasize about their futures and in the suicidal clients asked to do the same. This forcing often has a more material emphasis, as in the cases described earlier where ritual prescription requires that letters and other personal artifacts be used to bring the untouched out into the open. Yet, no matter where the emphasis, the conclusions of all these ritualistic processes are more or less identical: the secret becomes public knowledge, the sacred becomes profaned, and the potent becomes impotent. In this manner, the subjective time of the individual client or client system is transformed through ritual and becomes objective time. Rituals of leave-taking all involve a qualitative transformation of time; their preparation, organization, and finalization stages work to thaw that which is static, and thus allow the lives of individuals and groups to assume a more fluid and dynamic character where subjective and objective time more or less coincide.

In one sense, these kinds of ritually induced changes in therapy are but a final underscoring of the evidence presented by all the contributors to this book as well as authors of other books focusing on the role of ritual in therapy (e.g., Selvini Palazzoli, 1974; Van der Hart, 1983a) that successful ritualistic interventions produce transformations in the individuals and systems in therapy. In the leave-taking ritual complex just described and discussed, there appears to be another kind of transformation process at work, specifically that of a series of transformations in the relationship between the system in therapy and the systems conducting therapy. Taken as a whole, the evidence from successful rituals in therapy seems to suggest that all such therapeutic interventions involve the dialectical transformation of opposites. In the home ritual just examined the family itself, through its own leave-taking rite, emphasizes its transformation from a pathological, helpless system into a smoothly functioning, fully competent system. Through a series of rituals it becomes its opposite. This dialectical principle, we believe, is at the core of all successful therapeutic rituals.

In a related way, all successful therapeutic rituals are in one sense leave-taking rituals. Whether they are characterized as leave-taking rites, as in this book, or the rites of degradation, coronation, or masking described in our own work with families, all successful rituals include a leave-taking component. No matter how a ritual produces a thawing effect in an individual or culture frozen in time and space, its very nature as an instrument inducing transformation from stasis to fluidity must include some elements providing a bridge for the individual and the culture bearers to exit the former and enter the latter. This is just as true of the rituals successfully prescribed in twentieth century Euro-American therapy by agents of change as it was of the rituals, most probably conducted by shamans, which thawed the maladaptive cultures of prehistoric hunting and gathering bands, and thus allowed their bearers to bring about the agricultural revolution (Childe, 1952). In all these situations, the role of ritual as an instrument of change involved, in the final analysis, a transformation of the previously stalemated relations between material behavior (the signifying) and ideational behavior (the signified).

Conclusion

A book recounting successful leave-taking rituals in psychotherapy carries an implicit message about the benefits of rituals. This book, like much of the writing about psychotherapeutic rituals in recent years, is still an exploratory effort. Our combined experience with ritualistic interventions in individual, group, and family therapy is a short one. Many of us have not yet amassed a history of successes and failures with rituals in therapy since our experience is so limited. There is a very real danger of allowing our shared positive experiences with therapeutic rituals to override the caution we exhibit in relation to more traditionally established methods in psychotherapy. Therefore, it seems appropriate to conclude a book celebrating and discussing successful ritualistic interventions in therapy with some words of caution. First, it should be made clear that rituals are not always instruments of change either at the individual or group level. Freud (1907) was, perhaps, the first modern thinker to draw attention to the role of ritual in relation to the anxiety experienced by individuals and groups. He pointed out that performance of ritual by the obsessive-compulsive individual had very little to do with change. Indeed, the rituals performed by these persons in an attempt to deal with their own anxieties are a central component in their own inflexibility and resistance to change. The obsessive-compulsive individual expends a great amount of energy and exhibits great activity in performing rituals which accomplish nothing.

Similarly, Merton spotlighted the maladaptive role of rituals in social organizations. In his treatment of social structure and adaptation (Merton, 1961), he described how rituals performed in social organizations prevent people from attaining their agreed-upon goals. Bureaucracies are the performers *par excellence* of rituals in modern societies, and their devotion to ritualized procedures for attaining goals often works to prevent those goals from being attained. So it would indeed be naïve to suppose that the proper performance of ritual, in and outside therapy, always produces change in individuals or groups. It is apparent that there are very real qualitative differences to be found among the rituals of mankind, but our knowledge is not yet sophisticated enough to identify those components in ritual responsible for these differences. In view of this deficiency, it also seems highly appropriate to conclude with an even more cautionary note. As Van der Hart describes in the introduction to this book, psychotherapeutic rituals are being researched by Euro-American therapists working in a variety of settings. These, together with the evidence presented in this book, all lead to one inescapable conclusion; rituals are powerful instruments in therapy.

This message has rapidly spread during the past decade, and today there are many therapists actively engaged in learning how to make use of rituals. Some of this learning is vicarious and is, perhaps, aided by books such as this one. Some of this learning is more direct and takes place in workshops, seminars, and more clinical settings. Unfortunately, there are signs indicating that the consequences of some of this learning and the current interest in ritual are not good. Evidence already shows that some practitioners, especially those with little experience and minimal training, have been blind to the two-sided edge possessed by rituals as a means of influencing human behavior. In their enthusiasm for an instrument capable of inducing change in behavior—often dramatically and in a short period of time—some of these practices may inflict damage on clients.

Napier and Whitaker (1981) recently expressed some fear of the fetish for ''technique'' pervading some therapeutic circles today, and we share this fear. There appears to be a growing number of individuals working with clients and client systems who fail to realize that instruments like rituals, as well as other techniques, have their proper and improper uses in therapy. Used properly, they can produce the kinds of beneficial results recorded in this and other books on therapy. Used improperly, they may add to the suffering of clients and client systems already possessing too few defenses.

We would like, of course, to conclude this book with whatever advice about the proper uses of ritual our own practice has yielded. Unfortunately, our knowledge, as already indicated, does not provide sufficient background for advice. But it is our feeling that there is a kind of experiential intuition by which the proper use of therapeutic rituals can be guided. Though extremely difficult to define we feel that this particular kind of intuition has at least three components. Clinical experience with clients and client systems, to be sure, is one of them. Likewise, the kind of intuition this experience provides a therapist in interpreting the behavior of individuals and systems is of equal importance. Finally, we believe that the therapist should always be aware that she/he possesses instruments and techniques with extremely potent effects, both positive and negative. The ritual is like the scalpel or forceps of the operating theater. It can preserve or damage life. In the final analysis, its proper use as an instrument depends on the experience, insights, and timing of the practitioner: what clinicians often refer to as ''good clinical judgment.''

We have no patent solutions as yet. Those of us who contribute to books such as this one have not yet brought the state of the art to the point where textbooks can illustrate and prescribe the proper procedures for these instruments in therapy. Like pioneers in early somatic medicine, we are still very much in the process of experimenting with these instruments ourselves. In our attempts to develop and to work with such tools as rituals and culture, many of us are in the early stages of what promises to be a long struggle; a struggle to replace the dominant paradigm based on monocausal and linear thinking and practice with a more circular and culture-oriented approach to human pain and suffering.

References

Alexander, F. & French, T. M. *Psychoanalytic Therapy Principles and Application*. New York: John Wiley & Sons, 1974.

American Psychiatric Association. *DSM-III, Diagnostic and Statistical Manual of Mental Disorders*, Third Edition. Washington, D.C. Author, 1980.

Ariès, P. H. *Western Attitudes Toward Death: From the Middle Ages to the Present*. Baltimore: Johns Hopkins University Press, 1974.

Averill, J. R. Grief: Its nature and significance. *Psychological Bulletin*, 1968, 70(6), 721-748.

Bain, A. The Capacity of Families to Cope with Transition: A Theoretical Essay. *Human Relations*, 1978, 31(8), 675-688.

Bandler, R. & Grinder, J. *Patterns of the Hypnotic Techniques of Milton H. Erickson, M.D.*, vol. 1. Cupertino: Meta Publications, 1975.

Bascom, W. The Forms of Folklore: Prose Narratives. *Journal of American Folklore*, 1965, 78, 3-20.

Beattie, J. *Other Cultures*. London: Cohen & West, 1964.

Bibeb, Interview with Judith Rossner. *Vrij Nederland*, 1984, 45(24), 7, 10.

Bowlby, J. *Loss: Sadness and Depression*. London: The Hogarth Press, 1980.

Brinkgreve, C. & Korzec, M. *Margriet weet raad: Gevoel, gedrag, moraal in Nederland 1938-1978*, Utrecht: Spectrum, 1978.

Brinkgreve, C., Onland, J. H. & de Swaan, A. *Sociologie van de psychotherapie 1: De opkomst van het psychotherapeutisch bedrijf*. Utrecht, Spectrum, 1979.

Burger, A. Imaginaire confrontatie. In: J. W. G. Orlemans (ed.), *Handboek voor Gedragstherapie*. Deventer: Van Loghum Slaterus, 1978.

Childe, V. *Man Makes Himself*. New York: New American Library, 1952.

Creyghton, M. De betekenis van een dodenritueel. *Intermediair*, 1974, 10(34), 9-19. Also in: E. van der Wolk (ed.), *Het naderend einde*. Meppel: Boom, 1974.

De Swaan, A., Van Gelderen, R. & Kense, V. *Sociologie van de psychotherapie 2: Het spreekuur als opgave*. Utrecht: Spectrum, 1979.

De Vries, Mzn; rabbijn, S.Ph. *Joodse Riten en Symbolen*. Amsterdam: De Arbeiderspers, 1968 (reprint).

Elias, N. *Über den Prozess der Zivilisation: Soziogenetische und psychogenetische Untersuchungen*. Bern: Francke, 1969.

Erickson, M. H., Rossi, E. L. & Rossi, S. J. *Hypnotic realities*. New York: Irvington Publishers, 1976.

Erickson, M. H. & Rossi, E. L. *Hypnotherapy: An exploratory casebook*. New York: Irvington Publishers, 1979.

Ezriel, H. Experimentation within the Psycho-Analytic Session. *Brit. J. Phil. Sci.*, 1956, 1, 29-48.

Fakenheim, E. *God's presence in history*. New York: Harper & Row, 1970.

Fenichel, O. *The Psychoanalytic Theory of Neurosis*. New York: Norton & Co., 1945.

Fernandez, J. W. The Performance of Ritual Metaphors. In: J. D. Sapir & J. C. Crocker (eds.), *The Social Use of Metaphor: Essays on the Anthropology of Rhetoric*. Philadelphia: University of Pennsylvania Press, 1977.

Fields, S. Folk Healing for the Wounded Spirit II. Medicine Men: Purveyors of an Ancient Art. *Innovations*, 1976, 3(1), 12-24.

Firth, R. *Symbols: Public and Private*. London: George Allen & Unwin, 1973.

Fisch, J. M. *Placebo Therapy*. San Francisco: Jossey-Bass, 1973.

Fontenrose, J. *The Ritual Theory of Myth*. Berkeley: University of California Press, 1966.

Fordham, M. *Jungian psychotherapy: A study in analytical psychology*. New York: John Wiley & Sons, 1978.

Fortuin, J. Op verzoek van de overledene . . . Een onderzoek naar de uitvaart-gewoonten aan de hand van overlijdensadvertenties. In: G. A. Banck et al. (eds.), *Gestalten van de dood*. Baarn: Ambo, 1980.

Frank, J. *Persuasion and Healing: A Comparative Study of Psychotherapy*. Baltimore: Johns Hopkins University Press, 1973.

Freeman, C. P. Personality Disorder. In: R. E. Kendell & A. K. Zeally, *Comparison to Psychiatric Studies*. New York: Churchill Livingstone, 1983.

Freud, A. A Discussion of Dr. John Bowlby's Paper 'Grief and Mourning in Infancy and Early Childhood'. *Psychoanal. Study Child*, 1960, 15, 53-62.

Freud, S. Medusa's Head. *Intern. Journal of Psychoanalysis*. 1941, 22(69).

Freud, S. Totem and Taboo (1913). *Standard Edition*, XIII. London: The Hogarth Press, 1953.

Freud, S. Mourning and Melancholia (1917). *Standard Edition*, XIV, pp. 243-258. London: The Hogarth Press, 1957.

Freud, S. Obssessive Actions and Religious Practices (1907). *Standard Edition*, IX. London: The Hogarth Press, 1974.

Fromm, E. & Eisen, M. Selfhypnosis as a Therapeutic Aid in the Mourning Process. *American Journal of Clinical Hypnosis*, 1982, 25(1), 3-14.

Geertz, C. *Agricultural Involution*. Berkeley: University of California Press, 1963.

Geertz, C. Religion as a Cultural System. In: C. Geertz, *The Interpretation of Cultures*. New York: Basic Books, 1973.

Glover, E. *The Technique and Practice of Psychoanalysis*. Vol. 1. London: The Hogarth Press, 1974.

Goffman, E. *Asylums*. Garden City: Doubleday-Anchor, 1961.

Golan, N. Using Situational Crisis to Ease Transitions in the Life Cycle. *American Journal of Orthopsychiatry*, 1980, 50(3), 542-550.

Greenson, R. R. *The Techniques of Practice of Psychoanalysis*. Vol. I. London: The Hogarth Press, 1974.

Haley, J. *Strategies of Psychotherapy*. New York: Grune & Stratton, 1963.

Haley, J. *Uncommon Therapy*. New York: Norton, 1973.

Hodge, J. R. They that mourn. *Journal of Religion and Health*, 1972, 11, 229–240.

Homans, G. Anxiety and Ritual: The Theories of Malinowski and Radcliffe-Brown. *American Anthropologist*, 1941, 43, 163-172.

Hoppe, K. Persecution, depression and aggression. *Bulletin Menninger Clinic*, 1962, 26, 195-203.

Horowitz, M. J. *Stress Response Syndromes*. New York: Jason Aronson, 1976.

ICODO pamphlet, Utrecht, 1981.

Jackson, E. N. Grief and Religion. In: H. Feifel (ed.), *The Meaning of Death*. New York: McGraw-Hill, 1959.

Janet, P. *Les médications psychologiques*, vol. II. *Les économies psychologiques*. Paris: Félix Alcan, 1919. English edition: *Psychological Healing*, vol. I. New York: McMillan, 1925 (reprint: New York: Arno Press, 1976).

Janis, I. L., Malh, G. F., Kagan, J. & Holt, R. R. *Personality: Dynamics, Development and Assessment*. New York: Harcourt, Brace & World, 1969.

Janov, A. *The Primal Scream Therapy: The Cure for Neurosis*. London: Sphere Books Ltd., 1970.

Jones, B. *Design for Death*. New York: Bobbs Merrill, 1967.

Kemeling, J. Gezinsobservaties. *Huisarts en Wetenschap*, 1979, 22, 493-495.

Kempler, W. *Principles of Gestalt Family Therapy*. Oslo: Joh. Nordahls Trykkeri, 1974.

Kernberg, O. *Object-relations Theory and Clinical Psychoanalysis*. New York: Jason Aronson, 1976.

Kluckhohn, C. Myths and Rituals: A General Theory. *The Harvard Theological Review*, 1942, 35, 45-79. Also in: Lessa & Vogt (eds.), *Reader in Comparative Religion*. Evanston: Row, Peterson, 1958.

Kluckhohn, C. The Philosophy of the Navaho Indians. In: M. Fried (ed.), *Readings in Anthropology*. New York: Crowell, 1968.

Kluckhohn, C. & Leighton, D. *The Navaho* (rev. ed.). Cambridge: Harvard University Press, 1974.

Kramer, C. Ending Family Therapy. In: G. Berenson & H. White (eds.), *Annual Review of Family Therapy*. New York: Human Resources Press, 1981.

Kroeber, A. *Configurations of Cultural Growth*. Berkeley: University of California, 1944.

Krystal, H. *Massive Psychic Trauma's*. New York: International Universities Press, 1968.

Lamphere, L. Symbolic Elements in Navaho Ritual. *Southwestern Journal of Anthropology*, 1969, 25, 279-305.

Lawlor, R. Translator's Preface. In: R. A. Schwaller de Lubics (ed.), *Symbol and the Symbolic*. Brookline, Mass.: Autumn Press, 1978.

Leggett, J. (ed.), *Seizing State Power*. New York: Harper and Row, 1974.

Lévi-Strauss, C. Le Sorcier et sa Magie. *Les Temps Modernes*, 1949, 41, 5-27.

Lévi-Strauss, C. The Effectiveness of Symbols. In: C. Lévi-Strauss (ed.), *Structural Anthropology*. New York: Basic Books, 1963.

Lévi-Strauss, C. *Myth and Meaning*. New York: Schocken Books, 1979.

Levick, S. E., Jalali, B. & Strauss, J. S. With Onions and Tears: A Multidimensional Analysis of a Counter-Ritual. *Family Process*, 1981, 20(1), 77-84.

Lewis, I. M. *Ecstatic Religion: An Anthropological Study of Spirit Possession and Shamanism*. Harmondsworth: Penguin, 1971.

Lex, B. W. The Neurobiology of Ritual Trance. In: E. G. d'Aguili et al. (eds.), *The Spectrum of Ritual: A Biogenetic Structural Analysis*. New York: Columbia University Press, 1979.

Lifton, R. J. *The Broken Connection*. New York: Simon & Schuster, 1979.

Lindemann, E. The Symptomatology and Management of Acute Grief. *American Journal of Psychiatry*, 1944, 101, 141-149.

Linton, R. Revivalistic Movements. In: W. Lessa & E. Vogt (eds.), *Reader in Comparative Religions*. New York: Harper and Row, 1961.

Lo Kuan-Chung. *Romance of the Three Kingdoms* (transl. C. H. Brewitt-Taylor). Rutland, Vermont & Tokyo: Charles E. Tuttle, 1959.

Loewald, H. W. The Experience of Time. *Psychoanal. Study Child*, 1972, 27, 401-410.

Mailer, N. *The Executioner's Song*. New York: Warner Books, 1980.

Malinowsky, B. *The Sexual Life of Savages in North Western Melanesia*. London: Routledge, 1929.

Malinowski, B. *Coral Gardens and Their Magic*. New York: Dover, 1978.

Marris, P. *Loss and Change*. London: Routledge & Kegan Paul, 1974.

Meeuwisse, E. Th. F. & Van der Ploeg, H. M. Eens gegijzeld, blijft gegijzeld? De invloed van perspublikaties op de gevolgen van gijzeling. *Intermediair*, 1979, 15(30), 1-7.

Merton, R. *Social Theory and Social Structure*. Glencoe: Free Press, 1961.

Minuchin, S., Rosman, B. & Baker, L. *Psychosomatic Families*. Cambridge: Harvard University Press, 1978.

Moore, S. F. & Myerhoff, B. G. Introduction: Secular Ritual: Forms and Meanings. In: S. F. Moore & B. G. Myerhoff (eds.), *Secular Ritual*. Assen: Van Gorcum, 1977.

Munn, N. The Effectiveness of Symbols in Murngin Rite and Myth. In: R. F. Spencer (ed.), *Forms of Symbolic Action. Proceedings of the American Ethnological Society*. Seattle: University of Washington Press, 1969.

Munn, N. Symbolism in a Ritual Context: Aspects of Symbolic Action. In: J. J. Honigmann (ed.), *Handbook of Social and Cultural Anthropology*. Chicago: Rand McNally & Co., 1973.

Murray, D. W. Ritual Communication: Some Considerations regarding Meaning in Navajo Ceremonials. In: J. L. Dolgin, D. S. Kemnitzer & D. M. Schneider (eds.), *Symbolic Anthropology: A Reader in the Study of Symbols and Meanings*. New York: Columbia University Press, 1977.

Myerhoff, B. *Number Our Days*. New York: Simon & Schuster, 1980.

Napier, G. & Whitaker, C. *The Family Crucible*. New York: Harper & Row, 1981.

Ortner, S. B. On Key Symbols. *American Anthropologist*, 1973, 75(5), 1338-1346.

Papp, P. Brief Therapy with Couples Groups. In: P. J. Guerin, Jr. (ed.), *Family Therapy: Theory and Practice*. New York: Gardner, 1976.

Parad. H. J. (ed.), *Crisis Intervention: Selected Readings.* New York: Family Service Association of America, 1965.

Parad, H. J., Resnick, H. L. P. & Parad, L. G. *Emergency and Disaster Management.* Bowie, Maryland: The Charles Press Publ., 1976.

Parkes, C. M. Unexpected and untimely bereavement: A statistical study of young Boston Widows. In: B. Schoenberg et al. (eds.), *Bereavement: Its Psychosocial Aspects.* New York: Columbia University Press, 1975.

Peacock, J. L. *Consciousness and Change.* Oxford: Basil Blackwell, 1975.

Pollock, G. H. Mourning and Adaptation. *International Journal of Psychoanalysis*, 1961, 42, 341-361.

Raapis Dingman, H. Over doden niets dan goeds: Verslag van een rouwtherapie. *Tijdschrift voor Psychotherapie.* 1975, 1(1), 11-20.

Rabkin, R. *Strategic Psychotherapy.* New York: Basic Books, 1977.

Rachman, S. Emotional Processing. *Behaviour Research and Therapy*, 1980, 18, 51-60.

Ramsay, R. W. Grief Therapy (Film). Psychologisch Laboratorium van de Universiteit van Amsterdam, Afd. Persoonlijkheidsleer, 1975.

Ramsay, R. W. Behavioral Approaches to Bereavement. *Behavioral Research and Therapy*, 1977, 15, 131-135.

Ramsay, R. W. Rouwtherapie: De Gedragstherapeutische Behandeling van Pathologische Rouwproblemen. In: J. W. G. Orlemans (eds.), *Handboek voor Gedragstherapie.* Deventer: Van Loghum Slaterus, 1979.

Ramsay, R. W. & Happée, J. A. The Stress of Bereavement: Components and Treatment. In: C. D. Spielberger & I. G. Sarason (eds.), *Stress and Anxiety*, Vol. 4. Washington, D.C.: Hemisphere Publications Corp., 1977.

Raymond, F. & Janet, P. *Névroses et Idées Fixes*, vol. II. Paris: Félix Alcan, 1898.

Reichard, G. A. *Navaho Religion: A Study of Symbolism* (second edition). New York: Pantheon Books, Bollingen Series XVIII, 1963.

Rey, Y., Martinez, J-P, Meiring, F. & Burille, P. Ein Therapeutisches Ritual: Vom 'Familiengeheimnis' zu den Nicht Gemeinsam Geteilten Geheimnissen. *Familien-dynamik*, 1981, 6(1), 44-58.

Rosen, S. (ed.), *My Voice Will Go With You: The Teaching Tales of Milton H. Erickson.* New York: Norton & Co., 1982.

Rosenblatt, P. C., Walsh, P. & Jackson, D. A. *Grief and Mourning in Cross-Cultural Perspective.* New Haven, CT.: Human Relations Area Files Press, 1976.

Rosman, B., Minuchin, S. & Liebman, R. Family Lunch Session, *American Journal of Orthopsychiatry*, 1975, 48, 846-853.

Rubinstein, T. H. Personal Communication, 1977.

Seltzer, W. Multisystemisk Tilnaerming i Behandling av Anorexia Nervosa. *Fokus paa Familien*, 1983, 1, 3-15.

Seltzer, W. Treating Anorexia Nervosa in the Somatic Hospital: A Multisystematic Approach. *Family Systems Medicine*, 1984, 2(3), 195-207.

Seltzer, W. & Seltzer, M. Material, Myth and Magic: A Cultural Approach to Family Therapy. *Family Process*, 1983, 22, 3-14.

Selvini Palazzoli, M. *Self-Starvation: From the Intrapsychic to the Transpersonal Approach to Anorexia Nervosa.* London: Chaucer, 1974.

Selvini Palazzoli, M., Boscolo, L., Cecchin, G. F. & Prata, G. The Treatment of Children through Brief Treatment of Their Parents. *Family Process*, 1974, 13(4), 429-442.

Selvini Palazzoli, M., Boscolo, L., Cecchin, G. F. & Prata, G. Family Rituals: A Powerful Tool in Family Therapy. *Family Process*, 1977, 16(4), 445-454.

Selvini Palazzoli, M., Boscolo, L., Cecchin, G. F. & Prata, G. *Paradox and Counter Paradox.* New York: Jason Aronson, 1978.

Sierksma, F. *Religie, Seksualiteit & Agressie.* Groningen: Konstapel, 1979.

Siggins, L. D. Mourning, A critical survey of the literature. *Int. J. Psycho-Analysis*, 1966, 47, 14-25.

Skorupski, J. *Symbol and Theory: A Philosophical Study of Religion.* Cambridge: Cambridge University Press, 1976.

Sluzki, C.F., Migration and Family Conflict. *Family Process*, 1979, 18(4) 379-390.

Solomon, M.A. A Developmental Conceptual Premise for Family Therapy. *Family Process*, 1973, 12(2), 179-188.

Speck, R. & Attneave, C. *Family Networks.* New York: Pantheon, 1973.

Spiegel, J. P. Environmental Corrections as a System Process. In: W. Gray, F. J. Duhl & N. D. Rizzo (eds.), *General Systems Theory and Psychiatry.* Boston: Little, Brown & Co., 1969.

Steens, R. Het Toepassen van een Geritualiseerde Opdracht bij Echtscheidingsrouw: Complicaties. *Bulletin Interaktie Akademie*, 1982, 1(1), 30-39.

Ten Berge, H. L. De mannenschrik; over het motief van de verslindende vrouw in de mythische verbeelding. *Bzzlltin*, 1982, 10(92), 91-99, 121.

Tennov, D. *Psychotherapy, The Hazardous Cure.* Garden City, N.Y.: Anchor Books, Doubleday, 1976.

Ter Horst, W. *Het Herstel van het Gewone Leven.* Groningen: Wolters-Noordhoff, 1977.

Torrey, E. F. *The Mind Game: Witchdoctors and Psychiatrists.* New York: Emerson Hall, 1972.

Turner, V. W. *The Forest of Symbols: Aspects of Ndembu Ritual.* Ithaca: Cornell University Press, 1967.

Turner, V. W. Myth and Symbol. *International Encyclopedia of the Social Sciences*, 1968.

Tyhurst, J. S. The Role of Transition States—Including Disasters—in Mental Illness. In: *Symposium on Preventive and Social Psychiatry.* Washington, D.C.: Walter Reed Army Institute of Research, Walter Reed Medical Center, 1957.

Tylor, E. B. *Early History of Mankind.* Chicago: University of Chicago Press, 1964 (original edition: 1878).

Van der Hart, O. *Overgang en Bestendiging: Over het Ontwerpen en Voorschrijven van Rituelen in Psychotherapie.* Deventer: Van Loghum Slaterus, 1978.

Van der Hart, O. Problematische Gezinssituaties: Over de (Her)Organisatie van Gezinnen met Psychiatrische Moeilijkheden. *Maandblad Geestelijke Volksgezondheid*, 1980, 35(9), 764-786.

Van der Hart, O. Personal communication, 1981.

Van der Hart, O. *Rituals in Psychotherapy: Transition and Continuity.* New York: Irvington Publishers, 1983a.

Van der Hart, O. Commentaar op 'Het Toepassen van een Geritualiseerde Opdracht bij Echtscheiding'. *Bulletin Interaktie Akademie*, 1983b, 1(2), 83-85.

Van der Hart, O. & Defares, P. G. Gezinstherapie 1978. In: *Handboek Hulpverlenen en Veranderen*, Second edition. Deventer: Van Loghum Slaterus, 1978.

Van der Hart, O. & Ebbers, J. Rites of separation in psychotherapy. *Psychotherapy: Theory, Research and Practice*, 1981, 18(2), 188-193.

Van der Velden, K. (ed.), *Directieve Therapie I*. Deventer: Van Loghum Slaterus, 1977.

Van der Velden, K. (ed.), *Directieve Therapie II*. Deventer: Van Loghum Slaterus, 1980.

Van der Velden, K. & Van Dijck, R. Wat is Directieve Therapie? In: K. van der Velden (ed.), *Directieve Therapie I*. Deventer: Van Loghum Slaterus, 1977.

Van der Velden, K. & Habekotté, S. Vaak, kort en eventueel op ongelegen tijden. In: K. van der Velden (ed.), *Directieve Therapie II*. Deventer: Van Loghum Slaterus, 1980.

Van der Velden, K., Van der Hart, O., Van Dijck, R. Positief Etiketteren. In: K. van der Velden (ed.), *Directieve Therapie II*. Deventer: Van Loghum Slaterus, 1980.

Van der Zee, M. *Inhoudsanalyse van één rouwtherapie.* Psychologisch Laboratorium van de Universiteit van Amsterdam, Afd. Persoonlijkheidsleer, Internal Report, 1978.

Van Dijck, R. Modellen in psychotherapie. In: K. van der Velden (ed.), *Directieve Therapie II*. Deventer: Van Loghum Slaterus, 1980.

Van Gennep, A. *Les Rites de Passage.* Paris: Emil Mourry, 1909. English edition: *The Rites of Passage.* London: Routledge & Kegan Paul, 1960.

Van Gogh, V. *The complete letters of Vincent Van Gogh, Vol. 3.* Greenwich, Conn.: Graphic Society, 1958.

Van Peursen, C. A. *Cultuur in Stroomversnelling: Strategie van de Cultuur.* Amsterdam: Elsevier: 1975.

Volkan, V. D. Typical Findings in Pathological Grief. *Psychiatric Quarterly*, 1970, 45, 255-273.

Volkan, V. D. The Linking Objects of Pathological Mourners. *Archives of General Psychiatry*, 1972, 27, 215-221.

Volkan, V. D. 'Re-grief' Therapy. In: B. Schoenberg et al. (eds.), *Bereavement: Its Psychological Aspects.* New York: Columbia University Press, 1975.

Volkan, V. D. *Linking Objects and Linking Phenomena.* New York: International University Press, 1981.

Volkan, V. D. & Josephthal, D. The Treatment of Established Pathological Mourners. In: T. B. Karasu & L. Bellak (eds.), *Specialized Techniques in Individual Psychotherapy.* New York: Brunner/Mazel, 1980.

Vrolijk, A. Re-Grief Therapy: A Concrete Proposal. *Gedrag*, 1980, 8, 317-331.

Waardenburg, J. Symbolic Aspects of Myth. In: A M. Olson (ed.), *Myth, Symbol and Reality.* Notre Dame/London: University of Notre Dame Press, 1980.

Wallace, A. *Culture and Personality*. New York: Random House, 1961.

Watzlawick, P. *The Language of Change*. New York: Basic Books, 1978.

Watzlawick, P., Weakland, J. H. & Fisch. R. *Change: Principles of Problem Formation and Problem Resolution*. New York: Norton, 1974.

Weber, M. *Economy and Society*. Berkeley: University of California Press, 1979.

Weiss, R. S. Transition States and Other Stressful Situations: Their Nature and Programs for Their Management. In: G. Kaplan & M. Killilea (eds.), *Support Systems and Mutual Help*. New York: Grune & Stratton, 1976.

Whitaker, C. Psychotherapy of the Absurd with a Special Emphasis on the Psychopathology of Aggression. *Family Process*, 1975, 14, 1-16.

Wilson, P. J. The Outcast and the Prisoner: Models for Witchcraft and Schizophrenia. *Man N.S.*, 1978, 13(1), 88-99.

Winnicott, D. W. Transitional Objects and Transitional Phenomena: A Study of the First Not-Me Possession. *International Journal of Psycho-Analysis*, 1953, 34, 89-97.

Worden, J. W. *Grief Counseling & Grief Therapy*. New York: Springer Publishing Co., 1982.

Wouters, C. & Ten Kroode, H. Informalisering in het rouwen en in de omgang met doden in de snijzaal. In G. A. Bancks et al. (eds.), *Gestalten van de dood*. Baarn: Ambo, 1980.

Zeig, J. (ed.), *A Teaching Seminar with Milton H. Erickson, M.D.* New York: Brunner/Mazel, 1980a.

Zeig, J. Personal communication, 1980b.

CONTRIBUTORS

MAARTEN DORMAAR, M.D.
Department of Psychiatry
Limburg State University, Maastricht, Netherlands
Regional Institute for Ambulatory Mental Health Care
Maastricht, Netherlands

JOS EBBERS, R.N., M.S.W.
Department of Social Psychiatry
Regional Institute for Ambulatory Mental Health Care
Amsterdam South/New West, Netherlands

BERTHOLD P. R. GERSONS, M.D.
Department of Psychiatry
Utrecht State University
Utrecht, Netherlands

SONNY HERMAN, M.A.
Department of Clinical Psychology
University of Amsterdam, Amsterdam, Netherlands
Jewish Institute for Social Work
Amsterdam, Netherlands

GEORGE A. SARGENT, Ph.D.
National University, San Diego, California, U.S.A.
The Family Center, Vista, California, U.S.A.

WENCKE J. SELTZER, M.A.
Child and Adolescent Psychiatric Unit
The National Hospital, Oslo, Norway
Department of Pediatrics

Index

Now Available From
Irvington Publishers Inc.
740 Broadway N.Y., N.Y. 10003

ADOLESCENT SUICIDE: With a New Preface

by Jerry Jacobs, 1980.

Suicide ranks among the leading causes of death in adolescents. In this pioneering work, sociologist Jerry Jacobs fills a lack in the existing literature of suicide by dealing with the patients' own accounts of their lives and their reasons for taking the final step. The book was written to give the reader a better understanding of how an individual comes to believe that suicide is "the only way out." It offers case histories in depth, a critique of the existing literature, criticism of existing theories and methods of suicide prevention, and suggestions as to what can be done to help prevent suicide.

"Cogently criticizes current sociological and psychoanalytical theories of suicide ... his skepticism regarding traditional theories and practices with suicidal patients merits considerations."—*Library Journal*

Contents: *Theories of Suicide:* Durkheim and the Etiological Approach. Modern Day Followers. Psychiatric Explanations of Suicide. Conclusions. *Theoretical Methodological Orientation:* Life as a Sacred Trust. Central Hypothesis. The Sample. Methods of Data Collection. A Case History of an Adolescent Suicide Attempter. Excerpts from the Verbatim Account of a Psychiatric Interview. The Use of Suicide Notes as a Source of Data. *Findings and Interpretation of Data:* A Comparison of the Nature, Number and Sequence of Events in the Lives of Suicide Attempters and Control Adolescents. Behavioral Problems. Disciplinary Techniques. Adaptive vs. Maladaptive Behavior. Broken Homes. Constructing the Bridge between Considered and Attempted Suicide. *Conclusions and Implications for Suicide Prevention.* Problems with Existing Perspectives. An Alternative Outlook. Potential Uses of the Author's Formulation for the Detection of Suicidal Persons.

147 pages $26.50 cloth
$12.95 paper